EARLY CHILDHOOD EDUCATION SERIES
Sharon Ryan, Editor

ADVISORY BOARD: Celia Genishi, Doris Fromberg, Carrie Lobman, Rachel Theilheimer, Dominic Gullo, Amita Gupta, Beatrice Fennimore, Sue Grieshaber, Jackie Marsh, Mindy Blaise, Gail Yuen, Alice Honig, Betty Jones, Stephanie Feeney, Stacie Goffin, Beth Graue

(continued)

Language Building Blocks

◆ Essential Linguistics for ◆
Early Childhood Educators

Anita Pandey

Foreword by Eugene García

TEACHERS
COLLEGE
PRESS

Teachers College, Columbia University
New York and London

Excerpt from *Creating Florida's Multilingual Global Workforce*, edited by E. García, S. Fradd, & O. Lee (1998) is reprinted with permission from the Student Achievement Through Language Acquisition part of the Florida Department of Education.

Published by Teachers College Press, 1234 Amsterdam Avenue, New York, NY 10027

Library of Congress Cataloging-in-Publication Data

Pandey, Anita, Dr.
Language building blocks : essential linguistics for early childhood educators / Anita
    Pandey ; foreword by Eugene García.
      p. cm. — (Early childhood education series)
    Includes index.
    ISBN 978-0-8077-5355-2 (pbk. : alk. paper)
    ISBN 978-0-8077-5356-9 (hard cover : alk. paper)
      1. Language arts (Early childhood) 2. Education, Bilingual. 3. Linguistics. 4. Language
    and culture. I. Title.
    LB1139.5.L35P37 2012
    372.6—dc23   2012025838

ISBN 978-0-8077-5355-2 (paperback)
ISBN 978-0-8077-5356-9 (hardcover)

Printed on acid-free paper
Manufactured in the United States of America
19   18   17   16   15   14   13   12   8   7   6   5   4   3   2   1

For Amit, Sarika, and Sahara

Contents

Foreword

I admit that linguistics is not my cup of tea. In that way, I am like the teachers reporting that the discipline of linguistics is too esoteric or too theoretical for their work with children. But as someone who subscribes to the tenets of a developmental psycholinguist and engages in applied research on bilingualism and second language acquisition in U.S. schools, I have to admit that a basic understanding of the linguistic foundations of language is becoming more critical. I have noted over and over again in my own work that English language proficiency is associated with academic proficiency in our schools.

More significantly, children speaking their home languages and dialects are likely to meet in formal venues designed for learning and broader domains of education called schools, usually as their home language(s) are nearing formative developmental stages. Those who organize and serve to implement the intervention in those venues are asked to address these language circumstances and augment the initial stages of language development in those domains deemed important in the schooling enterprise, such as new phonologies, morphologies, syntax, semantics, discourses, and literacies that are characteristic of the schooling process. Whether the education enterprise succeeds or fails is a result of the partnerships between the child's caregivers and her/his educators. A mismatch of languages and cultures can prove to be a significant challenge for students who begin their education not knowing the language of the school.

It is to this challenge—the bridging of home and school, with a focus on linguistic foundations—that this volume makes a valuable contribution. That contribution is not primarily from any new theoretical or conceptual treatment of these bridges, but from the background knowledge and, most significant, the practice aspects of designing, constructing, and utilizing those important bridges. This is good news for all educators and the children they serve. But it is of critical importance to those educators taking on the challenge of teaching students a new language and addressing associated achievement gaps. These educators are asked to develop new linguistic forms in educational contexts that require children to utilize new forms in order to engage in broader contexts of learning (such as learning math, social studies, and other content).

This volume is not only a guide for these bridges; it is a substantive resource for all educators entrusted with the expanded development of the academic languages of schooling for diverse populations of students. The great value of this resource is that it offers numerous "bridging" reflections, strategies, and specific instructional interventions. It is a must for any educator who needs to understand the significant link between language and achievement in schooling contexts.

This volume recognizes that the United States is a country of incredible socio-linguistic diversity. This trend of ethnic and racial population diversification is most evident in young and school-aged children. California has already been transformed into a minority/majority state; 52% of California's students come from "minority" categories and 25% are identified as non-English-proficient, and in less than 20 years, 70% of its students will be non-White/non-Hispanic and one half will speak a language other than English on their first day of school. Nationwide, White, non-Hispanic student enrollment has decreased by 19% since 1976 (García & Frede, 2010).

A portrait of educational vulnerability has been a historical reality for cultur-ally and linguistically diverse children in the United States. Such groups (African Americans, Mexicans, Mexican Americans, Puerto Ricans, Cubans, Chicanos, Latinos, Southeast Asians, Pacific Islanders, Filipino, Chinese, etc.) are linguisti-cally and culturally heterogeneous. However, a significant record of educational underachievement has generated programs, research, and a wide range of intel-lectual discussion regarding the "at risk" circumstances of these populations. The contemporary educational "zeitgeist" embraces excellence and equity for all stu-dents. This is best reflected in the 1983 National Commission on Excellence in Education report, A Nation at Risk, and the national goals legislation, Goals 2000, reauthorizations of the Elementary and Secondary Education Act—known as the Improving America's Schools Act of 1994 and No Child Left Behind Act of 2001.

Each of these policy articulations pays particular attention to the under-achievement of linguistically and culturally diverse students. The major thrust of any educational effort aimed at these populations has been centered on identifying why such populations are not achieving and how schools can be "reformed" or "restructured" to meet this educational challenge. It is evident that the nation cares about these students, recognizes their historical and present profile of educational underachievement, and is acting to enhance their achievement at national, state, and local levels. At the core of educational discussion of these circumstances is always the language and literacy "issues" affecting these students, hence the value of language building blocks.

This volume speaks to important issues education must concern itself with for all students. In particular, this book speaks to educators of our growing linguistically and culturally diverse student populations and the circumstances they encounter in becoming academically proficient. I am unaware of any other volume that addresses this interaction of language with a particular focus on "linguistics."

—Eugene García,
Arizona State University

Acknowledgments

Without the assistance of many, *Language Building Blocks* would not have come to life. First and foremost, I wish to thank Marie Ellen Larcada for her availability, guidance, and persistence; Dr. Eugene García for his expertise; and Dr. Sharon Ryan for her research insights. Jennifer Baker, Meg Hartmann, and other members of the dedicated TCP team worked tirelessly. TCP Director Carole Saltz's words inspired me to challenge theory-centric accounts of linguistics. Merci beaucoup! The ideas in this book were pilot-tested in Project ABCDE (**A**ccelerating **B**altimore **C**hildren's **D**evelopment through **E**ducation) funded by the U.S. Department of Health and Human Services, so special thanks are due to Michelle Plutro, Sharon Yandian, Mary Gunning, Barbara Patalics, Barbara Bartels, Mary Darrow, Lynne Coven, Bickram Janak, and Rhonda Jackson.

My parents, Mr. R. and Mrs. S. Pandey, lifelong role models, deserve a big *dhanyevaad* for constantly pushing me and for providing me with a childhood rainbowed with the myriad colors and hues of culture and language as we moved from Asia to Africa to North America.

I learned much from the educators I had the good fortune of interacting with during the course of this project, including Jon Reyhner, Loui Reyes, Richard Jeffries, Judy Stone, Brad Herling, Laura Jockisch, Vicki Nevin, Rebecca Anderson, Nicole Patton-Terry, John Farris, Matthew Anderson, Elise Allen, Sammy Hung, CC Cohen, Denise Barnes, Gretchen Goode, and Yvonne Cox. My colleague, the late "Dr. J" (Robert Johnson), who couldn't wait to take me to lunch when I completed my manuscript, motivated me, as did Alexander Morel, Drs. Anjali Pandey, Terry Osborn, Braj and Yamuna Kachru-ji, Craig Scott, Adele Newson-Horst, Brett Butler, Mbare Ngom, Dolan Hubbard, Ella Stevens, Paul Greene, and the Naraharisetti family. *Muchisimas gracias* to Charles Buckner, Amit Kapadia, Pat Tessner, David McCoy, Alaina Elder-Corrêa, Karen Prengaman, Gregory Hartzler-Miller, and Dr. Zekeh Gbotokuma, for painstakingly reviewing drafts, and to publishers (Navajo Times, Charlesbridge, University of Illinois Press, Cultural Survival); my colleagues Drs. Dorothy Strickland, Debora Wisneski, Rossana Boyd, and Achilleas Kostoulas; students (Ebony Collins, Shanna Green, Sachet Timilsina, Michael Hallmen, Anjolie Anthony, Adain Palmer); children; teachers; and parents who readily gave of their time and expertise. Last but not least, to Sarika (Singing Bird), Sahara (Helper), and Amit, I extend my sincerest *Shukriya* for permitting me time away to attend to this "baby." I look forward to hearing about your experiences with *Language Building Blocks* (languagebuildingblocks@gmail.com).

Introduction

Think left and think right and think low and think high. Oh, the things you can think up if only you try!

—Dr. Seuss, *Oh, the Thinks You Can Think!*

Enya sat quietly and beamed as her father read *Goodnight Moon* in French to her preschool class. Enya speaks English and French. Her mother is from Ireland and her father is from France. Her classmates were focused, without needing any intervention. "French is a familiar language to several of the children," observed their teacher, Judy Stone. After the reading, Enya's father had "only positive comments about his experience." This activity allowed him and his daughter to celebrate their heritage language in a predominantly English-speaking classroom.

Next, David's mother read the story in Romanian. According to the teacher, "The magical aspect of this reading was that David, who sat at his mother's feet, echoed each Romanian word she spoke. We discussed ahead of time how I would read a page in English and then she [David's mother] would read the same page in Romanian," the teacher continued.

This anecdote, from Canada, illustrates

1. The pride children who speak another language feel when we welcome use of their home language in the classroom
2. How and why to involve families in the classroom
3. The value of focusing on language by varying the language of instruction, and teaching children handy expressions in other languages early on
4. How quickly young children learn vocabulary and appreciate diversity when we integrate other languages

Quality early childhood education (ECE) starts with a firm foundation in language—and not just the dominant language. The bulk of PreK–3 instruction/ learning has to do with mastering language, the language of oral and (e-)written communication or, in linguist Jim Cummins's terms, basic interpersonal communication skills (BICS) and academic language (Echevarria & Graves, 2007).

1

This is because language is the backbone on which academic content clusters. For PreK–3 educators to perfect the art of instruction, an understanding of the science of language, including its anatomy, production, and use is essential. Children spend most of their time acquiring (unconsciously), processing (subconsciously), and consciously learning language. Indeed, it is precisely through their language, specifically their use of words, and, gradually, longer stretches of language that children learn how to communicate. Vocabulary is the primary vehicle for PreK–3 content, collaboration, and agency (Beach et al., 2010; Marzano, 2010).

"I'm impressed with the way linguistics breaks down language in a way that most of us don't learn in school," observed 2nd-grade teacher Pat Tessner. Indeed, this is the goal of linguistics. This book was written with this in mind, to open up language and make it more meaningful, readable, and analyze-able to teachers and children. When children dissect and compare languages (i.e., sound-by-sound, letter-by-letter, word-for-word), learning is more hands-on, inclusive, inquiry based, learner centered, and mathematically sound.

One semester I was invited to teach an Introduction to Linguistics class at a university in Virginia. Some 30 students enrolled for the course. I was delighted to see so many interested in linguistics. Until then the students I had worked with had had a basic knowledge of another language or a working knowledge of linguistics. Before classes started, I planned my syllabus around the book that had been used in the course previously. Most of my students turned out to be K–12 teachers who were instantly put off by the notations and requested a "better book." I couldn't locate a suitable one, so I drew from a variety of resources, yet many were disappointed that they had purchased a book we barely used. I learned a valuable lesson in resource selection that semester. *Language Building Blocks* is designed to fill the gap in PreK–3 teacher preparation resources.

WHAT THIS BOOK OFFERS

PreK–3 professionals need a book that demonstrates the practical value of linguistics; 4th- to 12th-grade teachers also can benefit from this resource. In this text, I have attempted to make linguistics engaging and relevant to educators, using easy-to-understand terms and focusing on linguistic areas directly applicable to PreK–3 instruction. In my view, a book like this is desperately needed for teacher preparation and professional development.

Language Building Blocks illustrates how to integrate key language concepts and learning principles in the PreK–3 curriculum, instruction, and assessment. It provides teachers with requisite language skills and tools they need to effectively implement curricular standards (see Chapter 9). The Common Core (State) standards, for instance, is essentially a linguistic rubric that uses specific language building blocks to gauge on-grade competency. Take the "language standards" for

Kindergartners (Common Core State Standards, 2010, p. 26). Children are expected to form regular plural nouns orally (i.e., by correctly adding and pronouncing 's' and 'es'). To do so, not only must they learn about the different sounds of plural –s (depending on the sound that precedes it), they must also be made aware of word-internal sound changes (e.g., how the 's' in house becomes a 'z' in houses), necessitating knowledge of both phonology and morphology. They are also expected to use high frequency nouns and verbs (i.e., demonstrate their awareness of grammar or word function—see Chapters 1 to 9). Like the other standards, primary indices for the "reading standards for informational text" (p. 14) for 3rd-graders are tied to individual language building blocks. For "craft and structure," for example, they must know how to segment "academic" and other words and phrases (i.e., morpheme-by-morpheme).

Teacher-friendly features include Teacher Voices (TVs), Children's Voices (CVs), and Parent Voices (PVs) segments; reflection questions; and visuals (also see the Resource Guide). PreK–3 educators have multiple resources at their disposal, so what does this book offer that others don't? It focuses on the backbone of PreK–3 instruction and learning, namely, language, a tool that both enables and mirrors *agency* and other core competencies in PreK–3 and beyond. Most of us are preoccupied with connecting the curriculum, instruction, learning, assessment, and standards, among other requisites (e.g., professional development). Linguistics is a viable solution and a means to navigate and bridge multiple areas in PreK–3. This book illustrates how language analysis is the missing link in PreK–3 and offers multiple ways to systematically integrate other languages inside and outside the classroom. Using the language (as) building blocks approach recommended, teachers can watch children's cognitive, interpersonal, math, and other skills grow without having to overhaul the curriculum.

THE BOOK'S ORGANIZATION

According to the book's thematic structure Chapter 1 outlines the value of linguistics to PreK–3 educators. Chapter 2 introduces language units (e.g., phonemes) that allow for a more systematic phonics approach to effectively gauge and grow children's phonemic awareness and other core competencies. The rags-to-riches story of English that follows in Chapter 3 offers a more meaningful and hands-on approach to vocabulary, reading, and spelling/writing. The story also clarifies why we must look back to move forward and provides a quick tour of PreK–3 terms English borrowed from other languages. Chapter 4 proposes that we count on the mathematics in language and teach PreK–3 math and science using (multi)language units, instead of numbers alone. Math lessons are demonstrated to provide the perfect opportunity for children to learn about word functions (i.e., grammar) and logic (i.e., meaning). The *multilingual math* approach proposed is the first of its kind and bound to enhance multiple PreK–3 skills. Children who know Latin-based languages like Spanish will have an easier time learning math and science. Additional advantages of early exposure to language diversity are discussed in Chapter 5. Chapter 6 takes a global approach to language in the classroom by sharing the international language of food—offering nourishment and heightened global awareness through *functional bilingual vocabulary*. An overview of language acquisition processes, and how they inform instructional best practices, follows in Chapter 7. How linguistics helps teachers provide enhanced services to children with special needs is the focus of Chapter 8. Chapter 9 provides a step-by-step linguistic approach to reading, alongside strategies to integrate the WIDA/PreK–3 English Language Proficiency Standards. The focus of Chapter 10 is technology and digital language and linguistics, which makes this book particularly timely. Chapter 11 reiterates the importance of linguistics by demonstrating its value in revealing power relationships in the PreK–3 classroom and discussing how investigations of language in multiple contexts gives us a more accurate picture of *agency*.

Learning to engage children while drawing on their talents and enriching their lives is what drives most teachers. As we work to build better futures for children, families, and communities everywhere, *Language Building Blocks* urges you to explore language—the most effective means and end to this endeavor.

ACCOMPANYING RESOURCE GUIDE

The Resource Guide is available at www.teacherscollegepress.com. (The Guide will also be available, along with appendices, on languagebuildingblocks.com.) In it, parents and instructors share their experiences with language building blocks through supplemental visual aids. For a linguistic breakdown of the Common Core (State) and Content Standards, and hands-on activities that enhance phonology, reading, and content for PreK–3 teacher educators, alongside further readings for each chapter, please contact the author at languagebuildingblocks@gmail.com.

CHAPTER 1

Language ABCs: Introductory Phonetics, Phonology, Morphology, Semantics, Syntax, and Discourse

Well then . . .
Bring your mouth this way.
I'll find it something
It can say.

—Dr. Seuss, *Fox in Socks*

Q and U are stuck like glue!

—Sarika, age 5

"Ariyana starts with 'A,'" said Ariyana's grandmother. "No, Grandma, it starts with 'R'!" 4-year-old Ariyana insisted as she hummed the alphabet song. "Listen. /ari-ana/," grandma continued. "Hear the /a/ -A sound at the beginning?" "It took me a whole year to teach Ariyana just one of the sounds 'a' makes," reported Ariyana's grandma. "The only letter she learned right away was 't'—for tootsy!" Could the letter-based alphabet song often sung in the United States delay *phonemic awareness*; that is, children's recognition of individual letter sounds? Ariyana knows the alphabet song and can identify the letters by name (e.g., *ei* for 'a,' and *ar* for 'r'), which explains why she insists that her name starts with the letter 'r.' Like most preschoolers, this 4-year-old has trouble differentiating between letters and sounds. Or perhaps, in her mind, the letters and sounds are similar. 'T' and the affiliated sound (/t/) are easier for Ariyana, very likely because of the similarity between the name of the letter 't' and the sound it makes (/t/, the first letter in *tee*). To teach *phonemic awareness* to children like Ariyana, you might have to help them unlearn what they've already learned (e.g., the alphabet song). This example prompts us to ask, "What's the point of the alphabet song, and do we need a new one to help children learn some or most of the sounds individual letters make?" If the goal of this song is to teach letter sequence, how important is sequence? Note that the letters rarely are used in the sequence in which they're s(tr)ung, at least not in English. In languages like Hebrew and Greek, in contrast, the letters coincide with numbers, in chronological order, so sequence is important.

This chapter explains why a knowledge of linguistics is essential for ECE professionals. The primary objectives are to provide teachers with a comprehensive understanding of language and outline the value of understanding language and using linguistics in the PreK–3 classroom. Linguistics is first defined and its value to ECE illustrated. Next, language building blocks, the nuts and bolts of linguistics, are outlined, namely, phonemes, morphemes, words, sentences, and discourse—in order of increasing size—and their relevance demonstrated.

WHAT IS LINGUISTICS?

What is linguistics, and what's the point of studying it? I first heard the word *linguistics* when I was 8 years old. We were driving up a potholed road to a quaint grammar school in Ado-Ekiti, a rock-hilly town in southwest Nigeria. The car passed a beautiful clay-roofed house and my father observed, "A top linguist lives there! Got his PhD from Edinburgh." From that day, I wondered what a linguist did. It wasn't until my undergraduate years that I finally understood and grew to love linguistics.

Linguistics is the scientific study of LANGUAGE, using a building blocks approach that deconstructs language systematically. Capital letters are used here to refer to LANGUAGE as a universal medium of human expression, including Inuit, spoken in Alaska, and English, used worldwide. Some features are common to more than one language. Examples include the short and long 'a' sounds used in Hindi and English. Concepts, too, such as birth, death, money, honor, and marriage, for instance, often are shared across languages. Regardless of how they're phrased, they point at cultural similarities. Nevertheless, we must recognize that languages do differ, as they embody speakers' (sub)cultural beliefs, and that each language has unique features. No language is inherently better than another; each is ideal for the purposes for which it is used. In short, languages mirror what is *culturally significant* to speakers. In Hindi, for instance, the term *malai* refers to the skin or thin sheet of cream that settles at the top of recently boiled or hot milk. *Malai* is considered the best part of milk in many Indian households, and a variety of main dishes and desserts are made with *malai* (e.g., *malai kofta* and *ras malai*).

Linguistics traditionally is broken down into the following areas: *theoretical* and *applied*. The former focuses on incremental, or smaller-to-bigger, language units, and corresponding fields of study, termed *phonetics and phonology, morphology, syntax,* and *semantics*. Applied linguistics, as the name suggests, uses theories of language to account for how language is used in different contexts. Areas that fall under applied linguistics include sociolinguistics (the study of language variation), discourse analysis, language acquisition, and computational linguistics. Textbooks in introductory linguistics tend to be organized around successively larger language building blocks, namely, phonemes, morphemes, words, sentences, and discourse, in that order. Few emphasize applied linguistics, which is of direct relevance to instruction and learning, and much more likely to interest teachers and other nonlinguists. For this reason, this book carefully integrates both areas and demonstrates their relevance.

LANGUAGE BUILDING BLOCKS

Now that we know what linguistics means and how it enhances ECE, let's take a look at the language building blocks linguists use. These are diagrammed in Figure 1.1 and include *phonemes* (the sounds of the language), *morphemes* (the smallest meaningful language units), words, phrases, clauses, sentences, and discourse, from smallest to largest.

Since phonemes are the smallest, they are at the top of the pyramid. Language units also could be visualized as links of varying size. Since each could be meaningful, semantics, the branch of linguistics responsible for meaning, cuts across language levels, as shown in Figure 1.1. Since meaning is context specific and culturally nuanced, it is tied to *pragmatics* or *discourse analysis*, the area of linguistics that focuses on social etiquette. Pragmatic or politeness norms determine how language is interpreted. For instance, a caller who asks, "Is Jen there?" is (indirectly) asking to speak with Jen. If the context (i.e., a phone call) is unspecified,

Figure 1.1. Language Layers and Building Blocks

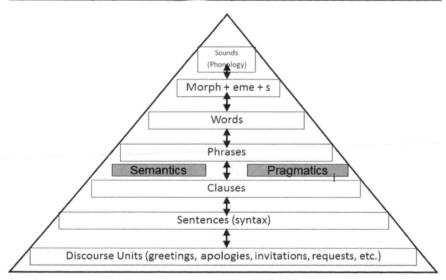

this question might be interpreted literally, that is, as an inquiry as opposed to a request. Semantics and pragmatics are yin yang-like. Joining a conversation without seeking or requesting a turn, for instance, is considered neither disruptive nor rude in some cultures (e.g., East Indian and Latin American), where overlapping turns are acceptable. In contrast, in the United States these are considered interruptions. Children in the United States are expected to wait their turn.

Phonemes

Languages have distinctive sounds, termed *phonemes*, yet it's sometimes hard to hear and/or produce sounds not used in the language(s) we speak. Nevertheless, many languages have identical sounds, especially if they're related or belong to the same (language) family. French and Spanish, for instance, have more sounds in common than Chinese and French. This is because Chinese is a tonal language. In contrast, romance languages are syllable-timed; each syllable has more or less the same beat. English is stress-timed, meaning that different syllables receive variable emphasis, so some parts of a word or sentence are stressed (i.e., sound louder).

In some contexts, single sounds can be meaningful. For instance, in southern Nigeria, when used as a suffix in Nigerian English, Yoruba, and other local languages, /o/ signals respect. When attached to a name (e.g., Nike O), it means respected or honorable. Interestingly, in Gaelic, the same sound in front of the surname is also meaningful. "O'Hara," for example, means grandchild of Hara (Comrie, Matthews, & Polinsky, 2003).

Discourse

Don't underestimate discourse! Discourse is another very important language unit. It makes language longer or larger than the sentence, including paragraphs, e-mail, preliteracy, and visuals. A basic understanding of discourse helps us to (1) understand and appreciate cultural and linguistic differences, (2) more effectively instruct children, and (3) partner with diverse families.

In linguistics, stretches of language that collectively serve distinct functions are termed discourse units or speech acts. Examples include apologizing and requesting. In cultures that consider directness and aggression impolite, these usually take the form of longer utterances or multiple sentences, as opposed to U.S.-preferred brevity (Pandey, forthcoming). In the more discrete Chinese and Indian languages, open declarations of love, such as the expression, "I love you," which many American parents frequently say to their children, are unconventional.[1] Different turn-taking practices also reflect discourse variations.

Given the large numbers of minorities entering U.S. and Canadian schools, we should pay particular attention to *discourse differences*. These include variations in expressions of politeness and respect (i.e., stated versus implied meanings) and in language format and length. The sound *fthoo fthoo* (which is how Greeks describe the act of spitting), for instance, communicates superstitious Greek speakers' polite attempts to ward off the evil eye. After providing a compliment, many say *fthoo fthoo* (e.g., "Oh, she's so pretty, *fthoo fthoo!*"). Some say, "Spit on it!" (accompanied by gestures) to communicate this belief. Telugu speakers say *thoo thoo*.

Apologizing openly is not a universal discourse feature, which explains why not all children say "excuse me" after they burp. Most southern Nigerians apologize when they hear someone sneeze. "Why?" you might ask. The local (e.g., Yoruba) equivalent of "bless you" is *"Ekpele (O),"* the same word for sorry and other expressions of sympathy. As noted earlier, the sound /o/ is an honorific. It conveys respect and often is tacked to the end of names and titles. Many Nigerians say "sorry" where Americans are more likely to say "Excuse me." Thus, they might come across as overly apologetic or not confident when they simply are trying to be polite. In East Indian cultures, apologies generally are reserved for unknown persons (i.e., strangers in the Western sense). Among friends and family, indirect apologies (i.e., expressed nonverbally or through made-up actions) are more frequent. The same goes for giving thanks. In fact, both thanks and apologies are considered distancing and formal.

Preschool instructors in the United States spend a considerable amount of time teaching children to be independent and literate (i.e., to read and correctly hold a pencil and move the eyes and hands from left to right). These preliteracy behaviors mirror mainstream discourse practices, which frequently put minorities at a disadvantage. A focus on child-rearing practices reveals different discourses at work (see Heath, 1983). Discourse analysis offers easy-to-use tools to investigate power and other variables (see Chapter 11).

WHY STUDY LANGUAGE?

Given that language is at the heart of practically every human endeavor, studying language as it is used in different settings (e.g., in the PreK–3 classroom and the home) and by individuals and communities gives us insights into human behavior. When we study someone's language, including how the person uses it in everyday exchanges, we get a better picture of that child and his or her family or community (see Chapter 5). We also understand what prompts children to use specific sounds, stress and intonation patterns, sentences, and even gestures or other nonverbal signs. One's language, including the way children pronounce certain sounds and/or words, as well as the terms and expressions they use in speech, mime, read-alouds, and/or (e-)writing, could be used to identify (sub)cultural and social backgrounds, interests and, in some cases, even the geographical setting(s) in which individuals might have spent most of their time. Often, it's not so much the geographical location as the people we spend time around that influence our speech habits.

Language constitutes the bulk of PreK–3 content. As shown in Figure 1.2, language—through speech, reading, and writing, for instance—is at the center of the PreK–3 learning wheel, driving curriculum, standards, instruction, learning, assessment, and even professional development (PD). For this reason, ongoing language analysis is essential for ECE professionals and even children.

Given the increasing sociolinguistic diversity in our schools and neighborhoods, linguistics is, in fact, a necessary component in ECE and PD. After all, language is the foundation of (pre-)reading and content area knowledge. Even math, science, and social studies are best conveyed through content area language. Cognition and critical thinking are mirrored in language. Spoken and written language (termed "literacy") are indices of learning and proficiency in practically all areas in PreK–3. By the same token, the language of individuals with language and/or learning "disabilities" is generally symptomatic of difference(s). Special educators with knowledge of linguistics are, therefore, in a better position to assist "special" populations, who make up a growing group. In short, linguistics is of value to all educators, so key and relevant aspects of language can and should be integrated into PD and ECE courses, including (Early) Childhood Development

Figure 1.2. Language Components, PreK–3

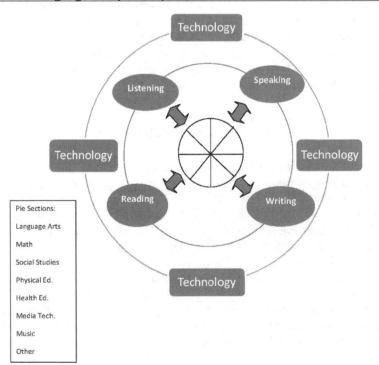

and/or Human Development; Assessment in Reading; Processes in Reading Acquisition; Parent, Family, and Community Involvement; Children's Literature; and Special Education. Subsequent chapters discuss how to incorporate linguistics in engaging and relevant ways.

Using linguistics in the PreK–3 classroom requires drawing children's attention to the sounds (phonemes) specific letters make, as well as to meaningful word parts (morphemes). Doing so teaches children and families to do the same. In short, making children language-conscious is key to early literacy and content mastery. Knowledge of linguistics makes this goal attainable, since the medium is also the message in PreK–3. A language-centered approach to PreK–3 is therefore proposed, premised on the idea that you cannot separate content from language.

WHY LINGUISTICS FOR PREK–3 TEACHERS?

Imagine what our world would be like without language. This oral, nonverbal, visual, and written medium is what we use to communicate, connect, and engage with others. Language makes us human; it is the hallmark of our humanity. For many of us, talking (sometimes subconsciously), humming, singing, signing, and/or writing help us to create, envision, and express what we have in mind, and to think through matters that interest and affect us. It therefore follows that the more languages we know, the more knowledgeable we are likely to be about cultures and contexts or locations in which specific languages are employed.

Language defines us. We are, in effect, what we speak (e.g., American, Chinese, Korean, and so on). German philosopher Johann Fichte observed, "*Die Sprache eines Volkes ist seine Seele*" (Language is the soul of a people). Language reflects our world view. For instance, we have names for concepts and relationships we consider important. Take, for instance, the terms "stranger," "privacy," and "personal space" in American English. Words with the same denotations and connotations (i.e., extended meanings) are absent in languages like Yoruba, Igbo, Hindi, and Urdu. In fact, in Nigerian English, "stranger" has the opposite meaning; it refers to a friend. A Nigerian who announces that he "has a stranger" is either explaining why he is tardy or requesting time off to nurture a friendship. In relationship-focused cultures, such discourse is perfectly acceptable. Imagine a Nigerian child's reaction to stranger-danger lessons.

In communal cultures, it's not impolite to ask personal questions (e.g., "Are you married? Do you have children?") Similarly, no single word is used to refer to "grandmother" in Hindi and Urdu; the words *nani* and *dadi* refer to maternal and paternal grandmother(s), respectively. In short, two distinct relationships are recognized, captured in two separate words, instead of via a single label and relationship. In these languages, the distinction between paternal and maternal is considered important enough to necessitate lexical differentiation or two distinct words for two distinct familial relationships. This explains why there are many more words for family in the languages used in communal cultures than in languages used in nuclear family settings. In general, in communal cultures, extended families are emphasized over and above nuclear families, so many more words are used to capture specific family relationships.

Language also aids and mirrors human thought. In short, language fosters critical thinking—whether in speech, writing, some other visual form, or via a mix of media. In many ways, language is our walking and talking DNA. It identifies us almost instantly. How many would agree that some of us sound different, depending on whom we are speaking to, how well we know the people, what we are talking about, and so on. How we utter specific sounds, and how we stress different syllables and words, varies, depending on a number of factors. In fact, some of us have a distinctive accent, which could prompt positive or negative judgments about our social class or standing, our level of education, and our racial, national, and cultural background (see Chapter 5).

Familiarity with the phonemes of English is, therefore, beneficial to teachers for a variety of reasons. First, such knowledge could help us to systematically compare the sounds used in different languages and to identify the phonemes of other languages that our students might speak or understand. Knowing how to produce specific sounds and words in different contexts would help us to more efficiently assist our students and others to quickly and successfully articulate specific sounds (e.g., ask versus aks). This is where a basic knowledge of phonology comes in handy. In phonology, we learn where in the mouth (and exactly how) specific vowels and consonants are produced. Using this information, we can instruct our students to correctly produce challenging sounds and words. For instance, if a child says "berry" for "very" (and Spanish speakers frequently conflate these sounds), you could train her to produce /v/ by biting her upper teeth into her lower lip, "like this" (demonstrate). Both (/b/ and /v/) are voiced consonants and involve the lips. The difference lies in the lips (bilabial = both lips for /b/ and part-lip-and-part-teeth for /v/), and in the air passage and amount of air flow involved in each (i.e., *plosive* versus *fricative*). Pronouncing /b/, which is a plosive, involves air being trapped momentarily behind closed lips before being (suddenly) released in *explosive* mode, generally signaled by the smacking of the lips, yielding /p/ and/or /b/, depending on whether the vocal folds vibrate (e.g., for voiced sounds, the rightmost partner in a sound pair) or not. The vocal folds vibrate for both /b/ and /v/. Not surprisingly, /b/ is an easier sound for children than /v/. Similarly, /d/ is easier than /r/ (see Chapter 8).

Knowledge of *phonetics* (study of human sounds) and of *phonology* (language-specific sounds) is also vital for success in reading and writing, as evidenced by the success of the phonics approach (see Lane & Pullen, 2004). The phonetic alphabet captures the different sounds that individual letters make; for instance, short 'a' or the schwa /ə/ in words like "another," long /a/ as in "arm," the diphthong ei for the 'a' in "angel," aw for the 'a' in "all," and ɛ for the sound 'a' makes in words like *anything*. A sound-based alphabet song is bound to be more instructive than the conventional alphabet song through which we expect children to learn the letters and the sounds that individual letters make. It's also presumptuous to assume that mere exposure to written text through books and resources will guarantee success in reading and writing.[2] Some teachers ask children to read for 15 minutes daily, yet assessments of the impact of this practice on their reading and writing skills are lacking. While likely to generate interest in literacy, and to assist children in committing certain words (i.e., spellings) to memory, such contrived attempts at reading are best supplemented with linguistic approaches. Sound and word segmentation (i.e., phonetics and morphology), for instance, facilitate meaning-making and spelling, and are therefore prerequisite skills.

With a knowledge of phonetics, morphology, and syntax, in particular, teachers could distinguish between dialects and/or correctly identify features, including dialect differences in languages other than English. For instance, Latin Americans pronounce the 'c' in *gracias* (the Spanish word for "thanks") as /s/ (i.e., /grasias/), while the phoneme *th* (/Ө/ in phonetic script) is used in Spain (i.e., /graӨias/). Since Spanish is widely spoken in the United States, teachers could inquire about and share examples from Spanish and other languages in use in the community. To do so, pay careful attention to children's speech, reading, writing, interaction styles, and listening habits, including dual language learners (DLLs). Observe how they hear/process, read, write, and/or interpret language. Since language unites us, identifying differences in language use is educational in and of itself.

Comparing sounds, words, and other features across languages is characteristic of linguistics, and is also exciting. In addition to helping us become global citizens, this exercise helps us develop a better ear and eye for our own and other languages. In Hindi, for instance, spoken in India and by East Indians in the United States, United Kingdom, Canada, and elsewhere, 'z' is not part of the sound system of the language and usually is replaced by 'j.' Knowing this could help us train a Hindi-speaking child to say "zebra" instead of *jebra*.[3] Linguistics teaches us to compare languages, so we can understand why a Spanish- or French-speaking child might say "(I) have seven," a direct translation of the equivalent expressions (i.e., [Yo] *tengo siété años* and *J'ai sept ans*) in Spanish and French, respectively, instead of "I am seven." By studying the component parts of language (i.e., language building blocks), and engaging in language comparison, we also learn that the subject is optional in Romance languages like Spanish and Italian. We could then make children aware of notable differences, in the event that they drop the subject or start an English sentence with a verb, for instance.

This enhanced understanding of language that linguistics provides us with (O'Grady et al., 2004) enables us to observe the workings of language in children's individual and collaborative speech and writing and in PreK–3 resources. Using this information, we can offer individualized and developmentally appropriate instruction (see Chapters 7 and 8), where each child's language drives instruction, learning, and assessment. For these and other reasons, linguistics is invaluable for PreK–3 professionals.

SUMMARY AND APPLICATIONS

This chapter opened by defining linguistics, outlining language ABCs or components used in linguistics, and sharing how they enhance PreK–3 instruction. Chapter 2 further explores the value of individual language building blocks. With knowledge of linguistics, PreK–3 educators recognize that language is the cornerstone of instruction, learning, and assessment, and that language is a diverse yet universally important construct. Linguistics helps us conceptualize, study, and scientifically segment language. Through a focus on language, we can observe and identify individual and group language and literacy practices and develop a better understanding of learning behavior(s) and more.

How can knowledge of linguistics help us be more responsive to our students? First, remember that language permeates all areas of PreK–3, so the best way to help young children is by building their (multi)language skills. Linguistics helps us conceptualize language in tangible terms and systematically segment language into meaningful parts. Through careful language analysis, young children can master core PreK–3 skills in step-by-step mode, as demonstrated in subsequent chapters. This process helps PreK–3 children master interpersonal skills, vocabulary, content, and reading relatively easily.

Recommended actions:

Pay close attention to *language use* in your classroom and beyond.
Reflect on the structure and functions of language in your classroom (e.g., in different lessons and interpersonal exchanges).
Observe each child's language use and identify individual language needs.

After reading this book, you will find that you will be able to meet the needs of culturally and linguistically diverse children promptly and more effectively. You will have a better understanding of the term *cultural diversity* (mirrored in language), and of language varieties and strategies, and will know exactly what to emphasize with each child, without having to rely on other personnel.

CHAPTER 2

Sound Essentials
A Sound Start Beyond Phonics

Today is your day!
Your mountain is waiting.
So . . . get on your way!

—Dr. Seuss, *Oh Baby! Go Baby!*

You don't have to be an English learner to be baffled by the complexity of the English language. How many times have children asked: "Why do we put an 'h' in "hour" (yet pronounce it like "our"), a 'z' in "is," a 'k' in "knife," and 'gh' in "right"? What do we say to the Spanish-speaking child who says and reads "mother" like "moth" + "-er" and "love" like the second half of "st-ove"? English spelling oddities are endless. This chapter discusses the classroom applications of phonetics and phonology, morphology, and grammar (syntax).

A SOUND START TO ENGLISH LETTER SOUNDS

Research shows that children have an easier time reading languages with phonetic alphabets (McGuinness, 2004). In Hindi and Spanish, for instance, each letter corresponds to a single sound (and both share sounds and morphemes from Sanskrit, the mother language).[1] In contrast, the 26 letters in English represent many more than 26 sounds. 'A,' for instance, makes at least six sounds. Even more confusing is the fact that a single sound can be represented by different letters. For instance, 'c,' 'k,' and 'q' make the same /k/ sound (e.g., cactus, kit, and quick), leaving children wondering why we need all three. *Homophones*, words that sound alike but are spelled differently (e.g., wait/weight) are common, further complicating English. Problems with sound representation are further compounded by multiple accents. Is it any wonder, then, that many children, including those proficient in English, struggle with reading and writing?

The sounds some words make in isolation sometimes change when they are used alongside other words. For instance, "of" is pronounced /of/ or /ɔf/ in isolation and /əv/ in context. In some English words, selected sounds change through

15

word extension (e.g., electricity → /ilektrisiti/). With knowledge of phonology, we can highlight and explain internally and externally motivated sound changes resulting from *letter blending*. For instance, plural [-s] and the [-ed] past tense ending (e.g., cats, dogs, dresses; and talked, rained, and accepted) each make three possible sounds (-s, -z, -əz/iz, and -t,-d, and -əd/-id, respectively), depending on the sound that immediately precedes them. Drawing children's attention to (high-frequency) sound changes will help them master pronunciation and spelling. This is especially important for DLLs, who are likely to find varied pronunciations of a single suffix confusing.

External (i.e., social) factors like geography also can modify sounds (see Chapter 5). Most English speakers use 50 or more sounds, depending on their dialect. The greatest sound variation is found in vowels. In fact, vowels are primarily responsible for differences in accents. For instance, fifty is pronounced in some regions and social circles as /fifti/ (Standard American English), /fi:fti:/ (through a characteristic southern vowel lengthening process), and /fiti/.[2] Even after children recognize that individual letters make different sounds, much work remains.

Phonics Through Phonology

"But /l/ doesn't sound like 'el'!" complained my 4-year-old when her older sister, "tired of waiting for the correct answer," answered her own question, "What sound does 'l' make?" "/l/," she responded. Making the jump from English letter names to sounds the letters make isn't easy for most children. Phonics instruction is designed to help children connect sounds to print, yet teachers struggle with teaching *phonemic awareness* (Allington & Baker, 2007). Linguistics, specifically phonetics and phonology, equips early childhood educators with the missing building blocks for phonics instruction, namely, standard representations of individual vowel and consonant sounds and information regarding their production.

Since not all sounds have equivalents in print, how is one to teach children phonemic awareness? To do so, one must first identify each vowel and consonant sound, know how it's produced, and capture or represent each in print, as children are more likely to learn sounds when they can both hear and see them. Educators must be familiar with and use a standard representation, like the International Phonetic Alphabet (IPA).

The IPA. Few educators are familiar with the phonemes of English and their phonetic symbols, or with the IPA, which inventories all human consonant sounds. Phonemes are critical tools in this day and age of linguistic diversity and are the missing link to successful reading and writing. While some phonemes are not used in English, such as the vibrating or trilled /r/ in Spanish *perro* (i.e., dog), the IPA provides a standard representation for each sound, clarifies where in the mouth each is produced and how (i.e., place and manner of production), and familiarizes us with similar and different sounds in use in other languages.

Familiarity with phonemes and the IPA is essential. First, it helps us understand why some children produce un-English sounds in certain words (e.g., the pharyngeal /kh/ of Arabic instead of the unaspirated English /k/ in "king"). Second, it helps teachers differentiate between close and exact sounds, and phonetic versus non-phonetic writing systems. For example, many Spanish-speaking children inadvertently pronounce the English letter 'd' using the Spanish phoneme /ɗ/, as in "would." Drawing attention to differences in (associated) phonemes would help children learn specific sounds. Indeed, using our knowledge of phonemes and/or the IPA, we can help children produce correct sounds when they use incorrect ones (which might very well be used in their primary languages, for instance).

The IPA also provides a blueprint for language-specific phoneme identification; linguists have created similar charts for the phonemes of each language. Create individualized charts containing the phonemes each child produces. These are especially helpful in teaching children who have trouble with selected sounds. This way, you can visually identify problematic sounds and other-language equivalents or approximations and monitor children's phonemic awareness.

Phonics Isn't Phonology. Phonics approaches tend to oversimplify vowel sounds. Categorizing vowels into *short, long, soft,* and *hard* fails to capture the full range of English vowel sounds and differences in their production—key to language-literacy mastery. Classifying vowels as *long* and *short* is also unhelpful because not all long vowels involve lengthening of a short vowel. Distinguishing between *short vowels, common long vowels, ambiguous vowels,* and *other vowels* (Invernizzi et al., 2012) is challenging. Further, terms like *blends, digraphs,* and *graphemes* (Invernizzi et al., 2012) make phonics unduly complicated. How, for instance, is a child to differentiate between digraphs and blends? How about *inflected endings, (un)accented final syllables,* and *harder suffixes,* terms Invernizzi and colleagues (2012, p. 320) use? How should we teach vowel digraphs (e.g., ee, oo, oa, ie)? Each can make multiple sounds, and not all are diphthongs.[3] What is a child to think? Children prefer order and precision. Using phonology, we can teach children sounds more systematically and relatively easily. For example, they can learn which vowels literally add up in diphthongs (e.g., e + a = /eə/ as in "ear").

Making sense of English phonology through countless vowel–consonant spelling patterns is cumbersome. Relating grapheme patterns (e.g., CVC, like "rat," vs. CVCV, "rate") to sound differences could get complex, generating multiple lists and flashcards (see Lane & Pullen, 2004). Second graders, for instance, could receive over 40 lists in a 4-month period (Invernizzi et al., 2012), yet few learn the sounds, spellings, and/or meanings. (Most try to memorize them.) Third graders typically have to master 53 "sorts," each with puzzling spelling patterns that are enough to make anyone's head spin. That the focus is on *spelling*, which is largely nonphonetic in the case of English, adds to the learning burden. One 3rd-grader was asked what she had learned from these sorts announced, "Pretty much nothing!" "You could still learn the words without putting them in categories or spelling them right," observed another.

Phonics, therefore, provides an incomplete picture of English phonology. Since sounds, words, and spellings are emphasized all together, phonemes do not get the individual attention they deserve. Moreover, few teachers provide symbols for each sound or encourage children to use their own, and even fewer focus on (sound) physiology. Therefore, phonics approaches tend to be overly complicated. Studying language from the bottom up, starting with just sounds (i.e., phonology) and progressively focusing on larger language units (e.g., sentences) in incremental mode, as is proposed here, is highly recommended. Supplementing and/or teaching phonics through phonology is both easier and more effective. Phonology allows us to systematically represent the sounds English letters make, and evaluate and grow children's phonemic awareness and vocabulary relatively quickly—before they have been given a list of words (many unfamiliar) to classify by spelling.

Indeed, a more comprehensive understanding of *decoding* (i.e., sound-to-letter-to-word meaning and sentence-and-contextual/extended meaning) comes from linguistics, specifically phonology. Phoneme-based phonics instruction helps children: to identify, distinguish between, and correctly pronounce individual sounds.

Children compare sounds orally and visually and work from their personal pronunciations toward standard English. For instance, in "root," "book," and "floor"—each containing the digraph oo—children see, as well as hear, how oo produces three different sounds: the diphthong in "root," the high back rounded vowel in *book*, and the mid-back rounded vowel in "floor." Phonetically, they are represented as /rut/, /bʊk/, and /flor/. The /ʊ/ is produced with rounded lips (i.e., corners protruding outward) and the tongue raised high[4] at the back of the mouth (hence the height designation, followed by the location in the mouth). For the /o/ or /ow/ (O'Grady et al., 2004) in "floor," the tongue rises midway at the back. The main difference between /u/ and /ʊ/ is length, captured in the terms *tense*(ness) and *lax*(ness). Tense vowels are longer. In the end, it's easier to explain print–sound correspondences and discrepancies using phonology, as opposed to phonics, plus you use fewer terms.

English Phonemes. Think sounds, not letters! Letters are visual representations of speech sounds. The different sounds (i.e., phonemes) English letters make are captured in Figure 2.1. (Phonemes are typically placed between slanting lines).

Sounds and sound pairs for which corresponding letters are missing in the English alphabet include

- Diphthongs (i.e., dual vowel sounds): aj, au, ɛə, ɛj/ei, ia, iu, ou, oi, uə, u∧ (e.g., one)

- ʃ or š = sh = s + h
- ʧ or č (ch = c + h), θ (th = t + h)
- ḏ (pronounced the, as in "that." This sound was a letter in Old English; that was written ḏæt, like it sounded)
- ʤ (d + ʒ), as in "jump"
- ɫ (just a hint of an "l"; called a "dark" /l/, as in "bottle")
- ʔ a sudden temporary glottal stop, as in Hawaiʔi
- ŋ (n + g, as in the suffix -ing; e.g., walking)

As shown, English has many more sounds than our 26-letter alphabet might lead children to believe. The words we write and their spellings are standardized versions of centuries of English usage. The texts of the Middle Ages are virtually unreadable for today's educated English-speaking adult. Why? Because English spelling hasn't kept up with changes in pronunciation, so it is not the best guide to phonics or phonology.[5] When we learn the sounds the written words once produced, early literature is easier to read (see Chapter 3). Young learners of English are still learning the names of letters, and sight words are few in number. When a child does not see (letter-like) representations of possible sounds, she is likely to be confused. In short, the absence of phonemic equivalents (in writing) is problematic. To ease reading, we must offer children a tool that captures the sounds they hear, say, and see (i.e., phonemes or a phoneme chart).

Phonetic writing is in partial use in classrooms today. The inventive spellings approach encourages children to write what they hear, yet what they hear is sometimes unintelligible. One 2nd-grader wrote, "Do not smoch!" What would a 7-year-old know about smooching? Ah, it was not "smooch" he was referring to, but "smoke." Had this child learned a standardized representation for his sounds, he would not have had to choose between the many alternative spellings of the target word (e.g., *smoke, smoak, smoch, smowk*—among the many choices he might have envisioned).

Pronunciation spellings provide a clearer illustration of what children actually hear, enabling teachers to anticipate reading and writing problems, and to build bridges to correct pronunciation and conventional spellings. Phonetically writing sounds permits easy and precise identification of sounds and eases pronunciation, vocabulary, and spelling instruction by providing teachers and children with a shared frame of reference.

Consonants Versus Vowels. Phonemes are separated into vowels and consonants. The distinction has to do with their production. For consonants, the tongue makes contact with different parts of the mouth. For this reason, consonants are described in terms of two axes: place (in the mouth) and manner (i.e., the nature of the contact between the tongue and other organs; see the International Phonetic Association (IPA) online). Place-wise, consonants include:

Figure 2.1. The Sounds of English and Corresponding Letters

Letter	Corresponding Sounds	Graphemes/Letter Combos
A	æ, ɔ, a, ə, ɛi, ɛ, ɚ, iɚ, ɛə, silent a	æpple, ɔl (all), arm, ən (an), ɛip (ape), ɛni (any), iɚ (ear), fair, eagle
B	b, silent b	book, rabbit, rub, dou(b)t
C	k, s, č, sh, kh	cat, (be)cause, cent, excite, chin, chéf, Loch
D	d, j, t, silent d (for some)	do, educate, talked, Wednesday
E	ɛ, ee/e, iə, ɛi, ɛa, silent e	elf, ev(e)ry, very, key, near, queue
F	f, v	fish, lift, stuff, off, of
G	g, j, f, silent g	give, magic, laugh, li(g)ht
H	H, silent h	hat, that, (h)eir (from French)
I	i, ai, ə, i, ɛə	India, ice, position, Rita, air
J	j /ʤ/	jam, jump, pajama, raj
K	k, silent k	kite, racket, knife, know
L	l, ł, silent l	lime, sell, tilt, walk
M	m	mama, ma'am
N	n, ŋ	no, none, nun, singing
O	w, au, ə, o, oi, uə	one, owl, done, on, oil, poor
P	p, f	pie, phone, elephant
Q	k	queen, queue
R	r	road, bored, star

Figure 2.1. The Sounds of English and Corresponding Letters (continued)

Letter	Corresponding Sounds	Graphemes/Letter Combos
S	s, š, z, ʒ, silent s	sit, fist, sits, sure, nose, usual, island
T	t, č, θ, ɖ, d, š/sh silent t	tin, picture, thing, the, Kindergarten, -tion, listen
U	u, ʊ, ʌ	cute, put, run
V	v	voice, dove, loaves
W	W, silent w	west, saw, wrestling
X	ɛks, k, gz, z	x-mas, X-box, excite, exist, xylophone
Y	y, i	yellow, worry
Z	z and ʒ	zebra, azure

Bilabials (i.e., use both lips: /m/, /p/, and /b/)
Labio-dentals (i.e., involve one lip and the teeth: /f/ and /v/)
Dentals or *interdentals* (/Θ/ and /ɖ/ or /dh/)
Alveolar (tongue against the gum ridge: /n/, /t/, /d/, /s/, /z/)
Post-alveolar or *palatoalveolar* (i.e., right behind the alveolar ridge:
        /ch/, /dʒ/, /sh/, /ʒ/)
Palatal (tongue touching the hard palatte: /j/, as in "yes")
Velar (tongue touching the velum: /ŋ/, /k/, /g/)
Glottal /h/ sounds

In regards to *manner*, consonants can be:

Plosives or *stops* (i.e., sounds you can't hold; hence their explosive-ness: /p/,
        /b/, /t/, /d/, /ch/, /j/, /k/, and /g/)
Fricatives (sounds you can hold: /f/, /v/, /Θ/, /ɖ/, /s/, /z/, /sh/, /ʒ/ or /zh/)
Nasals (i.e., air passes through the nose: /m/, /n/, and /ng/ or ŋ)
Liquids or *laterals* (/r/ and the clear /l/ in leaf, and the dark (velar) /ł/ or a
        hint of /l/ in "milk" and "cool")
Glides, approximants, or *semivowels* (/j/ and /w/), which are produced like
        vowels (without the tongue touching any organ), yet function like
        consonants—at the boundary of the syllable (versus at the nucleus)

Many websites (e.g., YouTube) demonstrate how specific phonemes are produced and could help children produce challenging sounds. All children are technically *language learners*, so many have trouble producing certain sounds (see Chapter 7). Remember that your mouth is a sound lab, and the tools you need to teach children are literally at the tip of your tongue! When children learn to track their tongues, the sounds they produce are their own. This act of discovery is sure to excite them and might even get them to compete with one another—making animal sounds (Sterne, 2002), for instance.

Vowels are produced entirely by the tongue making different gymnastic moves without touching any organ. They are therefore described on the basis of tongue location (front, mid, and back) and height (high, low, and mid). Height generally is mentioned first, followed by location and, for some vowels, lip aperture. When teachers know how vowels and consonants are produced, they can offer children easy-to-follow directions and explanations.

TONE, STRESS, AND INTONATION

Suprasegmentals refer to sounds above segmental sounds (i.e., larger than phonemes). They include tone (pitch variations), word stress, and intonation (sentence-level stress). In tonal languages, different tones convey different meanings. For example, the Chinese word *ma*, depending on the tone used, could mean mother, horse, question, and yelling. However, speakers of stress and syllable-timed languages (like English and French, respectively) have a hard time hearing tone differences. Imagine how hard it must be for Chinese students to realize that tone is relatively unimportant in English.

Stress and intonation are meaningful in English. Word stress clarifies part of speech. For example, "record" is a noun when the first syllable is stressed (RE-cord), and a verb when the second is stressed (re-CORD). We hear stress as emphasis, higher pitch, or loudness—uttered with rising intonation. Direct questions in English, for instance, typically end with stress on the final word. Contrast the following:

1. *Bring* your backpack.
2. I'd *like* you to bring your backpack.
3. Could you bring your *backpack*?

How does a child know that the first is a directive, the second an indirect request, and the third a direct request? These differences are conveyed through stress and intonation. Punctuation also signals intonation. Exclamation marks, for instance, convey excitement. Double or triple exclamation marks indicate extreme excitement—best dramatized (verbally). Variations in stress and intonation could confuse children whose primary languages differ in suprasegmentals. In Czech, Hungarian, and Finish, for example, word stress is fixed, always on the first syllable. With knowledge of phonetics and phonology, you could easily contrast suprasegmental features and grow children's phonemic skills.

Rhyming words that differ in a single sound are called *minimal pairs*. They are minimally different (e.g., *roar* and *soar;* Invernizzi et al., 2012). Language-specific phonemes are identified through minimal pairs, via a simple process of sound substitution. Using minimal pairs, we quickly can draw children's attention to different sounds and train them to create words. Observe how quickly they infer language rules (e.g., frequently used suffixes, which many (over)extend, yielding words like "bringed" and "badder").

Phonemes, as you'll soon discover, change the meaning of words. The only difference between "mad" and "sad," and between "milk" and "silk," for instance, is in the initial sound. Minimal pairs teach children to experiment with language and identify distinctive sounds.

Dr. Seuss's books encourage readers of all ages to play with language. They persuade the tongue to perform acrobatics and to master specific sounds (i.e., phonemes) at the same time. Minimal pairs play a key role in introducing readers to the phonemes of English in a musical and comical context. In *If I Ran the Circus,* Dr. Seuss uses many examples, including "not" and "lot," and "moon" and "Foon" (a Dr. Seuss creation). The titles of some Dr. Seuss's books also contain minimal pairs. Examples include *Daisy-Head Mayzie.*[6] Through minimal pairs, children can (1) focus on sounds, (2) distinguish between them, (3) see that many words in English that don't look alike rhyme (e.g., "fox" and "socks"), and (4) learn how two or more sounds and words can create a memorable story.

Even nonsense words like "Snuvv" (secret strange hole, which rhymes with "glove") are instructive (Gathercole, 2006). Children quickly recognize that there is no limit to our word power and that they, too, can create words. They get to experience firsthand the musicality and creativity of language. *On Beyond Zebra* suggests that the English alphabet is restrictive. The following verse, for instance, emphasizes the difference between 's' and 'z' through the minimal pair "see" and "z(ee)" (i.e., /si/ and /zi/):

> In the places I go there are things that I see
> That I never could spell if I stopped with the Z.

In addition, minimal pairs instill good writing habits in children, encouraging them to write what they hear, create, and see (a sure way to connect speech to writing), and to stretch the alphabet. The many minimal pairs in Dr. Seuss's books ease sound, word, and content recall. Additionally, repetition, visual and textual meaning, the economical sentences, and humor help children commit words and storylines to memory. Dr. Seuss's books therefore enhance children's phonemic skills and more. In short, non-phonetic spellings are easier to master when presented in easy-to-recall, contrastive, minimal-pair verses.[7]

ASSEMBLING AND UNPACKING WORDS

The lion's share of PreK–3 learning has to do with vocabulary mastery (Marzano, 2010), and since a large vocabulary is a prerequisite for successful reading, knowledge of morphology, the science of word construction, is essential. Marzano (2010) lists the words children have to learn in PreK–12 and observes that even "if all 3,948 basic terms were addressed in grades 1 to 3," we would have to teach "948 . . . each year" (p. 10). Teaching all of these words would be time-consuming and "daunting" (p. 10) so we must train children to learn words on their own. Dissecting words along *morpho + logic + al* lines (i.e., meaning-part identification) is engaging and exactly what they need in order to learn the thousands of words they must know by 3rd grade, as well as to enhance their literacy, reasoning, problem-solving and math skills (see Chapter 4).

Morphology-based vocabulary instruction makes scientists of children because they discover the component parts of words and are constantly constructing and decoding words. With the exception of idioms, words can be pieced together and disassembled relatively easily, as this section demonstrates. Word assembly is meaningful, and, best of all, kid-friendly. By segmenting words and using the smallest parts to create more words, children learn (i.e., build, decode, and retain) many more words more quickly. Early exposure to the jigsaw puzzle composition of words presents children with a hands-on and systematic vocabulary-learning mechanism. When children are able to dissect words into smaller meaningful parts, their listening, speaking, reading, and writing skills demonstrate visible improvement, and they have an easier time piecing reading (and writing).

Morphemes

A *morpheme* is the smallest meaningful part of a word. Morphemes are identified using curly brackets. *Morphology* ({morph} + {logy}) is the study of word composition. Morphemes or meaning units that can stand on their own are termed *free morphemes, roots,* or *stems* (i.e., other parts can be attached to them but are not required; e.g., *child*). Those that must be attached to other parts in order to make sense are called *fixed* or *bound morphemes* or *affixes*. They include prefixes (e.g., un- in *unusual*), infixes (rare in English), and suffixes (e.g., -ish in *childish*).

Add two or more free morphemes together and you get compound words (e.g., *gingerbread* and *strawberry*). You could start by segmenting names, including yours. For example, ask children if they know anyone whose name contains a *Mac* and/or a *Ben,* as in *Ben-Gurion.* Then share how *Mac* means *child of . . .* in Scots, and *Ben* means *child of . . .* in Hebrew (Comrie, Matthews, & Polinsky, 2003). Similarly, the name *Gruberova* refers to Gruber's daughter, in Czech. When you share examples, children are more likely to want to explore their own language, and will quickly infer its structure and recognize that languages share features.

Morphemes vary in length from single phonemes (like plural -s in *cats*) to more than one sound. *Allomorphs* is the term for morpheme variants (e.g., *a* vs. *an* for singular indefinite nouns and the irregular plurality indicator -es, as in *dresses*, pronounced /əz/).[8] Most words longer than one syllable can be segmented. The road sign "oversize load" contains three morphemes:

over + size + load

1   2   3

"Softsoap elements" is divisible as follows:

Soft soap element s

Marzano (2010, p. 7) reports that children acquire mostly basic terms in PreK–2. In grades 3 to 5, they encounter the most "academic" (i.e., content) words, 2,398 to be exact. In his view, DLLs would benefit from instruction in both basic and content words and "all students" should benefit from "instruction in more advanced terms" (p. 7). To decode words, children need not only *phonemic awareness* (via phonology, as proposed earlier), but knowledge of word parts (i.e., morphemes/ morphology). Morphemes are vital language building blocks for vocabulary, content, and literacy enhancement. We must focus on the anatomy of words and teach children to (dis)assemble words—beyond letter sounds—early on. Children should be able to identify and add and subtract parts to decode words systematically, without having to memorize endless lists.

Vocabulary Instruction

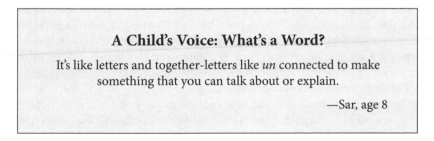

A Child's Voice: What's a Word?

It's like letters and together-letters like *un* connected to make something that you can talk about or explain.

—Sar, age 8

A strong vocabulary is essential for success in listening, reading, speaking, and writing. Vocabulary is the most important language unit in PreK–3, since words enable children to learn even more words and, through them, content—in English and other languages. In addition, words can communicate more than one meaning (in different contexts). Thus, they are powerful content capsules. Given the importance of vocabulary in PreK–3, the next four chapters emphasize task-based PreK–3 vocabulary instruction.

Children must know at least 3,000 words by the 3rd grade (Marzano, 2010), during which time children begin to get tested using state assessments. These tests typically emphasize math and reading—contingent upon phonemic awareness, vocabulary, and grammar. Therefore, offering purposeful and ongoing vocabulary instruction is key. Since different content areas are best learned through *content words*, ensure that children are continually learning and using new vocabulary. Such continuity is important both inside and outside the classroom and not merely during the time devoted to language arts.

There are many ways to teach vocabulary (Marzano, 2010). You could provide or elicit synonyms, illustrations, examples, verbal/written definitions, and roots and/or affixes, so that children can use these clues to decode (i.e., {de} + {code} = unlock) the meanings of words containing familiar parts. The most effective approach, as demonstrated, is the last-mentioned, which teaches children to segment words, morpheme-by-morpheme. Use the word lists in Marzano (2010) to create meaningful vocabulary-building exercises. By showing children how to break apart words, you'll be providing them with a new pair of eyes or reading glasses. This exploratory approach creates curious and independent learners who have fun guessing.

Examples

mono + lingua + ual (mono = 1 & bi = 2), lingua = language, and,
     in Greek, -ual refers to the quality of being
bio + graph + y

Derivation and *inflection* are the two most common word-creation processes. *Derivation* is the process through which one word class is derived from another. Take the word *derivation*.[9] It comes from the verb "derive." In short, it is the noun or nominalized form, created through the addition of the suffix -tion. *Inflection* refers to the process of adding stems to create words without a change in word class. Be sure to demonstrate how both processes work.

Children are never too young to learn how to decode words. Dissecting words is, in fact, one of the most exciting games you could have children play. Accompanied by visuals (e.g., pencil boxing of morphemes in books and worksheets, math manipulatives and dramatic play), this activity is bound to engage. Children will also learn to predict (i.e., probability, a key math skill) while constructing words. They will master math and meaning faster when you show them how to add and subtract word parts (e.g., un- in *unlock* and *untie*). Key concepts like opposites will also be easier to differentiate, including "either" and "neither" *(= no + either)*, which even 9-year-olds frequently misuse, un*less*, of course, a morpheme has a different meaning in another word! When my 7-year-old burst into tears after I told her that her smile was "priceless," for instance, I discovered that she interpreted "-*less*" negatively because the words with -*less* that she had encountered (e.g., use*less*) used it in a less-than manner. Sharing how languages like Hindi teach opposites faster using *paired morphemes* is also instructive.

Use activities that require children to segment words into smaller, meaning-ful (i.e., "full of meaning" versus "mean-ing-less") parts. Time them and offer incentives. You'll find that children learn more when they dissect words; they literally engage in discovery. Provide visuals and explanations, so children learn to partition words along mean-ing lines. Children who segment words are more likely to look for and de code letter–meaning patterns.

Sharing the (historical) roots of PreK–3 words (see Chapter 3) and the most frequently used stems (see White, Sowell, & Yanagihara, 1989) organized by word class, for instance, helps children quickly identify morphemes. According to White, Sowell, and Yanagihara, "With just four prefixes, un-, re-, in-, and dis-, one could cover approximately three-fifths of the prefixed words (58%)" (p. 303). They report that the first three prefixes account for 51% of prefixed words, while "three inflectional suffixes, -s/-es, -ed, and -ing, account for 65%" (p. 303). "In light of this," they continue, teachers "would do well to concentrate" on these three.

Example

The following vocabulary exercise (www.frog.com/catalog/samples/FP-050/10.jpg) might suggest that only compound words are segmentable into meaningful parts:

Which word is two little words?

A. Helper
B. Children
C. Football

Meaning wise, each is divisible into two smaller parts: help + -er; child + plural; foot + ball.

Morphemes Across Languages

All languages contain morphemes (e.g., *porque = por + que*; *porquoi = por + quoi* = for + why/*why* in Spanish and French, respectively). Core meanings are shared across languages. "Mama, *fire* and *light* are alike!" shouted my 8-year-old when her friends shared the Spanish and Russian words they used for "firefly" (luciérnaga and светляк/swεθliačo/, respectively, which draw on "light" where English uses "fire" or "lightning" [bug]). The kinds of meanings different languages convey and how they do so reveals much about users' culture or what they value. Many names in Dagaare, a Ghanaian language, for example, recognize and praise God and defy death.

Examples

*Mwini*diayeh = God has accepted
Deli*mwini* = lean on God
Angtuong*mwini* = Is there anyone stronger than God?

Note the morpheme *mwini* (God) in all three. While Dagaare appears relatively complex, packing a lot of information in a single word (like Swahili and many other African languages), its morphemes clarify meaning(s). When free and bound morphemes are presented as roots and stems, children have an easier time identifying them. Show them how roots can grow in both directions, left and right (e.g., un-friend-ly), while stems are added to just one side (e.g., root + s). You'll find that children enjoy segmenting words in storybooks. They are also more likely to create their own words (e.g., *mider*, which a 4-year-old proposed when asked for "a word like driver." "It's a Dr. Seuss word for a driver of babies!" she announced). With some help, even preschoolers should be able to play word lego (i.e., identify and circle roots and stems).

Note that morphemes are not the same as syllables. They sometimes coincide, as in many compound words, where each individual part is both a syllable and a morpheme (e.g., *pig tail*). Some words contain bisyllabic (i.e., two-syllable) morphemes. Responsible, for instance, would be segmented as follows: respons(e) + ible; the first meaningful part/morpheme contains two syllables. Also, just because a word contains easily identifiable parts that make sense on their own (e.g., the syllables *moth* and *er* in *mother*), does not mean that each part retains the same meaning as it does in isolation. The "moth" in "mother" differs from the noun *moth*. Some children will find such anomalies confusing. By getting children in the habit of segmenting words, you'll create memorable learning moments, so keep pencil in hand (and erase when you're done).

Even the names of several languages are segmentable and reveal much about the culture(s) that use them. In Bantu languages like Zulu, for instance, the prefix ki- means language. *Kiswahili* then refers to the Swahili language. The prefix wa-, when added to Swahili (i.e., *Waswahili*), refers to the people of the Swahili Coast. *Swahili* refers to the culture of the Swahili people. Similarly, *bhasa* in *Bhasa Indonesia* refers to language. Incidentally, *bhasa* is the Sanskrit, Hindi, Gujarati, Punjabi, and Urdu word for language. You can trace language relatedness through morphology. Morphemes could be pictorial, as well, as in the case of Chinese and children generally have an easier time learning these.

Using Morphology with Word Up™

Word Up™ is an author-created, vocabulary-building and sequencing game that emphasizes the math in words. It can be played using just English or a mix of languages. A form of "complex block play" (Reed, Hirsh-Pasek, & Golinkoff, 2012, p. 30) found to enhance math, it is ideal for advancing multiple skills, including math and vocabulary. To get started, you simply need 20 or more Lego or other blocks (plastic or wooden). Use blocks that vary in size and color to teach additional concepts and measures. Unifix cubes, math manipulatives that link on one side, are also usable. Affix strips of paper or blank mailing stickers on two or more sides, so children (or adults) can write on as many sides as are visible. It's best to place the blocks on a raised surface, such as a table, so that children can assemble and read words at eye level.

Now you are ready to draw or write word parts and math symbols on the blocks. Individually or with kids' help, write roots, common stems, and math symbols on the blocks. The children who play with these modified blocks should have as many parts to work with as possible. It's a good idea to leave some blocks blank. This will enable the children to fill them up with pictures, words, or affixes of their choosing (if they decide to), while getting some writing practice. Next, invite children to play with and (co-)assemble the blocks containing word parts and math symbols on them. Alternatively, invite children to write on their blocks after they have created things. They can then extend their creations using applicable suffixes (e.g., car + s – cars).

Watch what words and geometric shapes they construct. Invite them to create words using parts you provide or to extend words they have heard or seen. Try tailoring blocks to specific readings and/or themes. After reading *Snowy Day*, for instance, you could teach weather words, specifically winter words, and show PreK–1 children how *snow* = *snowy* minus (-y), or *snowing* minus (-ing), and so on. For older children, provide synonyms, such as "slush" and "sleet," and invite them to share words for snow(y) elements in other languages they know. A follow-up task could take the form of sets and (comparative) bar graphs. Not only will children come away with insightful language- and culture-specific terms for which English lacks equivalents, but they'll be doing math. Invite children to combine words or roots from one language with affixes from another, yielding code-mixed forms that bilinguals frequently use, such as "limpiaring" = *limpiar* (Spanish for "clean") + ing. This way, children also learn the meanings of similar-sounding words in English, such as "limp." Indeed, many English words sound like other words in several languages. Through this exercise, everyone will add to their vocabulary. You do the math!

Use Word Up™ to teach children counting, and sequencing, science, and other concepts and vocabulary. Devise focused Word Up™ tasks based on story-lines or science stages, such as the life cycle of a butterfly, growth (from seed to plant), and so on. An example follows:

$$E_1 g_2 g_3 \rightarrow c_1 a_2 t_3 e_4 r_5 p_6 i_7 l_8 l_9 a_{10} r_{11} \rightarrow \text{pupa} \rightarrow \text{butter} + \text{fly}$$

Children will get to play with cognitively and linguistically stimulating blocks, and have fun while (co)constructing words and more. They could paste pictures on some of the blocks or on sheets they can attach to a neighboring wall (with the blocks in front), adding visual props. Websites like www.kidsbutterfly.org/life-cycle provide instructional pictures. You also could use Word Up™ to teach *sequencing* in reading(s) and writing. Chronologically chart—on sheets you place on Word Up™ blocks—historical events like the Civil Rights Movement, timelines, works by artists, etc.

Invite children to first read, then segment word parts in (age-appropriate) books using pencil. From these and/or online resources, they could select the bare bones (i.e., segmented words) to build using Word Up™. Then they could add and subtract parts using math symbols. Book titles (e.g., *Mapping Penny's World*) could be fractioned as follows:

Mapp + ing + Penny + 's + World

Juice boxes, food containers, and cartons could be covered with paper and used in place of, or in addition to, blocks. Adding these to the mix will also yield blocks of varied sizes and shapes. Such variety will allow children to create more artistic spaces while practicing comparison and measurement words like *tall(er/est)*, *shorter, smaller*, and *long(-er/-est)*. Using Word Up™, four Head Start centers successfully taught roughly 120 young children to build and read words (some code mixed) in English and Spanish (Pandey, 2008).

Semantics

"Mama, how do you spell *meet*?" asked my 2nd-grader. "Not the meat that you eat. The meet when you meet together." Her provision of the context helped me determine which spelling to provide. Children respond best to language that makes sense. While it's a good idea to use simple (monosyllabic words) with PreK–3rd-graders, sometimes you have to use your judgment. Unlike "take away," for instance, the term "minus" fails to communicate the action involved. You are likely to find that PreK children respond more favorably to the former even though it's longer. Just because young children hear meaningful language and/or predominantly high-frequency words does not mean that they can't understand more complex language.

Children's ability to interpret language that is often more complex, linguistically and cognitively, than what they typically produce (i.e., age- or grade-wise) and/or hear evidences their sophisticated meaning-making or semantic skills and the fact that understanding precedes speech production, reading, and writing (see Chapters 7 and 9). Many young children, for instance, understand sarcastic language even though they might not have heard the word "sarcastic" or been introduced to sarcasm through example or instruction, reflecting sophisticated linguistic and cognitive skills. For example, when an 8-year-old observed, "Mama, I want to be like Tina—thin," and her mother responded in a serious tone in Urdu, "*Bus cookies aur mithai khate jao*" ("Just keep on eating cookies and sweets"), the child pouted and responded, "That's mean!" Indeed, language can be both a weapon and a harmony-infuser.

Words and sentences are sometimes misconstrued, particularly in the absence of cues. For instance, for homework, my 5-year-old had to circle rhyming words in a 1919 poem, "Indian Children," by Annette Wynne, and illustrate it. I read the poem out loud to ease understanding. When she exclaimed, "I don't want to be Indian anymore!" I asked her, "Why?" "Because it says they are like woods and they had no churches," she responded. "Where? Show me?" I prodded. "It just does!" she insisted. I found myself instinctively crossing out the word "Indian" and replacing it with "Native American." At that point, she burst into tears and said I had "ruined" her homework. In vain, I tried to explain why "Native American" was a better choice, yet suddenly realized my awkward position (I had inadvertently challenged her teacher).

How do young and impressionable minds process both stated and unstated meanings? This example is a perfect reminder of the power of language—of how words, sentences, and their organization (e.g., for comparison and contrast) communicate subtle or not-so-subtle messages. Even without analyzing the poem word-for-word, most would agree that semantics or meaning—the essence of language—is encoded in the different units, and that it is only by paying careful attention to each, and to their relative ordering, that we accurately interpret meaning(s). In short, like words, sentences are meaningful. Conditional sentences like, "Unless you . . . , then . . . ," for instance, impose conditions. In English, sentence-initial and sentence-final positioning contain the most important content. Therefore, language units, while separable size-wise (i.e., into phonemes, morphemes, etc.), work together to convey meaning. Systematic language analysis of the kind linguistics entails, therefore, is essential for PreK–3 teachers.

Idioms

"When my teacher told me to 'sit down' and 'sit up' at the same time, I was very scared and confusing [sic]," lamented a Bangladeshi participant at the 2008 All India Conference on Linguistics. Amelia Bedelia books instruct children on idioms and other ambiguous language units. They would learn, for instance, that idioms cannot be segmented word-for-word, and that many language units have more than one meaning.

Grammar and Syntax

Modern English has word-order restrictions. Some languages (e.g., Hindi) allow for scrambling (i.e., random ordering) of words, as was the case in Old English (see Chapter 3). You could teach young children grammar rules explicitly or indirectly (see Chapters 4 and 6). Math word problems, for instance, contain at least one verb (e.g., solve, draw, and round [to the nearest 10th]). For every math concept, you could identify corresponding nouns, and every math problem necessitates action/verbs. Similarly, recipes teach children the primary parts of speech, including nouns, verbs, adjectives, and prepositions (e.g., pour runny batter into 17- x 14-inch pan and bake at 350 degrees), as well as imperative sentences.

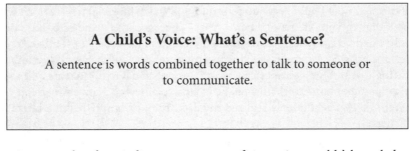

A Child's Voice: What's a Sentence?

A sentence is words combined together to talk to someone or to communicate.

An example of an indirect assessment of 4- to 6-year-olds' knowledge of nouns, verbs, and adjectives is the Denver Language Assessment used by many pediatricians.

A Child's Voice: Why Nouns and Verbs?

Nouns and verbs help communication. [They] tell you like what you're doing. Nouns fit in the biggest suitcase in the world. A verb is what a noun does.

Once again, as with interpersonal and literacy skills, a large vocabulary facilitates sentence construction. Sentences enable children to communicate novel ideas and to expand their vocabulary and knowledge faster than other language units. Using the word lists Marzano (2010) provides, create meaningful grammar activities, as children are expected to have mastered at least 3,000 words by

3rd grade, when children are tested. Not surprisingly, their math and reading are assessed—both facilitated by strong language, specifically phonemic awareness vocabulary and grammar skills.

Could knowledge of grammar facilitate vocabulary instruction and learning in PreK–3? This section will attempt to answer this question. Most of us are all too familiar with *grammar,* rules that yield complete, correct, and acceptable sentences. In linguistics, the subfield that examines sentence structure is *syntax.* At this level language-specific and universal rules (i.e., applicable to all languages) operate, as researched by theoretical linguists. In many ways, then, *grammar* and *syntax* are synonymous. Both emphasize the rule-governed nature of language; *grammar* through the distinctiveness of word functions, syntax through a focus on sentence ordering (e.g., subject-object-verb in Hindi vs. subject-verb-object in English).

For a while, and especially in the 1960s and 1970s, *parts of speech* were emphasized. Sanskrit grammarian Pāṇini deserves credit for identifying these functional word categories, the basis for grammar. Latin and Greek scholars quickly adopted them, identifying eight parts of speech (nouns, verbs, adverbs, adjectives, prepositions, conjunctions, determiners, and interjections). Since most of the words PreK–3 children learn are nouns (roughly 61%, as contrasted with 22% verbs, 11% adjectives, and 3% adverbs) (Marzano, 2010), it makes the most sense to focus on these using a functional approach (see Chapters 4 and 6).

When we introduce children to grammar (i.e., sentence-level word usage), we not only enrich their vocabulary, we also fine tune their phonemic skills. How so? When they can differentiate between "use" as a noun and as a verb, for instance, they have technically learned two words. In addition, since "use" belongs to different word classes (e.g., /jus/ vs. /juz/, respective noun and verb forms in speech), children learn to pronounce one-and-the-same-word differently, depending on *how it is used in a sentence.* Grammar-focused lessons could prompt them to pay closer attention to sound, sequence, and spelling. So whether we explicitly focus on grammar (i.e., use terms like "grammatically correct") or use an inductive approach to teach children grammar (without reference to "grammar"), we must be sure children understand the terms we use and the concepts they communicate (e.g., that words perform specific functions in sentences). "What's "grammatically?"" asked a 3rd-grader puzzled by the test question "Which word is *not* grammatically correct?" "My teacher never used that word!" When the question was rephrased (i.e., the term "grammatically" was eliminated), she promptly identified "runned" as the correct answer. This example suggests that grammar terms could, in fact, confuse young children, and that the words we use to assess learning must be familiar. By drawing children's attention to the building-blocks composition of sentences, we can systematically build their vocabulary and other requisite skills, yielding confident, creative, and critical communicators.

SUMMARY AND APPLICATIONS

Knowledge of phonetics, phonology, morphology, syntax, and semantics makes PreK–3 teachers more effective, as outlined here. Phonetics and phonology make letter–sound differences easier to explain to children than phonics-based approaches, which tend to offer endless spelling patterns. Teachers also must be able to explain sound-, word-, and sentence-level changes and differences (e.g., across language units and languages) so children correctly identify (i.e., hear, then read) and produce (in speech and writing) sounds, words, and meaningful sentences.

Recommendations:

Use phonemes to differentiate between letters and sounds.

Use phonetic spellings and a sound-based alphabet song to ease pronunciation, reading, and writing in PreK–3.

Engage children in identification, substitution (using minimal pairs and morphemes), and assembly of variable-size language units. Most children do so subconsciously (see Chapter 7), yet making them conscious of this knowledge is instructive, as language becomes their primary toolkit.

Invite children to play with language through language-focused activities. Children are more likely to enhance their vocabulary and grammatical awareness, and to use language creatively when they observe and analyze, and then segment it in a lockstep manner.

Carefully evaluate and/or pilot test resources to minimize bias. Be especially attentive to language. Use a checklist.

Integrate language units from other languages, so children develop a keen interest in language (diversity) and discovery and "learn to learn" and "make sense of their experience" (Darling-Hammond, 2012).

With knowledge of phonology, morphology, grammar, and semantics, early childhood educators can build core skills from the ground up and offer children logical explanations, as they explore their world through language(s).

CHAPTER 3

Literacy and Multiskills Enhancement Through the History of English

"My goodness! My gracious!" They shouted "My WORD!"
"It's something brand new! It's AN ELEPHANT-BIRD!!"

—Dr. Seuss, *Horton Hatches the Egg*

English is weird. "Pearl" should be spelled P-U-R-L, like "curl"!

—Sarika, age 7

"Mama" is from Sandscript [Sanskrit].

—Sahara, age 5

Have you ever wondered why so many stories in English open with "Once upon a time"? When was the last time you opened a conversation this way? This idiomatic expression was the English translation of the opening line of popular fairy tales and fables from German ("*Es war einmal*," Brothers Grimm), French ("*Il était une fois*," e.g., Charles Perrault), and Danish ("*Der var engage*," Hans Andersen). It dates back to the 1380s (Madden, 2006). By the 1600s, when the oral storytelling tradition was alive and well in England, it became the standard opening line. Its continued use in children's stories prompts us to ask why some archaic PreK–3 English expressions have survived. Knowing where specific English sounds, letters, words, and sentences came from could make vocabulary, reading, and writing easier for young children, as demonstrated in this chapter. This knowledge will also make early English literature (e.g., Edward Lear's poetry) more meaningful and enjoyable

Third-grade readings like "The Problem Princess" (Sneller, 2001) date back to the 16th century and would make more sense to children if we provided relevant linguistic (i.e., historical) information about the arrival of Christianity and Latin words in England. This way, children could decode such words as "angered," "buried," "church," "Catholic," "tombs," "beheaded," "religion," "plots," "plotting," "powers," "prisoner," "Protestant," "scared," "spells," "feared," and "witch" relatively easily. Unusual idiomatic expressions like "raise an army" and "bring about peace," and sentences like "She could even order to have Elizabeth put to death," would be easier if the words used were introduced in their proper historical and cultural-geographical (i.e., war-, religious belief-, and superstition-based) context. So would complex sentences that mirror the marriage of statehood and Christianity (e.g., "She was afraid that the English would not come back to the Catholic church.")

As children explore the lands to which English has traveled, and the diverse cultures and languages that have flavored it along the way, they will learn many more words, discern learnable patterns in sounds and spellings, and expand their knowledge of geography, social studies, and science.

Indeed, English is an international language, the first of its kind. In the course of its worldwide travels, it has added much to its long lineage. The goal of this chapter is to give you a flavor of this nomadic language at different time periods, including the role reading and writing have played, and to demonstrate the PreK–3 instructional value of its history.

WHY EXPLORE LANGUAGE HISTORY?

To many, English is Greek to the ear and the eye. Through the years, most of us have learned not to be misled by English spellings. Yet, can we blame new readers for reading and writing the way that they speak? Research shows that English readers lag behind readers of most other languages (Fortson, 2004; McGuinness, 2004). Reading scores for DLLs point at even greater discrepancies. August and colleagues (2009) report that only 7% of DLLs in 4th grade scored at or above the proficient level on the National Assessment of Educational Progress in 2007, as contrasted with 36% of monolingual English speakers. That English spelling is nonphonetic and, therefore, tricky has much to do with the difficulty many DLLs experience reading and writing English. As discussed earlier, many English letters sound nothing like we might expect, and, to add to the confusion, the sounds some letters make change in different environments. For example, 'c' is /k/ in "cat" and "brick," but /s/ in "ice" and "excite," /ch/ in "rich" and "champion," and /sh/ in "champaign." Such inconsistency makes English particularly challenging. How is a child to deduce the correct sounds and spellings? Knowing a bit of its history could help children spell.

Imagine if you didn't know your history. You'd be clueless about your identity. The multiple benefits of language history for core competencies in PreK–3 and beyond cannot be overemphasized. Learning about the changes English has undergone is of immense value to teachers and children alike. Not only do we develop a better appreciation for language and cultural diversity, globalization, and language contact—given the many languages that have fed into English—but we are in a better position to help all children, including DLLs, master English. Comparing English sounds, words, and other language units from different time periods enhances our understanding of English (and other languages) and helps us provide more satisfactory answers to children's spelling and other language-related questions.

Words and grammar are also most meaningful in their proper (i.e., historically storied) context. When teachers weave in interesting aspects of language history to explain the many exceptions to the rule, children are more likely to master unusual pronunciations, spellings, idioms, grammar, and discourse features. Since children respond best to hands-on instruction, they're more likely to learn the nuances of English when they explore its history. Moreover, the story of English is action-packed; it's bound to interest children and to help them become better spellers, readers, and writers. When we share this fascinating story with children, we also provide them with a firm language-literacy foundation. Knowing the history of English helps us contextualize (language) instruction, as we understand the reasons for its peculiarities.

ENGLISH AS AN INTERNATIONAL LANGUAGE

Did you know that most English words for family members came from Sanskrit, the oldest written language? "Sugar" and "candy" are from Hindi,[1] and kid from Scandinavian languages. "School" and "paper" came from Latin, another descendant (like most European languages), and "cookie" and "dollar" from Dutch. "Son" is Swedish, so now you know that Anderson[2] means Ander's son! Children might be interested in knowing that "chocolate" came from Nahuatl, the language of the Aztecs,[3] through Spanish, and "banana," "bug," "monkey," and "okay" from African languages. "Cent" and "dime" are originally French, as are most English words for social conduct, including "art," "theater," "etiquette," and "manners" (the PreK–3 synonym). English also adopted over 500 words from Spanish, including "cafeteria," "guitar," "tornado," and "vanilla" (Comrie, Matthews, & Polinsky, 2003).

"If you speak English, you know at least a bit of a hundred languages. Or more," observes Metcalf (1999, p. ix). English has borrowed from several languages, accounting for its complexity, as demonstrated in this chapter. It's composed of so many that even if we were to take out just the non-British words and sentences, there'd be no English left (Ehrlich, 2000; Pyles & Algeo, 1993). To borrow a term from billiards, other languages have "put some English" on the rolling and expanding rubberband ball we call English. Borrowed words and the widespread use of English worldwide explain why it has the largest vocabulary of any language (Crystal, 1997). Roughly 45% of English words came directly from Sanskrit and its Germanic descendants (German, Danish, Dutch, Norse, and Celtic languages) and another 45% from Latin, Greek, and French (around 23%). Roughly 1% came from Arabic, which, in turn, borrowed many terms from Spanish; 2% directly from Spanish, 2% from indigenous languages, and 5% from other languages, depending on the dialect in question. Not knowing exactly what was borrowed from which language poses a problem, unless we share the history.

A CONCISE HISTORY OF ENGLISH SPELLING

Four major periods of language history are identifiable, namely: Old English (OE, prior to 1100), Middle English (ME, from roughly 1100 through the Renaissance of 1500–1650 to 1800), Early Modern English (EME, the 19th century), and present-day English (PDE). English has changed so much since the OE period that most mistake OE for a "foreign" language.

Children might be just as surprised to learn that in OE word order was flexible (i.e., not the subject-verb-object sequence of today), and that several OE words had suffixes no longer used and some words had different meanings. For instance, "nice" originally meant "not nice." Given its Germanic roots, OE sounded like German and/or Danish. "Good," for instance, was pronounced with a long /u/, as in German. Now you know why it's spelled this way! Each letter corresponded to a single sound: 'A' was Æ/æ (termed *ash*) and written exactly as it sounded (e.g., "Ælfred"). So was the /ð/ in ðat (i.e., *that*). Modern English has retained the /ð/ sound in words like "the" and "that," but not the phonetic spelling, making English harder to read today. OE words like "girl" (from Anglo-Saxon *gyrl* where 'y' was pronounced like short 'i') could help children understand why 'y' is a fish*y* letter (i.e., pronounced like /i/ here and /ai/ in *sky*)!

While English pronunciation has changed so much as to make OE harder to understand today than Spanish, the spelling has remained virtually unchanged, accounting for reading and writing difficulties. With the exception of a handful of letters (C, F, H, J, Q, V, and W), our capital letters date back to the 14th century and come from the Greek alphabet (i.e., A for alpha, B for beta, D for delta) through the Roman church (Schmitt & Marsden, 2006). The Romans added C and Q, as variants of 'K,' so now you can understand why most words with 'c' and with 'q' sound like /k/. The word "capitals" comes from Latin *caput* (head). Lowercase letters were used subsequently because they were easier to write and took up less space.

English spelling was not considered problematic in the OE and for much of the ME periods because English was primarily a spoken language used by the non-elite, much like pidgins and Creoles are today (Pandey, 2005). In OE, for instance, since words were spelled like they were pronounced, varied spellings were common. *Merry*, for instance, was spelled at least five different ways in OE. Some 20 spellings of this word were recorded in ME, at the same time that Norman scribes"[4] introduced "new spelling conventions" (Schmitt & Marsden, 2006, p. 159).

Concerns about English spelling are not new. They were rampant in the time of Shakespeare and in the 17th and 18th centuries. Yet it wasn't until the 18th century that the spellings we use today came about. Reasons spelling rules suddenly appeared in this period include the growing importance of the Royal Chancery, an administrative department that sent documents all over England; the birth and growing importance of the printing press in and the political clout of London and the residents of south London. The proximity and role of the University of London and other private schools, and the publication of dictionaries, helped raise the status of English, which had been competing with the more esteemed French and Latin. These and other factors prompted English standardization, yielding spelling conventions enforced even today. Not surprisingly, since London was home to William Caxton's printing press, the London dialect of English, Received Pronunciation (RP), became the standard language in print and speech (i.e., standard British English).

By 1870, inconsistencies in English spelling were questioned by the English Philological Society and widely debated in *Transactions* (a journal) and newspapers like the *Academy*. Even Americans got interested and, in 1883, a list of new spellings was jointly approved by both countries. Spelling reform associations subsequently were formed. In 1898, 12 simplified spellings were adopted by the National Education Association (*tho, altho, thru, thruout, thoro, thorofare, program, catalog, prolog, decalog, demagog,* and *pedagog*). A Simplified Spelling Board appeared in 1906, with the support of President Roosevelt. It published a list of 300 simplified spellings (e.g., the slightly condensed *judgment* for *judgement*). However, the Board, and its publication, *Spelling,* disbanded in the 1930s. Since then, spelling reform efforts have been virtually nonexistent. Most have come to accept that written English must be consistent. Yet pronunciation has continued to change, making English confusing.

The emergence of American English as a recognized brand of English and of American spellings (e.g., *color*) represented a major breakthrough. The largest and most obvious changes to American spelling appeared with Webster's *Dictionary of American English*. It helped standardize American English (e.g., *aluminum* versus *aluminium)*. Some of Webster's spellings were also adopted in Britain (e.g., *music,* from French *musique,* replaced *musick*).

IS OLD ENGLISH A "FOREIGN" LANGUAGE?

Some of us might be surprised to know that English predates England by many years, and that Celtic languages and Latin were spoken extensively on the island for some 400 years before the birth of what we now call English. So English was once a "foreign" language in the geographical region that eventually became its home. Immigrants to the area called England brought it with them.

English most likely started in the Indian subcontinent, home of Indo-European languages—the largest family of languages. Sanskrit is the oldest recorded Indo-European language,[5] others being Latin, Greek, and German. By the

5th century B.C., the Indian linguist Pāṇini[6] had identified word roots, parts of speech, and other language components and rules—long before Latin and Greek grammarians and other scholars (Cardona, 1999). His research clarified the relationship of Sanskrit, the mother language, to related languages in both vocabulary and grammar. In fact, the earliest written records are in Sanskrit, making for a long and rich Eastern writing tradition that deserves mention. Some, like the Puranas (i.e., translated literally, "the Oldies" or "Ancient Wisdom"), the Upanishads, and the Vedas are from 3000 B.C.

The Indian Influence

Sanskrit loanwords in English include almost all the words for family (e.g., *ma(ma)/mother* from *mata*, *father/pa(pa)* from *pita*), reflecting a communal culture, and many others, including what we term "Arabic" numbers 0 to 10 (Burnett, 2002), *nam* (i.e., *name*), and *nama* for *named*—emphasizing identity, belonging, and kinship. While some, like "jungle," have retained their original sounds, many have been Anglicized (e.g., *Cashmere* versus *Kashmir(i)*, *eight* vs. /ath/, and *sabun* (soap) vs. *savon* and *jabón*, in French and Spanish, respectively).

Traveling from Indian through Europe, most notably Germany and the Danish Peninsula, English entered the area now known as England in the form of Gaelic, Cornish, Gothic, and other minority languages (much like Spanish, Korean, and Thai in the United States) that Celt immigrants brought with them before the arrival of the Vikings.[7] While little is known about the original inhabitants of this island, some believe the Basques (currently in southern Spain) were part of "this non-Indo-European culture."[8] The Romanization of the island followed, starting with an invasion by Julius Caesar in the summer of 55 B.C., and followed by that of Emperor Claudius (in 43 A.D.), planting the numerous Latin roots we see in English.

Danish, German, and Scandinavian Influences

Around 449, Indo-European "Germanic tribes" from Denmark and the Low Countries invaded Britain (Baugh & Cable, 1993), starting with the south and east and gradually moving north and west, except for the highlands. These groups are described by Bede in his *Ecclesiastical History of English* as the Jutes, Saxons, and Angles. The Angles apparently held the most power. Hence, the terms *Angli* and *Anglia* appeared in major place names and Latin texts (Baugh & Cable, 1993). The Germanic settlers apparently referred to their language as *Englisc*. *Engl* is very likely how they pronounced *Angle*, and *sc* was pronounced /sh/. The suffix -ish designated groups (e.g., *Dan-ish*, *Spanish*, *Finn-ish*, and *selfish*).

At that time, *Englisc* was the "vernacular" (Baugh & Cable, 1993, p. 49), the stigmatized speech of the working class, much like Black English Vernacular

(BEV) is in America today (Pandey, 2000).[9] The land and the people were referred to in OE as *Angelcynn* (i.e., kin of the Angles), and it was only around the year 1000 that *Englaland* (land of the Angles/England) was used. 'C' was pronounced as 'k' (e.g., *bæc* was *back*) and 'y' as short 'i,' as it still is. 'S' + 'c' (i.e., 'sk') was pronounced 'sh'[10] as in *scip* (ship) and *scyrte* (shirt). We can, therefore, distinguish between native (Indo-European) 'sh' words (like *shall* and *fish*) and words with 'k' and 'sc' that were borrowed from Scandinavian languages (e.g., *sky*, *skin*, and *scared*). Interestingly, *kin* was written the way it was pronounced, namely, "cynn" (i.e., "kin," a "sight" word). 'K' was not used in written OE, which might explain why 'c' represents both /k/ and /s/.

Knowing how influential Danish and German were at the time helps to explain why OE sounds a lot like these languages. English pronouns "she," "her," "they," "their," "him," "them," and the demonstratives "both" and "same," as well as almost all prepositions, are Scandinavian (mostly Danish) in origin. They include *till*, *fro(m)*, *at* (frequently used in the word *ado* in Shakespeare's time = at-do), "to" (also used in the surviving form *to and fro*), and "though" (from Old Norse). The verb *to be* and the hard-to-explain plural form *are* also came from Danish, alongside the adverbs *ever* and *seem*. Many of these Scandinavian words appear in the literature from that time (e.g., Chaucer's *Book of the Duchess*). "Lego" is also from Danish; *leg godt* means "play well" (Metcalf, 1999). This information helps solve part of our spelling puzzle. To this day, over 600 Danish place names are still in use in England and the United States (i.e., settlements). Many, like *Shelby*, *Derby*, and *Rugby*, end in -*by*, the Danish word for farm or town.

"Kindergarten" (i.e., a children's garden), spelled the German way, was borrowed from German. A teacher, Friedrich W. A. Froebel, first used it in 1840 (Metcalf, 1999). He believed children are like plants; they need water and tender care (i.e., fun and love) to flourish.

OE and ME differed in pronunciation and spelling; OE was written phonetically (e.g., "God," "we," "foot," "come," "hi:e" for "he," "aye" for "eye," "fisc" for "fish," "nay" for "no," "scip" for "ship," "to," benc" for "bench," "fyr" for what we now call "fire," and "wi:f" for "wife"). This is the case with many writing systems, and precisely why we consider writing an extension of speech (i.e., secondary literacy), and why we recommend language-rich environments for young children.

In OE, as in Sanskrit, new words were created by adding word parts, a process termed *derivation*, *extension*, and *compounding*. For example, "ear" + "hing" = "earhing"/earring, and "fisc + deag" = "fishdye," which is what the color purple was called because of how it was derived. The prefix with- (spelled *wiđ*) yielded up to 50 OE verbs. Of these, "*withstand* is the only one in use today, although in ME two new verbs, *withdraw* and *withhold*, were formed on the same model" (Baugh & Cable, 1993, p. 65). Our suffixes -dom (e.g., *kingdom*, which was pronounced and written in OE as "cyningdom"), -full (e.g., restfull), -scipe (pronounced *ship* as in "freondscipe" [i.e., friendship]), -some (spelled *sum*, e.g., *wynsum/winsome*, as well as *lonesome*), and -ness (e.g., *kindness, goodness*) have roots in OE. We can now understand how we came to use compounding (e.g., *laptop, freedom*[11]) and other forms of word extension to expand our vocabulary.

The 15% of OE vocabulary that survived continues to play a critical role today (Baugh & Cable, 1993). Take the word "Easter," for instance, borrowed from a Germanic festival. The value of "kinship" is reflected in the frequency of the OE term *kin* (i.e., "cynn"). OE vocabulary mirrored the communal culture of the times, one in which family, community, land (e.g., *plow* was *land*), and sustenance (e.g., terms for food, flora, and fauna, like *bloom* for *flower*, and words for war and survival) were important. Interestingly, "cynn" is the root in "cyningdom" (kingdom) and even in "cyning" (king), suggesting that kings were highly regarded—literally heads of the family/clan and that one's "cyningdom" was like one's extended family. The word "folc" (i.e., folk) also emphasized community and kinship (e.g., "cynnfolc" or kinfolk).

Interesting facts and lessons from OE include:

1. English was not always as challenging as it is today.
2. Many languages contributed to English, especially in the early stages. Like American English, English is an immigrant language—a granola bar of borrowed tongues. This information should increase children's interest in and respect for other languages, fostering language tolerance, mutual understanding, and cultural exchange.
3. Familiarizing children with the distinctive sounds, morphemes, and other features of the languages that have fed into English could help beginning and challenged readers, as the next section illustrates.
4. Knowledge of the history of English also helps children appreciate literature from the OE and ME periods and reminds us that no single group can lay claim to English; English belongs to *everyone*.

Classroom Applications of Old(er) English

Researching words and word parts from OE and later periods through a scavenger hunt of sorts, and borrowings from children's heritage languages, would make for an exciting cross-age and community project on language and culture. Social studies and language arts lessons could integrate segments of the story of English, battles won and languages and dialects that influenced today's English. You could draw on OE even in 2nd- and 3rd-grade math lessons. For instance, the fact that 85% of OE vocabulary was lost makes for an interesting 3rd-grade math problem. Children could identify Scandinavian, French, and Latin roots (i.e., word parts) in PreK–3 English words. Teach them to use basic addition and subtraction with word parts instead of numbers alone (e.g., *kind + heart + -ed + -ness = kindheartedness*). Numbers could be placed at the bottom of letters or word parts to strengthen math skills (e.g., $kind_1$ + $heart_2$ + $-ed_3$ + $-ness_4$ = $kindheartedness_5$). Invite children to propose words with similar endings. They will learn language and math at the same time. Use Word Up™, the whole-child game recommended earlier, to build words from different periods. Invite 3rd-graders to identify spelling differences between words in American and British English—enhancing dialect awareness, math, social studies, and spelling.

Explore the origins of well-known English nursery rhymes. "Ring Around the Ros(i)es," some argue, references the Bubonic Plague that killed most of the working class between 1349 and 1350. Invite children (and families) to research and share their families' stories. The outcome would be fruitful partnerships between the school and community.

THE GROWTH OF MIDDLE ENGLISH

Unlike OE with its distinctly Germanic flavor and opaque vocabulary, over 50% of ME words are from Latin and French. Some of our words, such as "consist" and "explore," could have come from either Latin or French.

Latin Words in English

Latin arrived with Christianity in the 7th century. This was followed by active church building and other missionary influences. At least 450 Latin and Latin-based words appeared in print in the later part of the Old English period. Examples include "altar," "angel," "ark," "candle," "mass," "temple," "hymn," "noon," "offer," "organ," "psalm," "palm," "pagan" (used for non-Christians), and "rule." The church also had a major impact on education, clothing, and food (cultural mirrors), as evidenced by the many other Latinate words that entered English. Examples include "box," "collect," "grammar" (i.e., rule-bound), "mat," "cap," "sock," "lily," "pine," "marshmallow," "pear," and "verse." Many have reproduced. The word "plant," for instance, started as the Latin noun *planta*. Shortly after that, the verb form (i.e., to plant) was formed with the addition of the suffix -ain (*plantain*).[12] "Planting" and "planted" soon sprouted. Many more Latin words entered English during the ME period, which explains why Latin terms make up a sizeable portion of grades 4–12 vocabulary.

Helping Children Learn Latin Words Using Spanish

Have you ever wondered why Spanish is considered a *Latin language*? Spanish is heavily Latin-based, if not the closest survivor. Strong similarities between Latin and Spanish suggest that, with proper instruction, children who know some Spanish and/or related languages (e.g., Italian, Portuguese) are likely to master vocabulary faster. They already know many Latin-based English words, so use of such languages could help all children learn key (mostly science) vocabulary. Indeed, integrating language history and vocabulary from other languages could make all the difference. Familiarity with and interest in other languages children know could help us accurately identify their base vocabulary and systematically enhance instruction. Using your knowledge of language history, develop each child's vocabulary, for instance, by emphasizing shared roots, thereby easing vocabulary acquisition for many DLLs and their peers.

Many Spanish words, including *alto* (loud), *carbón* (coal), *facile* (easy), and *significa* (mean), could even ease English-speaking children's mastery of polysyllabic words with these roots (e.g., *altitude, carbonize, carbonate, facilitate*, and *significant/ce, signification*). The Spanish word *isla* (pronounced /isla/), for instance, helps explain why *island* (from Latin) has an 's' (which was silenced when it replaced OE *igland)*. With a peer or child, leaf through a Romance language dictionary and identify additional Latin roots and stems in English. Early exposure to Latinate languages and guided exchanges with children familiar with them could jumpstart PreK–3 science vocabulary and more (even if the English equivalents are infrequent in PreK–3).

Predominantly English-speaking children stand to gain just as much as DLLs. Drawing children's attention to *other-language roots* in science and multicontent English words makes vocabulary acquisition more meaningful. Latin, Spanish, and French *fin* (end, last), for instance, is the root of English "finish," "finale," and "finalize." [The fin on a fish is from OE *finn* → from Old Norse *finn* → German/Swedish *finne*.] *Crudo*, the Spanish word for raw, shares the same root as the science term "crude" (i.e., unprocessed). Through language history and an awareness of the components of language, PreK–3 children (e.g., DLLs) can learn even complex words usually taught in later grades (see Chapter 9). *(La) fabrica*, the Spanish word for *factory* and *manufacture* is an example. It's an easy bridge to "fabric," "fabricate," and "manufacture."

French Words in English

English contains many French words and expressions. Over 10,000 French words entered English after the Norman Conquest of 1066 (Baugh & Cable, 1993). They include words for food (e.g., *baguette, croissant, gourmet, hors d'ouevres*); social order and timekeeping, such as *administration, ticket, chair, religion*, and *calendar*; social etiquette and fashion (e.g., *bouquet, color, petit*, and *music*); and many more. Some are nouns (*square, sum, river, ocean*); others are verbs (e.g., *arrange, chase, cry*, and *obey*), many reflecting rules for social conduct; and descriptors (*easy, practical*, and *pleasing*). The words "scent," "park," "squirrel," and "forest" were associated with the favorite "outdoor pastime of the nobility" (Baugh & Cable, 1993, p. 168). During this period, Italian was used by the French elite, opening the doors of English to Italian fashion (e.g., words like *balcony, design*, and *violin*). Longer French borrowings include *je ne sais quoi*, and *s'il vous plait* vs. plain "please" *(as in RSVP—deemed more formal and inviting)*.

At the start of the ME period, English was still the language of "the lower classes" (Baugh & Cable, 1993, p. 159). In contrast, for many years after the Norman Conquest, French was considered "the language of the educated and prominent" (p. 149). French was, therefore, the language of schooling, as was Latin. The few who could write knew Latin and were members of the upper class. They tended to use Latin out of habit, because of its "international character" (p. 149), and because it was relatively stable, unlike English, which was constantly changing. Similarly, the bulk of the literature until the mid-12th century was in French, as it was hard to sell materials in English. Much of the English literature prior to the 13th century, some of it ballads, was orally communicated and subsequently lost. This historical information, when shared with students, could help emphasize the value of both oral storytelling and writing.

The Hundred Years' War between France and Britain (1337 to 1453) generated in residents of England feelings of linguistic and other pride/patriotism (Baugh & Cable, 1993). However, what changed the fortune of English was the "Black Death," the Bubonic Plague of the mid-14th century. Most of the laboring class died, so an acute shortage of labor ensued, increasing "the economic importance of the laboring class and . . . the language they spoke" (Baugh & Cable, 1993, p. 139). By the 15th century, English was able to compete with Latin and French, once writers began to sell religious codes of conduct—in English—to the socioeconomically disadvantaged. This prompted well-known literary works by Chaucer (1340–1400) and others, raising the value of English. Changes to English were most obvious in this period.

Helping Children Master the French in English

Children identify and recall spellings and words relatively easily when we share interesting and meaningful tidbits about the words. For instance, telling children that the /ʒ/ sound in words written with 's,' like "treasure" and "measure," is French could help them identify similar words. When 'ch' is pronounced /sh/, the word is French, as in "chef" (Metcalf, 1999). When children see an accent on a vowel (e.g., chéf, French-style), they will know to pronounce the /sh/ and /e/ the French way. This might be a good time to share how accent marks function in Spanish (and perhaps even Portuguese).

Linguistics and knowledge of language history increase spelling efficiency and decoding (i.e., reading) in PreK–3. When you tell children, for instance, that *ville* is French for town (and the 'll' is silent in the non-Anglicized version), they have an easier time understanding why U.S. cities like Jacksonville contain this morpheme. Add the pronunciations for French names like *Louis* (where the final 's' is silent in French, as is typical for most final consonants and even some initial ones, as in *hotel*), and children get excited about identifying U.S. and Canadian locations (e.g., Louisiana, Louisville) settled by the French.

PRESENT-DAY ENGLISH

Today, English is like bottled water, consumed everywhere and flavored with lo-calisms. Educators should be interested in PDE and the future of English to pre-vent misconceptions regarding language proficiency and ownership. Given the frequency of accent discrimination (e.g., Indian and Spanish accents are typi-cally frowned upon while a French accent is usually admired), it's important to remember that accents could be deceptive. They could, for instance, mask the fact that many "second language learners" of English have a larger vocabulary than so-called "native speakers." Second, in our global world, increased contact between English and other languages has led to *Englishization*, as well as to two-way lan-guage exchanges.

English has continued to borrow from other languages—not just European languages. For instance, the all-American "ketchup" comes from Malay, through Chinese *kejap*, fish sauce (Ehrlich, 2000, p. 127). Much of the borrowing occurs as English is embraced by speakers of these other languages—giving it a truly inter-national flavor.

An adaptation of the *three circles of English* that linguist Braj Kachru identified (jalt-publications.org/old_tlt/files/96/oct/englishes.html) is in order, since tech-nology (e.g., through outsourcing) has given birth to a fourth circle, *hybrid English* (Pandey, 2010). Be sure to familiarize children with world Englishes (see Kachru & Smith, 2008) like Indian English (widely employed in this age of outsourcing), Nigerian English (increasingly important given energy needs and Nigeria's crude oil), and Caribbean English (helpful in tracing the roots of English-, Spanish-, and French-based languages, and in understanding Afro-Latin literature). Even a handful of heartwarming expressions could make a world of difference in chil-dren's lives and would give them a competitive edge in the future.

ADDITIONAL CLASSROOM APPLICATIONS

Use visuals to show children how English is quilted from multiple languages. Share and elicit examples of borrowed words. This is an excellent way to engage and in-clude all children, and affirm cultural pride, while helping them learn and become more linguistically aware.

Etymology is a valuable literacy prod. When, for instance, we consider the fact that some 1,150 English words begin with the Scandinavian 'sc' (i.e., /sk/), the role of other languages in English becomes starkly visible. In pairs or groups, invite children to list borrowed words and use them in sentences and stories—to help them to recall meanings and spellings. In addition, identify the Indian subcontinent, Scandinavian countries, and other countries on a map; discuss the nature and functions of early math (e.g., barter trading and cowries); and track climate change (through words) and migration (i.e., linguistically).

Invite children to categorize loanwords by function and to research additional examples (see Ehrlich, 2000). Familiarize children with common word-building processes—a fun way to teach the history of English and expand their vocabulary. Examples include *compounding, coinages* (e.g., *lego, zipper*), acronyms (e.g., IM), *trimming* (e.g., *tech* for technology, *zoo* for zoological garden), *extensions* (e.g., the tech web), and *sound change* (e.g., the /a/ and /o/ sounds in the French word for grape, *raisin* [pronounced /razon/], which became /ei/ and /i/, respectively [i.e., /razon/→/reizin/], explaining why we pronounce this French word differently).

Knowledge of these and other morphological processes should prompt children to pay closer attention to the words they encounter. Rather than providing them with PreK–3 words in these categories—where minimal learner involvement is required—elicit examples. Active child involvement is likely to yield more positive results. Invite children to study the vocabulary used in formal (e.g., wedding and recital) invitations. Do they contain more French- (e.g., *hors d'oeuvres, cocktails* vs. *snacks*) and Latin-based words, for instance? Ask them to explain the word choice.

The history of English gives children a lot to talk and write about. Children could enact the rags-to-riches story of English (or segments of the story) or stories of specific words, nursery rhymes, and/or spellings through performances reminiscent of Shakespearean theater. From Japanese *Bunrake* to Hopi ceremonial puppet theater to Russian puppetry and age-old Javanese *Wayang Golek* (Bauer, 1997; Buurman, 1988), theater has delighted children and adults the world over and developed their language, art, and more (Ewart, 1998). Invite children to co-author the dialog, create electronic or visual representations (Cary, 2004), rehearse, and even design and construct their own theater with blocks, cartons, fabric, and other materials. The instructional value of creative drama (Furrman, 2000; Hui & Lau, 2006) makes dramatization advisable.

SUMMARY AND APPLICATIONS

This chapter explained why English spelling doesn't resemble speech and reviewed the distinctive sounds, vocabulary, and structure of English in different time periods. Of what use is the history of English in the PreK–3 classroom? First, it could ease vocabulary and spelling. As you assign and review vocabulary, remind children that the spellings predate the pronunciations (hence the difficulty). Knowledge of history also enhances children's phonemic awareness.

With the massive borrowing and sound changes English has undergone, mastering it could be quite challenging, making it necessary for us to trace its roots and equip children with handy language-identification and analysis strategies. Indeed, language history is the key through which we can more effectively decode the English of the past and the present. For these and other reasons, familiarity with the English used in different time periods and locations is essential (see also Chapter 5).

As it stands, few teacher-training programs require linguistics, and survey courses rarely cover the history of English. All language educators would benefit from linguistics and language history, which could easily be integrated into reading courses and professional development. Exploring and sharing the history of PreK–3 words, spellings, and sentences, and inviting children and families to join in, is an excellent way to instill in each of us a sense of cultural pride, while highlighting the impact of cross-cultural contact. Such inclusive and linguistically diverse partnerships also make early learning more meaningful.

As illustrated, its multilingual ingredients have spiced up English and made it an international language—the first to acquire so many speakers worldwide. Through the action-packed history of this unique language, we could begin to realize our indebtedness to undervalued, endangered, and lost languages and cultures (e.g., Taino) that have contributed to English. Like an enormous tidal wave, English continues to pull from multiple sources, constantly changing direction and form as it attempts to cover new ground. Inviting children to predict future influences should be just as exciting.

CHAPTER 4

Language as $M_1A_2T_3H_4$ and Science

When Adding + Subtracting Words = Success

And will you succeed?
Yes! You will indeed!
98 and 3/4 percent guaranteed

—Dr. Seuss, *Oh! The Places You'll Go!*

If you take hands as place values, the highest number Americans can show on two hands is 55; the Chinese could flash a full 100.

—Hobson, *The Year I Smelled Like Milk*

U.S.-based children lag behind their peers in China, India, and many other nations in math and science. In one study, the U.S. "came in 48th out of 133 nations in . . . math and science" (Aud et al., 2010).[1] We must do a better job of preparing children in these areas as well. This chapter illustrates the math in language and offers language strategies to ease PreK–3 math mastery.

Both language and math are foundation skills. "Mathematics is a language," observed mathematician J. W. Gibbs. Similarly, language is mathematical, as illustrated earlier. Math uses universally understood symbols. While language is both an art (e.g., language-specific meanings) and a science, a fixed number of rules explain its forms and functions. Linguistics emphasizes the universal properties of language. Research shows that more PreK–3 teachers are using literature to make math more meaningful (Shatzer, 2008). However, despite its popularity, Nesmith and Cooper (2010) report significant differences in professionals' evaluations of recommended PreK–3 math-focused literature.[2] Their findings suggest that teaching PreK–3 math through literature raises more questions than test scores. For this and other reasons, this chapter proposes enhancing children's math skills by drawing on languages[3] in which math concepts are more intuitively mathematical in representation and using (comput + able) language units to teach math.

MATH IN DIFFERENT LANGUAGES

From the sounds, meanings, and visual representations of numbers to the words for basic math concepts and symbols, and the sentences and discourse used in PreK–3 math lessons the world over, noteworthy differences exist. These necessitate mention in a book aimed at illustrating the value of adding, subtracting, multiplying, and dividing language units for greater success in early math. Research suggests that language instruction plays a key role in enhancing children's understanding of math (Xin & Jitendra, 1999) and determining the rate at which they master specific concepts, as well as whether they enjoy math and develop what Dehaene (1997) terms *the number sense.*

Let's examine differences in the sounds of math. Gladwell (2008) reports that "pronouncing English numbers takes about 1/3 of a second versus less than 1/4 of a second for Chinese numbers" (p. 231). In Chinese, 4 is *si*, 7 is *qi*. Both the sounds and the words are shorter. They not only rhyme, but are minimal pairs (see Chapter 2). Their musicality and single-sound difference teach both phonemic awareness and vocabulary (i.e., recall). In short, the phonemic, lexical, and visually meaningful structure of Chinese facilitates Chinese-speaking children's mastery of numbers and basic math concepts. Gladwell (2008) identifies a third advantage speakers of languages with shorter sounds have when it comes to numbers, namely, a larger working memory, which translates to longer number sequences. In his words, "The prize for efficacy goes to Cantonese . . . , whose brevity grants residents of Hong Kong a rocketing memory span of about 10 digits." Unlike in Chinese, Japanese, and Korean, numbering in English is "highly irregular," observes Gladwell (2008), so "Asian children learn to count much faster than American children" (p. 229). No wonder Gladwell remarks, "When it comes to math, Asians have a built-in advantage." By age 5, "American children are already a year behind" (p. 250). In some languages, numerals also are inherently mathematical. Many are written in visibly mathematical mode— using self-evident representations that encode mathematical functions like addition, subtraction, multiplication, and even division and fractions. In Chinese, the numbers 1 to 4 literally add up (i.e., grow visually); 1 is a single line, 2 is two lines, and 4 has 4 sides. When larger numbers appear above smaller ones, as in the case of 12 to 19, for instance, their visual representation implies addition. When smaller numbers appear on top, multiplication is implied. For instance, 20 is two lines (=) atop 10 (+). It literally reads "2 tens" or "2 of 10" and tells children: 2 x 10 = 20 (or 10 + 10 = 20).

With numbers in the thousands, Chinese lists how many thousands, hundreds, tens, and ones are in each set. Such numbering is logical and intuitively mathematical. Young children exposed to these numbers should not only be able to correctly write the next few, even if they don't know Chinese, but to instantly compute them. By the time Chinese-speaking children learn how to say, read and/or write 20, they have learned addition, subtraction, and multiplication. Contrast this with children who know just English. Few U.S.-based 1st-graders can subtract, and multiplication and division are rarely introduced until the latter part of 2nd grade.

In some languages, *number logic* is visible in only a few numerals. In Hindi, for instance, the penultimate numbers in a sequence of 10 imply subtraction. For instance, 29, 39, and 49 literally mean "1 before 30, 40, 50" (i.e., the higher number) or X – 1. In Hindi and Urdu, some numbers imply addition or multiplication (e.g., 26 = *chɔ bis* = six 20; i.e., 6 + 20; 200 = *dho so* = two 100(s) = 100 + 100 or 2 x 100).

Some languages are more conducive to math than others. Math words are, in fact, easier to understand or more visibly mathematical in some languages than others. In Spanish, Portuguese, and many lesser known languages spoken by many PreK–3 children in the Unites States, the terms for basic math concepts, symbols and functions are high-frequency words widely used in everyday speech. Plus (+), for instance, is *mas*, which means "more"; minus is *menos* or "less"; times is *por* or "for"; and division is *entré*, which literally means "in(to)" or "inside," so *uno mas dos* literally means "1 more 2." It tells children to add 2 more to 1. Depending on the language in which math problems are phrased, children will either know exactly what to do or struggle with math because ironically, in many instances, the language obscures the math.

In the case of division problems presented in Spanish, the word *entre* is more meaningful and math-facilitative than the relatively infrequent and complex (two-syllable) word "divide," which few children hear outside class. *Entre* tells children to put one number "in(side)" another. Imagine how much easier addition and subtraction would be if we used the words "more" and "less" (opposites) instead of "plus" and "minus." A 7-year-old bilingual who was shown addition, subtraction, division, and multiplication problems from Spanish and who was familiar with the words used in them observed: "It's easier because the words (i.e., *mas, menos, entre, por*) tell us exactly what to do." Spanish *mas* (i.e., more or heavy) also makes the science concept and word "mass" more meaningful than "weight." Such terms might facilitate learning, especially for DLLs.

Fractions are similarly self-evident in Chinese. According to psychologist Fuson, "For fractions, we say three-fifths. The Chinese is literally 'out of five parts, take three.' That's telling you conceptually what a fraction is. It's differentiating the denominator and the numerator" (Gladwell, 2008, p. 230).

Interestingly, in Hindi and Urdu, range-indicative quantifiers and opposites are learned as compound word pairs and typically employed together. The expression *thora-bohot*, for instance, means less-more or a little-a lot and is used to convey indefiniteness (e.g., in quantity). It explains variation in anything and everything, from languages to airfare to religion.[4] How often do you use "plus," "minus," "times," and "divided by" in everyday conversation? The more mathematical nature of some languages is precisely what prompts Gladwell (2008) to describe math success as "cultural practice" (p. 231). In short, some languages communicate math more explicitly, and in all cases, language reflects culture and is more tangible than culture. Sharing math vocabulary from visibly mathematical languages with young children, as advised here, will

> Ease math and science for DLLs who use these languages, and for English-speakers
>
> Demonstrate and emphasize multiple approaches and perspectives to computation, communication, and problem solving
>
> Interest children in math, science, and language (including Latin and other languages)

Given that differences in languages could yield noteworthy differences in math mastery and performance, the benefits of a bilingual instructional approach should be even more apparent. Integrating languages with more meaningful math and science vocabulary in PreK–3 math lessons might help. Take *número par* and *número impar*, the Spanish terms for "even" and "odd numbers," respectively. Once children know that *par* refers to a "pair" or "couple" in Spanish (including the expression *a couple of words*), even those unfamiliar with Spanish will put two and two together (pun intended). They'll read that *par* refers to "two" and im- conveys opposition (e.g., as in *impatient*). Spanish speakers will very likely have an easier time decoding such terms since their form (i.e., morphology) spells out their meaning (i.e., (in)divisible by 2) and relatedness, unlike the odd (i.e., hard-to-decode and mismatched) English pair.

When Words Don't Add Up

Is it any wonder children who speak and/or write inherently mathematical languages have an advantage in math and science? Arguably, their math skills have just as much to do with language or culture (Gladwell, 2008) as instructional approach. According to Professor Fuson, math is "transparent" in some (Asian) languages. In her view, the linguistic difference "makes the whole attitude toward math different" (Gladwell, 2008, p. 230). "Instead of being a rote learning thing, there's a pattern" one can "figure out" (p. 230). Indeed, when children understand math language, they can readily apply it. Just as children's correct use of words implies mastery, the more words children use, the more—and the faster—they learn.

"Daddy, what's division?" asked my 5-year-old one evening. "Sharing," her father responded. "Oh!" she observed." "Then why don't you call it sharing?" As the following 3rd-grade math problem illustrates, sometimes language creates unnecessary confusion. The problem opens with a table listing the names and corresponding height of four American trees, two of which are mentioned in the following question: "What is the height of a tree that has a greater height than a giant sequoia but less than a Coast Douglas fir?" (Daily Spiral Review, p. 37). This question has no definite answer; the wording is ambiguous. How is a child to respond? For math, more than one answer is an anomaly. The question and the table do not correspond. The question implies variations in tree height (i.e., a numerical range), yet the table does not include a tree that is in between the sequoia and the Douglas fir in height. As this example illustrates, the language through which we present math problems must be clear.

For this problem to make sense, another tree must be added. The mathematical terms *greater than* and *less than* are not the best choices in this context (i.e., trees, not mass nouns, are the focus). More precise and age-appropriate comparatives like "taller" and "shorter" would facilitate understanding. Invite children to first plot the trees and corresponding heights on a cline, using associated descriptors:

tall (275)	taller (295)	tallest (321)
shortest (275)	shorter (295)	short (321)

Indeed, the language we use could either ease or obstruct (content) learning, so we should use terms that children will find clear. "Mama, what is this saying?" my 8-year-old asked, pointing to the following 3rd-grade math problem: "Describe each story as an addition story, a subtraction story, or a multiplication story" (Charles et al., 2009, p. 117). The wording is unclear. When I observed that I didn't understand what "describe" meant, she was shocked. "But you're a grown-up!" she exclaimed. "You should have learned this a long time ago!" I tried to explain that the word "describe" was unclear to me when used with "story," so I proposed two possible answers. In our quest to make math meaningful using storied context-building language, we should be careful not to make it unduly complex and/or imprecise. Here, "classify," "categorize," or "identify" are better choices than "describe," and "(math) problem" is clearer than "story."

STEPS TO SUCCESSFUL MATH INSTRUCTION IN PREK–3

Four steps for successful math instruction in PreK–3 are outlined below. Similar steps would work for other content areas.

Steps 1 and 2: Identify Math Language

Math and other content areas consist of *key concepts* and *applications*. Both have associated vocabulary. Before children can successfully apply core concepts, they must understand them. Identifying PreK–3 math concepts is, therefore, the first step. The second is identifying core vocabulary and other language units associated with each concept.

Numbers and math symbols (e.g., +, –, x, >, <, and =) are like words. A symbol-based math sentence uses numbers and symbols in varied combinations. Depending on which symbols you use and how, you can communicate different math concepts or meanings, which can be summarized in words and/or sentences. So you can teach math concepts using conventional, symbolic, and visual language, as shown below.

(1) 2 + 10 = 12
part 1 + part 2 = whole
(2) Ann got 10 cookies for her birthday and has 2 others in her backpack.
     part 1   +   part 2
How many does she have in all? = How much do parts 1 and 2 equal?

Of the two expressions, (1) is a "number sentence" (Charles et al., 2009, p. 33), (2) a word-based one. Most 4-year-olds would interpret the "and" in (2) to mean "plus," and the ending question as an invitation to calculate what the parts "equal." Both "sentences" have two parts. As with most subjects, children appreciate clear, logical, and visual explanations in math. Hands-on math with visual and/or other linguistic clarifiers works best for young children. It helps to segment parts of problems, as shown above. When PreK–3 math problems are phrased using words and clauses, as in (2), and/or visual cues, for instance, and are not purely numerical, they are generally more meaningful. Similarly, a subtraction problem could be presented using abstract numbers (i.e., 22 – 2 = 20) or in a more engaging manner. The alternative would present a scenario such as "Molly has 22 apples and her sister Ginger has 2 less. How many does Ginger have?" Visually, the parts would look as follows:

Molly has 22 apples and her sister Ginger has 2 less. How many does Ginger have?
part 1   –   part 2   =   Ginger's total

Such part-whole segmenting and diagramming of math problems is more likely to grab children's attention (1); help them process the problem relatively easily (2); and arrive at a logical solution (3). Children get to read different kinds of language, both conventional and numerical, and the visualization eases understanding of the concepts communicated.

You could teach comparison (e.g., *similar + ity* or *same + ness)*, a key math concept and linguistic skill, by asking children, "What's the difference between parts (1) and (2)"? When we use meaningful language (including visuals), math becomes easier. Indeed, language breathes life into math, as the following 2nd-grader's response to both versions indicates:

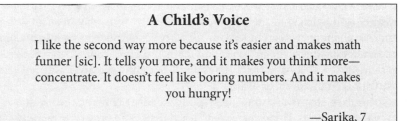

A Child's Voice

I like the second way more because it's easier and makes math funner [sic]. It tells you more, and it makes you think more—concentrate. It doesn't feel like boring numbers. And it makes you hungry!

—Sarika, 7

Indeed, conventional language adds meaning to numerals and other math symbols. Since numerical math is like a sentence, math problems, when phrased using words and sentences, alongside numbers, are like logical equations. In fact, children might find them easier to understand. Questions like, "How many more (buttons) did she buy?" are more engaging and explicitly directive-based than the symbol "=". Questions, are, in fact, more likely to teach children problem solving. Language then is the best mirror and measure of problem-solving skills in PreK–3, for example:

"Daddy, please give me more cookie math!" pleaded my 5-year-old daughter one morning, after I handed her some numerical problems. She was referring to the contextualized math problems her father gave her (e.g., "If Mommy gives you 8 cookies and you share them with Didi, Ayla, Shria, and Lauren, how many will you each get?"). This math was easier and more exciting and meaningful to her (see Schwartz, 1985).

Language also helps children to connect math concepts (often abstract) to real-world applications. When PreK–3 math and science are presented in a multiple modes—visually/storied (Schwartz, 1985); through symbolic and digital language; in words and sentences; or in a combination—children are more likely to learn key concepts and develop integrated skills. You could use multisensory math manipulatives or visuals, for instance, to teach mathematical measures and opposites (e.g., temperature, height, weight, length/width, etc.).

A thermometer (or picture of one) could help you teach a range of incremental (1–100 or 100 versus 50 versus 0) measures or math words like "hot," "warm," "cold," "high," "mid," "low," "top," and "bottom," as well as (-er/-est) gradations like "hotter," "colder," and "lower." Weight and weather words also make most sense in the context of numbers (e.g., 30 inches = heavy snow), and you could even touch on time (measured through the clock, calendar, and seasons) and related math and literacy concepts, such as sequencing (*before* and *after*).

"Communicating math concepts" and "making connections" are curricular objectives identified by Maryland's Office of Elementary Math and in many other states. Dr. Seuss does both successfully in *One Fish, Two Fish, Red Fish, Blue Fish*, where he uses finger counting, a meaningful and visual exercise, to teach numbers, and provides a shocking revelation ("He has eleven!") to help children compare, contrast, and recall digits. Remember that "young children learn and understand best from what they can see, touch, feel, and manipulate" (Eggers, 2010). Add "measure" to this list, and the role measure(ment) words play in math learning becomes even more evident. Indeed, in the early years, much of your focus should be on developing interpersonal skills and math and other content area vocabulary (Marzano, 2010). A look at your state's PreK–3 math objectives will reveal that vocabulary is emphasized, as it should be.

Vocabulary shapes and measures (pun intended) children's math and other skills in the early years. Using language to teach math, and providing rational explanations and visuals for math concepts, is more instructive than expecting children to infer abstract concepts from numbers. Learning the words for grade-appropriate numbers, besides being a necessary first step in telling time and reading the calendar, simultaneously teaches children the concept of shapes, directionality, relationships, and other math concepts and stimulates critical thinking. For grade 1, for instance, one of Howard County Public Schools' objectives for the 2nd quarter reads, "Use direction, location, and position words, right to left." For geometry, children's ability to "identify and draw open and closed figures and use the terms: inside, outside, and on" is emphasized. For the concept of probability, once again, specific words are listed; in fact, two out of the three objectives mandate use of specific words.

> Play games . . . to develop an understanding of the terms "impossible,"
>   "unlikely," and "likely."
> Make predictions . . . using the terms "likely," "unlikely," "certain,"
>   "impossible." (smart.hcpss.wikispaces.net)

Outline core concepts and associated vocabulary for grades 1–3 math and science. For each unit, (visually) identify and group core vocabulary into functional categories, namely, nouns, verbs, and "other" words. Then, with the help of your peers and students, co-create a list of synonyms. This will make core concepts and vocabulary easier. Like most content areas, math language consists of key concepts (nouns), associated verbs like "add," and quantity words (adverbs), so math lessons provide the perfect opportunity for children to learn about sentence logic (i.e., word functions or basic grammar, and, specifically, the primary parts of speech).

Dissect key words into smaller parts. This exercise is both math- and language-instructive. Math words like "addition," "algebra" (from Arabic *al + jabr*, the assembly of broken parts), and *geo + metry* (from the Greek roots *earth + measuring*), for instance, could be segmented to teach addition and subtraction, as well as language arts and social studies, all in one shot. You could integrate math and spelling history (e.g., the Indian roots of Arabic numbers; http://www-history.mcs.st-and. ac.uk/HistTopics/Indian_numerals.html). For instance, the word "addition" was first recorded in "The Crafte of Nombrynge," one of the earliest English language publications to mention math. Notice the math words in the following excerpt: "The first is called addicion, (th)e secunde . . . subtraccion. The thyrd . . . duplacion. The 4. . . . dimydicion. The 5. . . multiplicacion" (http://www.gutenberg.org/files/25664/25664-h/25664-h.htm).

Such activities would make language and math more meaningful and teach cultural awareness, comparison (a math skill), and spelling (i.e., recall of earlier versus current forms). In addition to vocabulary, some math problems use longer units, including sentences. These are typically declaratives and questions. Declaratives usually build the context for part of a math problem, as illustrated earlier. Statements could be instructive, and you could invite children to participate by sharing observations in one or more languages, such as "I spy 2 small(er), round, green/verde things. What could they be?" (e.g., limes). Through such exercises, children would learn measurement terms and to differentiate between colors, shapes, sizes, and numbers.

Either/or and wh- questions are the most common question forms used in math. For example, "How many/much ___?" (quantification) and "Who/Which is long/tall/short(er/est)?" (comparison/contrast). Some math problems are presented using directives (Learning Horizons, 2009). To respond correctly, a child must read and understand the core vocabulary and required actions. For example, including "color" and "circle." The measure word, "equal to," implies comparison, as does the conjunction "or," making familiarity with word functions key.

Step 3: Teach Math Using Meaningful Language and Language-Based Activities

Children learn what they understand. Clear, relevant language is key to understanding, especially when mathematical annotation is missing. In the following 3rd-grade math problem, children cannot tell from the visual alone what is being asked, since the point of intersection isn't circled. They therefore must understand the words used (e.g., *place*, *intersect*, and *point*).

Example

"Which best describes the place where these two lines intersect?" (Charles, 2009, p. 108)
A. Line
B. Point
C. Line segment
D. Parallel line

The lesson opens with the following definition: "A point is an exact position" (p. 242). For most 3rd-grade English speakers, "dot" is a familiar word, easier than the synonym "point" (and, in this context, even *position*). Providing "dot" alongside "point" or in place of it would expand children's vocabulary and ease understanding (since the answers to multiple choice questions are often clues), so use familiar language to transition children to mathematical language.

Have you ever taught math using language units instead of numbers? This section will show you how to use language(s) to teach key PreK–3 math concepts while simultaneously building children's analytic, problem-solving, and vocabulary skills.

Numbers, Computation, and Sequencing. Since phonemic awareness is one of the first things assessed and emphasized in PreK, why not introduce PreK math concepts by demonstrating how to blend and silence letters (i.e., addition and subtraction) to create sounds in high-frequency PreK–3 words (Richgels, 2001)? In short, invite children to play *language math* from the start. Having children count letters and sounds in words develops phonemic awareness, quantification, *and* spelling skills. For example, you could ask:

1.   Which letters make the /kw/ sound? [q + u = kw, e.g., *quick(ly)*]
2.   How many *sounds* does "two" have? Say/Write them (2 = t and long u)
3.   How many *letters* does "four" have? (4 = f, o, u, and r)
4.   How many *sounds* does "four" have? (2 or 3, depending on your accent: f o (r) or f o ə) How about "five"? (3 or 4: f ai v or f a ə v)

Fractions. Have you ever halved words, phrases, or clauses to teach fractions? For instance, invite children to circle specified word segments.

1/2 of booboo = boo
1/2 of bonbon = bon (French for candy/sweet and good)
1/2 of a dollar ($1) = 50 cents

Share examples from languages (e.g., Chinese) that present fractions logically, and fragment songs (e.g., the "Old School Bus"), idioms and expressions. For example, in Chinese "thanks" is xei xei (/shei shei/). It means thanks x 2 or "thanks, thanks." One "thanks" is considered curt, and 2 is a lucky number in Chinese. Engage children using such examples (e.g., "In which language(s) is it rude to say "thanks" once?" xei + xei = ?)

Geometry. One way to teach geometry is to have children look for shapes in the English alphabet, and in letters and characters from other languages. This exercise simultaneously shapes children's language and math/science skills. Teaching children to decode the shapes in geometry words (i.e., morphemes) is an important first step, as shown below.

Examples

tri + angle = triangle = 3 angles
hexagon = hex(a) + gon = 6 sides

Use letters with familiar shapes from English and/or other languages to teach shapes and congruence, while firming up children's knowledge of letters and other requisite language skills. The Greek letter *delta* is perfect for teaching triangles, and the Hebrew letter *samech* is shaped like a square. You could use Korean characters to outline parts of rectangles, ovals, and squares. One even resembles the Hebrew letter *chet*, and could lead to a fruitful session on similarities and differences in letters and sounds. You could even include the hexagonal STOP-sign.

Children might be fascinated to see samples of Ogham, a writing system of the Celts that uses only straight lines joined together by a vertical line across the top (as in Hindi and Sanskrit). To demonstrate curves and squiggly lines, use Thai and Tamil script. Tamil contains a letter *ah* written using three dots in triangle formation (like the 'k' in Tuareg). You could use it to teach the triangle shape and ask children to guess what they would see if they connected the dots.[5]

Letters and other language building blocks are ideal for teaching the concept of symmetry as well. Many writing systems (Coulmas, 1999) have symmetrical letters. Teach children to use vertical and horizontal lines of symmetry on symmetrical English letters.

Multilingual math is (doubly) instructive; include phonetic symbols and/or symmetrical letters from other languages to teach math concepts and global awareness. Berber, a north African language spoken by the Tuareg, for instance, is excellent for teaching symmetry and congruence. The ancient (Libyan) Tifinagh script in which it is written contains many familiar shapes, including a rectangle and circle, called *ler* (used for 'r'), a rectangle and circle split longitudinally in two equal parts, called *leb* (i.e., 'b' in Berber), a square split in four equal parts called *lert* (which represents the blended consonant sequence 'rt' frequently used in Berber), and *lakh* ('x') which is four dots in square formation.

Synonyms help teach the math concept of equality. For instance, *blizzard = snow + storm; outside = not inside; inside = within; left = west; right = east*. Once again, draw on other languages to teach equality and use visuals to highlight differences and commonalities.

Example

Russian B = English V
Russian H = English N
Russian P = English R
Russian A, K, M, X = English A, K, M, X

When words and other units of language are presented in math mode (i.e., equations), children can see and better understand the concept of number in language and math (e.g., boy = 1 male child; pair = 2). They also get to see the math in words or the mathematical composition of words (e.g., *sleet* = snow +

rain) and learn to decode math (concepts), alongside math operations and terminology, social studies, and other core PreK–3 content and vocabulary.

Measurement. Range-specifying words like "until" are excellent math
words for teaching comparison/measurement and other core math concepts. The
following word-based subtraction problem is an example: Tom sat still from 9
a.m. to 1 p.m. How long did he sit silent? This example also uses synonyms (i.e.,
sit still = silent/quiet) and instructs children on synonyms and language structure
(i.e., grammar; see Chapter 7). For instance, to correctly use "until," one must
specify the full range being measured. When children's attention is drawn to such
information, they are more likely to understand the meaning of "until" (i.e., the
range-bound definition of this mathematical term) and to pay closer attention to
words and the way in which they are ordered (i.e., the science of word combinations). In short, used appropriately, word-based math could help children develop both math and language awareness in one shot. An example of how you could
use words and sentences to teach the concept of measurement, while enhancing
phonemic awareness, vocabulary, and core language skills, follows:

Use > or < to indicate if one word is longer or shorter in sound than the other:

apple < camel
æ p ə l = 4 sounds ("pp" = 1 sound = p); k æ m ə l = 5 sounds
because → bikɔz (7 letters → 5 sounds)

Ask children why "because" has fewer sounds than letters. If they are unable
to explain, tell them au = 1 sound, namely, ɔ, and the final -e is silent in "because."
They'll be practicing math and language at the same time. Have them compare
word length using another language, preferably one spoken or understood by one
or more students in your class.

Math tasks (e.g., conversion from pounds/lbs to kilograms/kgs) based on
readings are contextualized and instructive. Few(er) children realize they are doing math. The result is *task-based multiskills enhancement*. Math problems could
be presented using more than one sentence.

Use readings that lend themselves to science and math in concert with specific weather words to instruct children on statistics and other math concepts. For
instance, provide children with a list of words for snow and ice, and variants from
Eskimo, and/or another language used in a cold climate, and have them compare
the vocabulary to English. One question might be, "Which language has more/
fewer words for snow?" Children will learn early on and see firsthand how language mirrors our world, including varied climate, and will come away with a
richer knowledge of social studies, a broader (bilingual) vocabulary, and a firmer
grasp of measurement and other math concepts. What's more, they'll probably
share and ask for more other-language words to satisfy their hunger for exciting
(science) "facts."

Comparison, Contrast, and Equivalency. Examples of how you could use words—from English and other languages—to teach this concept, while growing children's word power and intercultural awareness, follow:

Comparisons: length and meaning

snowflake > snow
snowflake > flake
snow < snowflake

Definition and inferencing

preschool = pre + school = before school
winter = cold (weather)
summer = warm(th)
frost = snow + ice
10 = ten = 2 + 2 + 2 + 2 + 2 = two x five
I'm sorry = I shouldn't have done that (indirect) = My bad (BEV form used
    in mainstream U.S. speech)
A bulge in your pocket = something's in it

Synonyms and homophones

equals = means – that is = the same
2 dimes + 1 nickel = 25 cents = a quarter (you could elicit the other
    meaning)
aftercare = after school day care
1 nickel = 5 cents
dozen = 12
number = digit
1 gallon = 4 quarts
un happy = not happy
mass = *meat* in Hindi-Urdu
"Two can do *twice* the work," said Turtle [to Anansi, the spider] = 2 times
    the work (*Anansi Goes Fishing*, 1993, p. 3)

Language equivalents (e.g., greeting, thanking, leave-taking expressions)

au revoir (French) = *awjo* (Gujarati, *we'll meet again*) = *adios* (Spanish) = bye
asante (Swahili) = *merci* (French) = *dhanyevaad* (Hindi) = *gracias* (Spanish)
    = thanks = *shukran* (Arabic)

por favor (Spanish, literally *for/as a favor*) = please = *s'il vous plait* (French, *if you please*)

de nada (Spanish) = you're welcome = *afuan* (Arabic) = don't mention (Indian English)

Idioms

sleep in = sleep longer
sit up = sit straight
I'm dead = I'm/I am (dog) tired
a piece of cake = easy (like eating cake)

The hallmark of spoken American English, idioms are excellent for teaching equivalence. Since idioms do not equal the sum of their parts, they stump many children, including DLLs.

Currency Exchange

Reinforce computation and equivalence using other currencies, particularly devalued ones like the *lira* (Italian) and Zambian *kwacha* (Bemba word for dawn), which run into billions and trillions. Invite children to convert money from one currency to another. This will sharpen their math and global (economy) skills, and help them learn more about their world.

Algebra, Patterns, Functions, and Statistics. Letters could be used to teach the concept of sets and statistics. Adding other languages helps to build children's math and language skills. You could add a Latin set, since English borrowed some letters from Latin. Invite your biliterate students or peers in other grades to create similar sets using another language, including related languages like Spanish, French, and/or Italian (vs. English). Assign children to research for examples online. You'll advance their technology skills as well.

Display word parts and math symbols in crossword-puzzle-format and create math problems around them. Show students how to make bar graphs, pie charts (of word classes), and picture graphs of words or word parts, based on their length and weighting, for instance (and ask questions like "Which language has more cold-weather words?" and "How many more?").

Probability. Probability is inseparable from language. Use a language-based visual to teach probability. Ask questions that practice math concepts discussed earlier while priming children for predictions, as follows:

How many letters does English have? (26; counting)
How many are vowels? (5; subtraction)
Imagine you are a scientist and you're getting ready to pick an English letter.
    How likely are you to pick a consonant? (very likely: prediction-based)

Since word stems have de-cod-able, predictable meanings, ask additional language-math questions. An example follows.

Example

"Beautiful" means "full of beauty." Circle the second part (syllable) of each word listed: "beautiful," "helpful," "hurtful," and "restful." Use each word in a sentence or tell/write what each means.

When children follow the directives a sequence of numbers and/or words communicates (e.g., add, subtract, divide, multiply, weigh, etc.), they decode the language in math. In short, most PreK–3 math problems require knowledge of math vocabulary. Children get to see that math is a language—it is communicative. They usually can infer that math symbols like =, –, and x are like verbs, while the symbol = introduces the end result or outcome. They have to decode symbols and key words before they can solve the "problems" presented.

Multilingual Math

Successful instruction is innovative and explanatory, inviting self-discovery (Darling-Hammond, 2012). Teaching children to count in more than one language is an excellent way to teach sequencing and more. Children could start by counting to 10 in another language in Kindergarten, 20 in 1st grade, 60 in 2nd grade, and 100 or more in 3rd grade. They will learn, for example, that not all languages have plural forms; some use adjectives to clarify amounts. For example, in Urdu, you say "1 pen" and "10 pen" (i.e., *ek/das kalum*). This might be the perfect opportunity to share a bit about the Mogul Empire, and the love story involving Emperor Shah Jahan and Queen Mumtaz. In this storied context, introduce computations pertaining to the construction of Taj Mahal (Taj Palace), including the amount of marble, time, and labor expended for Queen Taz (Taj in Hindi).

Children could share the meanings of their names, explore the roots, and learn comparisons/weight(ing). For example, in Arabic, Persian, Urdu and Hindi, *Khusrau* means "be happy" (*khus* = happy; *ra(h)u* = be). Children who hear/see *Khusrau*, the name of a shah/King in *The Arabian Nights* (Tarnowska & Hénaff, 2010) will better understand this and other stories where characters' names reflect their roles. They could learn to write their names in different languages and add up the characters/letters or sounds, learning math and language. Invite those who speak and/or read other languages to assist.

Inviting children to share how numbers are written in other languages is another way to involve and empower children. Seeing how 1 to 10 are written in Arabic, Hindi, and English will help children with comparison, yielding a lively lesson integrating math, science, and social studies. Children will be excited to learn that many Greek letters (English borrowed A, B, E, and many others) coincide with numbers (e.g., alpha = 1, beta = 2, Γ (gamma) = 3, I (iota) = 10; and P/rho = 100).

This exercise could jumpstart young children for calculus. They will also see that Greek letters are ordered differently (e.g., in Greek, Y comes before X). What better opportunity to teach sequence words (e.g., *first, next, before,* and *after)*? State mathematics offices could add such language-as-math exercises to their resource listings, advancing math, science, and language(s) simultaneously.

Step 4: Assess Math Learning in PreK–3

A week after she employed the steps proposed here, educator Pat Tessner reported positive outcomes. In her words, "I need to bring more language and discussion amongst students into my math lessons; and more math into my language lessons!" She periodically stops to check math comprehension and draws children's attention to the language in math. How? She asks open-ended questions. Questioning prompts inquiry, helping children scaffold language and content, as noted earlier. By tracing the steps they used to solve math problems (i.e., explaining their responses), children fine-tune their reasoning skills and math language (Chi et al., 1989). The end result is a more confident and vocal child who simultaneously develops:

> Critical thinking skills, including organizational, classification, logical reasoning, sequencing, inferencing, and problem solving (i.e., *whole child*) skills
> Stronger interpersonal skills through routine involvement in cognitively and linguistically challenging exchanges
> Advanced phonemic, vocabulary, sentence, and discourse skills

These skills are likely to positively impact children out-of-class, too (see Pandey, 2010), yielding multiskills development and lifelong learning in areas (e.g., reading) requiring similar skills.

A key question you should be asking is: "How much of math assessment = language assessment?" Ensure that your math assessments capture children's comprehension and use of both math and expressive language. Many math concepts and terms, such as sequence and weight, cut across PreK–3 content areas. They constitute key instruction/learning and assessment measures in math (counting), science (e.g., indicators of growth/stages), music (composition), health and PE (i.e., heart rate, warm up versus cool down), art, and literacy (beginning, middle, and end). Reading, writing, and even speech, for instance, are (culturally) sequenced.

Since it's hard to draw the line between math language and expressive language or language used to communicate math concepts, for all practical purposes language and math are intertwined. To adequately measure math learning, assessment must be tied to your curriculum and lesson plans—specifically, objectives and resources you use to teach and test math skills. In one school district, PreK–3 students' math skills are assessed in the following four areas:

1. Meets expectations in learning basic facts
2. Demonstrates an understanding of concepts
3. Applies problem-solving strategies
4. Applies effort

Arguably, all necessitate comprehension and use of language. While (math) language comprehension and use are implied in the terms *understanding* and *applies* in (2) and (3), respectively, (1) and (4) are vague. For instance, how is "learning" assessed and what are the "basic facts"? How about "effort"? How is it measured? Is it through amount of time expended? What if in-class time allowed for math is insufficient for a child to complete assigned problems? Does that mean the child's effort is less than satisfactory? While effort could be verified in class, out-of-class effort is less empirically measurable. In fact, all four measures could be rephrased using language that specifies exactly *what* is measured and *how*. Is children's ability to arrive at the correct answer automatically indicative of their understanding of key math concepts? Is their ability to explain how they arrived at the answer a better measure?

Pat Tessner finds that her students learn more (i.e., reflect) when she asks them to "tell how" they arrived at their answers. The different strategies students employ mirror their creativity and uniqueness. "Through retelling and discussion, they quickly learn," she observes, "that there is more than one way to solve a problem, and you can see whether they have merely memorized it or really understand it." In her experience, when first asked to "tell how," most instinctively erase their answers, as they generally assume they must be incorrect ("or else why would the teacher ask?"). She has, therefore, decided to move her eraser to the other side of the desk.

As demonstrated, language is a medium through which math could be taught relatively easily and innovatively. To effectively teach and measure PreK–3 math skills in the absence of language or language indices is problem + at(t)ic (pun intended). Drawing children's attention to the meanings (semantic/logical: agent versus action versus outcome) of specific words, sentences, and discourse structures in math lessons and learning resources is essential. By analyzing key words and listing their ingredients using visual mapping, and identifying synonyms, children improve their vocabulary and computation skills. Segmenting and blending sounds and words also help children advance reasoning, inferencing, and automaticity/recall required in math and other areas assessed. Language-math problems could prompt children to expand key language and math skills together. When, for instance, you ask children, "How many English letters make the /k/ sound?" you expect them to demonstrate that they are familiar with phonics and can sequence and add. In the process, you help them connect language and math, so language becomes the bridge to math, and vice versa. Children are more likely to comprehend and reflect in terms of abstractions—beyond words to summative content packaged in variable language units. Introducing the concept of sameness by presenting a math problem in two ways is an excellent way to teach children to think creatively and to recognize that just as different words convey a specific idea in conventional language, math problems can be written and solved in multiple ways.

Example

1/3 of *Ho ho ho* = ho
Ho ho ho ÷ 3 = ho

As shown, to master math, children have to first understand the language through which it is presented, specifically, the vocabulary associated with math concepts. Awareness of the math in language, and of the language in math, is essential.

Indeed, math activities could be more visibly *language exercises* and vice versa. *As* and *when* you build children's word power and enhance their oral language skills, you encourage them to vocalize, collaborate, participate, and reflect. For every math concept, as shown, we can identify one or more corresponding nouns, and every math problem necessitates action. Math word problems, for instance, contain at least one verb (e.g., *solve*, *round* to the nearest 10).

Children with strong vocabularies are better readers (Blachowicz & Fisher, 2010) and writers (Schecter & Cummins, 2003); they easily connect spoken language and print. They also grasp math and other core content faster and are more expressive (i.e., use varied language). Language-proficient children (e.g., bilinguals) are also more likely to be agents of *critical literacy* (Beach et al., 2010). Since math is a language, it offers multiple channels to the same destination (e.g., $2 + 2 = 4$; $8 - 4 = 4$, $2 \times 2 = 4$). By using different math equations, we teach children that, like *synonyms*, there are multiple approaches to math and problem solving. Make sure to double check that your math lessons reflect multiple perspectives.

Recommended actions to ease PreK–3 math and science include:

Provide explicit and hands-on instruction in *core vocabulary*.
Teach math and science using easy-to-understand language(s).
Use familiar terms (e.g., instead of inviting children to add prefixes and
    suffixes to *base words*, use the familiar term *root* instead. As one 3rd-
    grader observed, "I like *root* better because words are like plants—you
    can grow them and chop 'em up—they're alive").
Diversify math to make it more meaningful. For example, invite children
    to identify shapes for which English has no names. They could
    borrow shapes from other languages or create their own shapes
    and words (see Dr. Seuss's *On Beyond Zebra*). Take, for example,

the yin-yang symbol and the paisley (from the Indian *paisleaf*). The swastika is another shape that's frequently misunderstood owing to its misappropriation by the Nazis. It means good health or mark (*tikka*) of health (*swasth*) in Sanskrit, the source language, and Hindi. The four hands in this symbol signify the four directions of the world. In Lithuanian, it's the symbol for the sun (www.israelnationalnews.com/News/News.aspx/137650).

Draw on intuitively mathematical languages to teach PreK–3 math. As shown, the phonetic brevity of Chinese helps speakers recall many more (and longer) numbers.

For multiskills development, integrate math concepts and vocabulary in language arts (e.g., organize a geometry lesson around scripts or fabrics). Children could identify and count letters and shapes (e.g., the *Lakota star* and *bear paw* on quilts; see Wilbur, 2011).

SUMMARY AND APPLICATIONS

While earlier chapters illustrated the math and science in language by showing how language is divisible into mathematically computable parts, this chapter:

1. Emphasized the language in math
2. Proposed the use of conventional language and multilingual ingredients in PreK–3 math instruction

The goal was to demonstrate that PreK–3 math is as much symbolic as linguistic, and to propose that we build children's math and language skills simultaneously, using multimodality and multilingualism—scaffolding math through language, on the one hand, and strengthening phonemic awareness, (bilingual) vocabulary, and literacy through math, on the other. This math-as-language approach teaches math concepts through language computations that prompt language analysis and make learning more exploratory, integrated, language focused, and meaningful. As shown, when it comes to early math, language is both the medium and the message.

As shown, just as math is a language, so too is language a math/science. When we consider the fact that language uses math on a number of levels, including sound blending (i.e., adding and subtracting sounds), words (which requires us to compute morphemes), and sentences, the connections between math and language are even more apparent. Identifying and understanding the component parts of each help children add, subtract, divide, measure, and multiply to learn the whole. In sum (pun intended), language, like math, is log + ic + al.[6]

CHAPTER 5

Sociolinguistics
The Benefits of Dialect and Language Awareness

Some people aren't going to like the way you talk.

—Dr. Martin Luther King, Jr.

I wish we could do what they do in Katroo.
They sure know how to say "Happy Birthday to You!"

—Dr. Seuss, *Happy Birthday to You!*

"Do you mind children?" asked the lady with what sounded like an Irish accent. "Not at all!" responded the woman with a Chicago accent. I chuckled when I overheard this exchange at an airport. It speaks to the frequency of miscommunication arising from dialect differences, specifically vocabulary. In Ireland, a child care provider is a childminder. In the United States, by contrast, with the exception of some dialects (see Salley, 2009), "mind" in this context means to tolerate. Some examples of dialect differences are comical. For instance, "knocked up" means awoken in British English, and impregnated in American English. Some might find it funny that many Trinidadians start conversations and e-mail with "Good night," as a greeting.

Sociolinguistics, the study of language in use, provides us with an exciting and practical vehicle to better understand children and families (Chambers, Trudgill, & Schilling-Estes, 2002) and to meet and exceed individual language-literacy needs, as demonstrated here. Learning objectives include:

To illustrate the value of sociolinguistics in PreK–3
To promote early multilingual awareness
To optimize reading through bilingual/bidialectal resources
To illustrate how our language choices mirror our social identities
To discuss how social factors influence language use
To demonstrate the value of *code-switching*, *code-mixing*, and other bilingual communication strategies

How many times have you drawn conclusions about your students and other individuals on the basis of their speech, their reading habits, and/or their writing? Like it or not, we frequently are judged on the basis of our language. Studying individuals' speech/language habits or their language practices is particularly insightful. It is, in fact, one of the most reliable ways to understand individuals and to identify language biases. Studying the sounds, words, sentences or utterances, and discourse structures we employ in our own speech, as well as in our writing, also helps us to become more aware of the role language plays in individual identity and in communication (Hudley & Mallinson, 2010).

Awareness of our language peculiarities better prepares us for identifying and explaining others' language choices. This is because we are, by nature, social creatures; we must interact with others and, to do so, we must use language. When we address loved ones using nicknames or other terms of endearment (e.g., "pumpkin"), our words simultaneously convey our intent (i.e., communicative goal) and serve as communication outlets. Strategic language use necessitates a clear understanding of the social workings of language. Only then can we work toward greater intercultural success, as illustrated here. The goal is to create global citizens by equipping teachers and children with sociolinguistic skills. Understanding why children use the linguistic features that they do is a necessary first step in this endeavor. We begin with a review of key concepts in sociolinguistics.

LANGUAGE (IS) IDENTITY

"Mama, I always thought 'Hondurans' was 'Hundurasans,'" announced my 1st-grader one afternoon after she heard me say *Honduran*. We spent the next week learning the correct terms for individuals from different countries. I was pleasantly surprised to see how excitedly my 4-year-old matched roots and suffixes (e.g., -an and -i) in country words (e.g., Israeli). Explaining the exceptions (e.g., Canadian, which they argued should have been *Canadan*) was somewhat challenging, but at least my children learned many identity words. Social identity is reflected in language. As the engineer-turned-linguist Benjamin L. Whorf (1956) observed, "Language shapes the way we think, and determines what we can think about" (p. 5). Our language mirrors our affiliations or social networks, and our social identity. Language identity is like fine china (i.e., fragile). It needs to be nurtured. Hence, the need for additive language practices.

Many of us belong to more than one speech community (i.e., a group with a common language). Members share certain expectations regarding acceptable speech or language and criteria for participation. We might, for instance, belong to a predominantly female group of Avon sellers, as well as to a community organization (e.g., a church or temple) and an academic network (e.g., the National

Association for the Education of Young Children [NAEYC] or the Parent-Teacher Association [PTA]). Our speech/language likely changes in each.

Our language choices are almost always purposeful, and socially driven. They generally are dictated by shared language conventions or "rules" of engagement we imbibe early on—through a process termed *language socialization*. We know, for instance, that it is rude in American culture to ask questions of a personal nature to those we meet for the first time. In Indian and Nigerian culture, however, it is perfectly acceptable to ask "strangers"[1] if they are married and whether they have any children. While a Yoruba speaker's response to the second question might be puzzling (e.g., "Yes, about four [children]"[2]), the question would be culturally acceptable. Like sponges, we absorb the speech qualities of those with whom we spend (or have spent) a considerable amount of time. For this reason, we might start to speak, read, and/or even write like them (think of this as a form of language osmosis).

In addition, one or more social factors influence our speech/language. They include age, gender, social class, cultural identity or "ethnicity," location, communication goals, the relationship between participants (e.g., formal, informal, new, or longstanding), cultural norms and expectations, and the topic(s). The impact of these on one's speech and language is of great interest to linguists who study how individuals respond to different social influences. At any given point, one or more social variables could be more decisive.

Youngsters, for instance, more than those 30 and older are likely to use slang and novel vocabulary. Many young children use "like" as a filler in reported speech, as in, "I'm like, that's . . ." or "she like, gimme dat!" The latter is an example of a BEV-sentence containing slang.[3] BEV, a dialect, is also called African American Vernacular English (AAVE) or Ebonics[4] (Pandey, 2000; Wolfram & Schilling-Estes, 2006). Many terms that are widely used today, including *cool* and *awesome*, started out as slang before they mainstreamed (i.e., were adopted by the wider community). The colloquialism, "My bad" (i.e., "I'm sorry") is an example. Like the BEVisms, "I feel you," and "It's ALL good!" it, too, has been appropriated by the older generation.

The role of gender is evident in the speech and language many inner-city males and females employ in same-sex interactions. In a 2005 study, for instance, the author found that even in an electronic learning environment (Blackboard's™ Virtual Classroom), African American males consistently interacted with their male counterparts in BEV—even in simulated "classrooms." They employed terms like "dawg" and other seemingly offensive terms exclusively with other males. Unlike African American females, they occasionally used what on the surface appeared to be insults, and derogatory or taboo language (e.g., the N-word), to convey and cement their close relationship. Such conscious use of non-Standard English signals covert prestige. In other words, the speakers/writers feel confident enough to use an in-group language, and to let it be known that their language deviates from the norm.

In general, research shows that more males than females use nonstandard varieties of languages, and that more females than males hypercorrect or make a sudden and concerted effort to use "correct" or "proper" language when on guard. In other words, they associate Standard English (SE) with overt prestige. When attention is drawn to their speech or language, more African American males, for instance, admit to using what they often term "street language" or "slang" (i.e., BEV). They are also more likely to consciously use BEV.

The impact of social class on speech is best illustrated through a famous department store study conducted in New York City by the sociolinguist William Labov (1966). Labov observed that more privileged New Yorkers, unlike struggling residents at the lowest end of the social spectrum, consistently pronounced or articulated the 'r' sound whenever it appeared after a vowel (e.g., /ka:r/ versus /ka:(ə)/ or /kæ/ for "car").[5] He set about testing his hypothesis at three different department stores that, in his view, reflected a social class hierarchy in their clientele. They included Saks Fifth Avenue (for the upper class); Macy's (frequented by the middle class), and Klein's, a discount store. At each location, he elicited r-words ("fourth floor") from employees. He recorded whether their initial and subsequent utterances were *r-full* or *r-less* (e.g., /fɔrθ/ versus /fɔθ/ and /fɔəθ/). His hypothesis was borne out. Employees at Saks Fifth Avenue pronounced the /r/ right away at least 62% of the time and those at Macy's 51% of the time, while only 20% of Klein's employees uttered the /r/ the first time they said "fourth floor." They also recorded the highest incidence of *hypercorrection,* switching "upwards" when they were self-conscious.

Ethnicity,[6] another social variable, often is conflated with culture (also vague), geography, and race. More Jewish Americans, particularly those from the northeast, are likely to pronounce "coffee" as /kɔfi:/ than those with other "ethnic" affiliations in New Jersey and New York.

Speech and language can also differ based on geography. To some Memphians, for instance, the words *pin* and *pen* sound similar, unlike in other parts of the United States. This expanded homophone, then, like the regional terms "soda" versus "pop," is geographical. Also, many southerners tend to elongate their vowels, saying /ta:(r)d/ for "tired," /fou(ə)(r)/ for "four," and /oən/ for "on." This process of vowel lengthening or, in the case of the last two examples, of inserting an additional vowel (i.e., the schwa, /ə/) yields what sometimes is described as slower speech.

ACCENTS, DIALECTS, AND OTHER TERMS

At the 2011 Clinton Foundation gala concert, President Clinton jokingly thanked country singer Kenny Chesney for "coming so I wouldn't be the only person up there without an accent." What's an accent? Do you have an accent? How would you describe it? Has it changed? When, why, and how? How does a dialect differ from a language? Approximately how many dialects does English have? These are some of the questions this section addresses. Attempt to answer them before you read on.

An accent simply refers to the sound quality of your speech. This includes the way you pronounce phonemes, as well as your use of stress and intonation. Since it's literally impossible to conceive of speech without sound, we all have an accent. The moment you leave your country or the place where you spent most of your life, you are likely to be perceived as having an accent. Yes, like it or not, you become the one with the accent. So before you dismiss someone's accent, remember that you, too, might be viewed as having a "strange" or "thick" accent.

Differences in the specific sounds we use to speak a language yield different accents of Arabic, English, French, and so on. Examples of regional accents of English include Indian, Russian, Nigerian, Kenyan, Trini, and Jamaican accents (as in the song "Under the Sea" in Disney's *The Little Mermaid* and in the hybrid, patois-infused music of Bob Marley and non-Jamaican reggae artists like The Green and Alborosie).

On a national scale, one generally can distinguish between a northern and southern accent. These, however, are relatively broad categories. The more exposed we are to the speech varieties used in a specific geographical area, the finer the distinctions we are able to hear. Examples include a north versus south Indian accent, a northern Alabama versus southern Tennessee accent, and Yoruba- versus Igbo-accented Nigerian English. Hence, there are clear benefits to increased exposure to other languages and regions.

The more traveled we are, the more tolerant we are likely to be of language differences, and the easier it is for us to communicate. This is because we learn to focus on the content, instead of the accent. This is a valuable skill, as our ears, like our eyes, easily could deceive us into believing that people sound less intelligent just because they talk or write in an unusual or "funny" manner. When we celebrate our language differences, and view them as mirrors of cultural vitality, we learn something new and interesting, in addition to making an effort to understand someone.

In English, vowels are largely responsible for different accents. Take the word "box," which could be pronounced /bæks/ and /boks/. The different vowels yield what most would recognize as Standard American English and British English, respectively. The pronunciation /boks/ is RP, the Standard British English spoken by a mere 8%. Appalachian English (e.g., the Ocrakoke Brogue of the Outer Banks of North Carolina) is hard for many to understand primarily because of this.

Some accents are harder to place—regionally, socially, or otherwise. These generally are considered the most desirable. Many anchor persons have seemingly accent-less speech. Their accents are indistinct, leading some to believe that they don't have an accent. Imagine if we all spoke the same language and, what's more, if we spoke it the same way. Would communication be easier? An estimated 6,912 languages, including hundreds of dialects, are used worldwide (Lewis, 2009). Most are spoken in Asia, specifically India. Papua New Guinea boasts the greatest language diversity. Africa is home to over one-third of the world's surviving languages, with some 400 in Nigeria alone. Familiarizing children with the names of some of these languages is an educational exercise in itself.[7] Some languages, like Native American languages, are endangered. Few to no youngsters speak them. Recent efforts to revive many *lesser-used languages* reflect recognition of the immense cultural knowledge languages embody. Enduring Voices: Saving Disappearing Languages, for instance, is a project sponsored by the National Geographic Society to catalog languages on the verge of extinction. Teachers could access the site for class projects.

In the United States, a predominantly monolingual, English-using society, languages other than English are considered minority languages. *Heritage language* is another term used, emphasizing the cultural wealth of these languages. Few minority languages enjoy the institutional backing English does, particularly in English-only states like Arizona. The dominance of English in the United States might account, in large part, for the lesser use of other languages. The more time we spend using English, the less time available for other languages. Teachers, therefore, have a critical role to play in interesting children—and families—in language varieties other than SE (Pandey, 2010). One of the goals of this chapter is to recommend weaving different varieties into the curriculum—to mold global citizens from the start.

While language attitudes or the general perception of languages could change, these generally are influenced by political and socioeconomic considerations. For instance, while Russian was a language of great interest to many Americans during the Cold War era, today it is not as widely taught in the United States as Spanish (more "sellable"), French (still largely associated with fashion and class), and, increasingly, Chinese, Arabic, Korean, Farsi, and Urdu. The last five are receiving more attention in large part because of their "special language" designation from the Department of Homeland Security. In short, they are under scrutiny for reasons of national intelligence. Current interest in Chinese has much to do with China's politico-economic standing.

Lingua Francas, Pidgins, and Creoles

Although the United States has no designated official language—which comes as a surprise to many—English continues to function like a quasi-official language in the United States and is, in fact, the lingua franca or most widely used medium of communication. For this reason, proficiency in English generally increases one's market(ability) value in the United States. In more-multilingual nations that also have no official language, such as Nigeria, Pidgin English, a compact language that formed along major waterways—the primary trade routes in early colonial times—serves as the lingua franca. Not surprisingly, Atlantic and Pacific pidgins, the two major branches, contain elements from local languages and Portuguese (e.g., "pikin" for child, with a similar-sounding word in Old French and the term *pequeña* in Spanish, meaning small). The host language, the one that contributes most of the vocabulary and/or determines the sentence structure, is echoed in the name. For instance, the label Nigerian Pidgin English specifies the chief role English plays in it. These contact languages result from exchanges between speakers who have no shared medium of communication. Pidgins are literally linguistic salsas. It is both mind-boggling and fascinating to hear how the single word "for" could mean "in," "on," "at," "above," "below," "behind," "opposite," "on top of," "adjacent to," and "next to" in Nigerian Pidgin, as well as in most English-based pidgins. Such is their communicative power.

When a pidgin functions as a primary language, it is termed *Creole*. Examples include Western Caribbean Creole, spoken in Belize and Jamaica (called "patois" or patwa[8]), and Krio, spoken in Sierra Leone and Liberia. Creoles have a much more expanded vocabulary than pidgins. This is because they play a more expansive role; in addition to serving as link languages (i.e., lingua francas), they perform all the functions a primary language serves. Not all Creoles start out as pidgins. Some linguists contend that BEV started out as a pidgin, then became a Creole (through a process termed *Creolization*), and that it is currently at the next "phase," termed *de-Creolization*. During this hypothesized final stage, the contact language begins to more closely resemble the standard (language), which explains why SE and BEV are sisters.

Accents and Dialects

Varieties of a language are termed *dialects*. Like accents, dialects can vary by region, social class, or a combination of factors, depending on which social variables exert the greatest influence on users. Accents are just one area of difference between dialects and/or languages. While accent-level differences generally are confined to speech, they can be captured in writing as well (e.g., southernisms in southern U.S. literature).

Unfortunately, like accent, dialect has also come to be viewed negatively by the general public. Most nonlinguists think of dialects as substandard, "improper," and adulterated brands of a language. Ironically, many speakers of stigmatized dialects, including BEV, distance themselves from these dialects or deny using them. Many of these socially conscious individuals might use these dialects in their unguarded moments. This social assessment of dialects (as inferior) differs drastically from a linguistic definition.

From a linguistic standpoint, dialects share many features, and no dialect is inherently better than another. For the most part, speakers of SE understand those who speak BEV, and vice versa, even if they don't speak each other's dialect. The reason SE is considered a language, as opposed to a dialect, is because it's the accepted standard. It's been institutionalized and elevated to the status of a language. In contrast, BEV, despite its widespread use in popular culture (e.g., in music and by professional athletes) and by individuals other than African Americans, continues to be considered non-Standard English.

BEV is one of the most widely studied dialects. Despite its regional variations (e.g., New Orleans BEV versus Detroit BEV versus Prince George's County, Maryland BEV vs. Washington, DC BEV), as well as gender and social class differences, it shares features with southern White speech. The last-mentioned has to do with historical reasons, including the fact that most African Americans started out in the south, speaking southern speech, and it was only after the Emancipation Proclamation that African Americans migrated north and brought with them their speech. For this reason, the speech of many American residents (both Black and White) on the Eastern Shore of Maryland (e.g., Queen Anne's County) has features common to both BEV and southern American English. Some linguists, in jest, refer to the elongated vowel used by some southern Marylanders as the "Confederate 'A'" Examples include "five" pronounced /fa:v/ (with a long /a:/, as opposed to the relatively shorter diphthong /ai/).

In the international arena, major regional dialects of English include British English, American English, and Australian English, for instance. On a national scale, within these and other predominantly English-speaking countries, regional differences in language use could yield broad dialects such as southern American English or more specific regional dialects such as New England English and Boston English (famous for its diversity).

Dialects for Life and Death, Friend and Foe

Dialect differences are most visible at the word level. For instance, the words "borrow" and "lend"/"loan" are used interchangeably by many Africans, whose languages rarely distinguish between them. Speakers of these languages generally believe that "what's yours is mine."

Some words and/or sentences literally point to life and death (differences) in usage. For example, in Jamaican English, "She put to bed" means "She died" and/ or put someone to sleep (i.e., euthanized). In Nigerian English, the phrase is a euphemism for giving birth (i.e., life).

Dialect variations are not limited to English. Many Latino Spanish speakers, for instance, delete final consonants (e.g., *buena nóche* versus *buenas nóches*), and sometimes do so even in spoken and written English (e.g., *goo nigh* versus *good night*). While most refer to friends as *amigos/-as*, many El Salvadorians use the term *cheros/-as*, and some Mexicans use *compass* (from *compañeros/companions*). Children (*niños* in most dialects of Spanish) sometimes are called *patojos/-as* in Guatemala, *bichos/-as* in El Savador, and *cipotes/-as* in Honduras. In Argentina, Central America, and Spain, the respectful address form *usted(es)* (i.e., you) frequently is replaced by *vos(otros)*. In Peru (e.g., Lima lingo), the suffix *–ito* (like *–ita*, which means little one in names like An*ita*/little Anna) is frequently added to nouns (e.g., *mi Juanito*). Pets too are addressed using this endearing form (e.g., *mi gatito*/my kitten—even if it's grown).

Through examples from other languages, children can recognize that words are vital cultural clues. They reflect varied beliefs and conceptions of politeness. Hindi has a term, *sankoch*, for a form of self-discipline and hesitation that prompts polite Indians to decline food, beverages, and favors the first time they are offered. Indians typically expect their host to insist until they accept what is offered, unlike in the United States. For a child to have *sankoch* or be *sankochi* (as opposed to greedy) by politely declining a cookie, for instance, means she is well mannered.

When varieties have fewer than 5% cognates (i.e., shared words), they usually are considered distinct languages. They could be related (e.g., Romance) languages. More similarities than differences suggest that they are dialects. However, some "dialects" are not mutually intelligible and technically are separate languages (e.g., Cantonese, Mandarin [the standard], Wu, Hakka, and Xiang). Since "China" is "a single political and cultural entity" (Baron, 2000, p. 12), and they share the same script, they are termed "dialects."

Just as certain languages are labeled dialects for political reasons, the reverse is also true. Examples of languages that are really dialects include Hindi and Urdu (spoken primarily in India and Pakistan, respectively) and Bosnian, Serbian, and Croatian. While Hindi uses Devanagari and Urdu Arabic script, they have more in common than north and south Indian languages, and have borrowed extensively from each other. Yet, when India was divided in 1947, so were Hindi and Urdu. Similarly, when the former Yugoslavia split into Bosnia, Serbia, and Croatia, each was associated with a distinct language. In short, language and politics are intertwined.

Languages are considered more powerful and consistently held in high esteem. Since "language" labels are sociopolitically charged, some linguists describe a language as a dialect with an army and a navy. It goes without saying that those proficient in the standard dialect (i.e., speakers of a "language") are generally more successful. This might explain why far more elites are proficient in Standard English than in nonstandard varieties of English in the United States. Have you ever wondered, for instance, why speakers of BEV are rarely considered native speakers of English?

Bilingualism, Bidialectalism, and Code-Mixing

Bidialectalism, proficiency in more than one dialect, is a valuable skill and, like bilingualism, the foundation for global success in multiple senses. It is noteworthy, for instance, that the majority of preschoolers and Kindergartners in the United States use a language variety other than Standard English at home. English is emphasized at school, often at the price of the home language, accounting for identity crises and heritage language rejection or feelings of language inferiority and isolation. Latino and BEV-speaking PreK–3 children, for instance, make up a sizeable percentage of Early Head Start and Head Start programs. Familiarity with their home languages would help us better serve these children.

Research shows that bilingual and bidialectal individuals have an easier time mastering other languages, particularly if they maintain their home language (see Chapter 7). This includes improved reading in more than one variety, easier mastery of the social sciences, and more. Research also shows that, for many BEV speakers, Standard English is like a second language, and that instructional strategies that have helped DLLs also work with speakers of nonstandard dialects.

In a study that monitored SE acquisition by a group of BEV-speaking young adults from Chicago, for instance, the author (2000) observed that *contrastive analysis* (i.e., comparing dialect features) is instructive. *Heightened language awareness*—through observation, elicitation, contrastive analysis, and discussion—facilitated students' mastery of SE. In 6 weeks, students went from being monodialectal non-Standard English-using students whose performance on the Test of English as a Foreign Language (TOEFL) was initially comparable to that of low-level English learners, to strategic language users. The varieties consistently were presented side-by-side, instead of one atop the other, so that students would not assume that Standard English was "better" (p. 97). Differences were discussed, with students as partners.

When students replaced non-Standard English (in assigned resources) with just SE, as they were asked to, they noted that much was lost. In short, as this study illustrates, bilingual and bidialectal resources help develop "positive linguistic awareness" (Pandey, 2000, p. 106; see also Wolfram, Reaser, & Vaughn, 2008). Through bilingual/bidialectal activities and resources, children quickly discover that their lives are more colorful (i.e., each variety serves an important function in a particular *context*, and each colors life's palette). In short, while teaching children SE, we must counter language bias by encouraging bidialectalism/bilingualism.

We are ultimately responsible for the language attitudes children develop. Ensuring that children not merely maintain but expand their primary language skills while mastering SE is in the best interest of individuals, families, and communities (Jones & Yandian, 2002). Individuals fluent in more than one language variety have an intimate understanding of cultural nuances (i.e., they are bicultural). Since each serves key functions, individuals frequently switch between them. The result is *code-mixing*. A Coke ad in rural India uses code-mixing. If this ad simply said, "Enjoy chilled!" instead of, "Enjoy karo!" it would sound foreign to Indians. *Karo*, Hindi for "do," serves an emphatic function (i.e., You deserve it!). Code mixing persuades Indians to buy Coke by making the ad read like an invitation to a (Coca-Cola) party. The instructional value of code-mixing is illustrated next.

Multilinguals in multilingual nations are generally more linguistically secure. This is hardly surprising since multilingualism is considered an asset in these contexts and actively promoted. In addition, in these societies, *speech accommodation* through code-mixing/switching to nonstandard dialects is monetarily advanta-geous. Bilinguals enjoy a competitive edge and buy more for less. When vendors hear you speak their "language," you blend in (i.e., become one of them) and are unlikely to pay top dollar. However, when you sound like an outsider, some as-sume you can afford to pay more and therefore will charge you more.

In places where the majority speak another language, much of the upper class is fluent in nonstandard dialects, including Pidgin in Nigeria and Bazaar Hindi in India. Most freely use nonstandard variants in exchanges with those that are not as well off or as proficient in the esteemed languages. In contrast, few elites in the United States switch "downwards" in public, evidencing differences in societal perceptions of bilingualism, dialects, and even code-mixing.

BILINGUAL AND BIDIALECTAL LITERATURE

Literature containing more than one language variety is termed *bilingual litera-ture*. This section shares its instructional value. When children hear examples of different varieties in the classroom, they appreciate cultural diversity.

Bidialectal literature is readily available at public libraries and online. Exam-ples include works by Jacqueline Woods, Toni Cade Bambara, Richard Rodriquez, and Oscar Hijuelos. Salley (2009) brings French-flavored Louisiana lingo to life through Epossumondas (the Bayou possum), and Blazek (1997) celebrates Irish culture through Gaelic.

Family and community are celebrated in *We Had a Picnic This Sunday Past*. In this appetite-whetting book, the narrator, Teeka, shares how her family and friends enjoy a very special Sunday picnic. The main character is her Grandma, a dominant character, as is the case in many African American homes. The bond between Grandma and Teeka is evident from the start; Grandma takes Teeka to the picnic and even makes her a special dress for the occasion. The use of two dia-lects (SE and BEV) yields an exciting story about family, soul food, and fun. Teeka is fluent in both dialects and hops from one to the other in this rhythmic tale that captures the voice of a community. BEV, a necessary ingredient, authenticates and flavors the story.

It would have been disrespectful for Teeka and her cousin not to have echoed Grandma's frustration; hence, their observation, "*Hmph*, me and Paulette echoed"[9] (p. 7). *Hmph* generally is accompanied by a gesture of disappointment (e.g., a visu-ally depicted pout). In BEV, in addition to referring to the Sunday that just ended, "this Sunday past" expresses more than the SE equivalent (i.e., that it was a special Sunday). Public declarations such as, "Can't my boy bake himself some bread!" express Grandma's pride in her son. Interestingly, her "boy" (a term of endearment here) is a grown-up. In this book about sharing—everything, from one's food and home dialect to one's opinions—Grandma's call-and-response language (Smitherman, 1999) prompts participation; hence, the many tag questions she uses (e.g., "Don't he look just like a Moon Pie?" as opposed to a statement, "He looked just like a Moon Pie").

Student/family literature that uses one or more language varieties is equally instructive, as Schecter and Cummins (2003) demonstrate. In addition to involving community, such resources are authentic and often more relevant to linguistically diverse students. They mirror actual language use and add greater value to the classroom. Essayist Richard Rodriguez's biography comes to mind.

In *Hunger of Memory*, Rodriquez recalls his childhood as a lonely Spanish speaker in a U.S. Catholic school. Chapter 2, "Aria: Memoir of a Bilingual Childhood," shares his family's language practices and would interest PreK–3 children. (Mis)advised by his teachers, Rodriquez's parents give up their home language so their children will learn SE. "'Ahora, speak to us only en Ingles,' [Now, speak to us only in English] my father and mother told us" (Rodriguez, 1983, p. 453). Soon his parents stopped using Spanish and so did Rodriquez.

MULTILINGUAL MEDIA

Unfortunately, minority dialects are minimally used in mainstream children's media, and the depictions are rarely positive. The availability of DVDs increases the risk of children imbibing negative language stereotypes through repeated viewing (see Anjali Pandey, 2004). We must teach children to embrace language diversity, as this section demonstrates.

Like literature, multilingual media (e.g., movies, music, and student compositions) enhances children's language skills. In *Akeelah and the Bee*, for instance, children will hear Akeelah, a child from south Los Angeles, switch between SE and BEV. Invite them to identify and rephrase segments (e.g., the BEV compliment, "You go, girl!"), and explain why her language changes (e.g., she code mixes). How Akeelah prepares for a national spelling bee, with the help of professor Larabee, also will interest children. That she continues to jump rope between both dialects as she negotiates different relationships, despite Dr. Larabee's distaste for "the ghetto talk" she initially uses with him, is instructive. Akeelah offers Dr. Larabee a practical lesson in language bias. She makes this English professor realize that he has been harboring misconceptions about the language spoken in her neighborhood. In the process of drawing his attention to his own (language) prejudices, she makes Dr. Larabee aware, for instance, that many words he frowns at (e.g., *diss*) originated in the dialect he rejects and are in the dictionary. She educates viewers on the word factories of the street by highlighting BEV's creativity. Children will learn new words and come away with segmenting and spelling strategies. They will also learn that many English words are from other languages (see Chapter 3). Like Akeelah, they will develop a passion for words. You could also interest them in words from lesser known languages not mentioned in the film.

PreK children will enjoy HBO's bidialectal *Happily Ever After: Fairy Tales for Every Child*. Denzel Washington, Chris Rock, Whoopi Goldberg, and Samuel L. Jackson offer a *rappin' and rhymin'* special, as they term this linguistically face-lifted tale of *Mother Goose* (see also Colby, 2002).

Bilingual/bidialectal music, another excellent resource that builds phonemic awareness, vocabulary, and grammar, while illustrating the value of language diversity, is readily available online and on TV (e.g., MTV, BET). Many songs (e.g., Beyoncé's song "Irreplaceable," and Reggaeton songs) on Spanish TV and radio stations, use *Spanglish*, and mirror the singers' dual identity. Bollywood soundtracks often mix English with other languages. Some movies have code-mixed titles (e.g., *Thoda Pyaar, Thoda Magic* = A Little Love, A Little Magic, a children's movie). Even the children in this movie mesh English and Hindi. Musical fusions, like Bhangra, Chiac,[10] Soka/Chutney, and Zouk,[11] fuse languages and musical genres. Artists like Lamine Fellah (http://www.npr.org/player/v2/mediaPlayer.html?actio n=1&t=1&islist=false&id=154064928&m=154064921), Céline Dion and Marie-Jo Thério frequently mix languages. You might be pleasantly surprised by how many code-mixed songs your students know (and own).

ADDITIVE LANGUAGE STRATEGIES

Rodriquez's (1983) teachers subscribed to the unsubstantiated view that other languages interfere with English acquisition when, in fact, their facilitative role in subsequent languages (and vice versa) has been demonstrated. We must share this research with administrators, caregivers, and children. Denying children access to their heritage language(s) is damaging. In *Hunger of Memory*, Rodriquez is ashamed of his parents' English; he soon stops calling them *Mama* and *Papi*. Rodriquez's father experiences difficulty speaking English[12] and recedes into his shell. His poignant silence mirrors the negative impact of forced language change on this once-very-close-knit family. Rodriquez and his family were happiest when they used Spanish alongside English. With the switch to English, they lose their closeness and their shared voice ("Spanish").

When students feel uncomfortable using their primary languages at school, they are linguistically insecure. Many imbibe a linguistic hierarchy in which English is consistently at the top. Some educators, medical practitioners, and even parents still believe that a second language slows down learning. We therefore must take time to emphasize the benefits of language diversity.

To Rodriquez, rejection of Spanish was the price he had to pay to be "American." He did not have the opportunity to experience the benefits of bilingualism.

His book conveys a nostalgia for his home language, suggesting that he regretted having to give it up for English. In *Cool Salsa*, a bilingual collection of poetry, Oscar Hijuelos recalls how he interpreted "Hispanic" as "his panic" (at being unable to speak English fluently).

Ironically, even today, years later, many teachers continue to impart the (questionable) message that English is the all-important American language and rarely encourage bilingualism early on, and not just for DLLs. Some of us also send the message that dialects other than Standard English are inferior. We must expose children to other language varieties and demonstrate their value. Occasionally, we hear that the home language should be "encouraged," yet additive language strategies rarely are provided. Peregoy and Boyle (2001) mention the case of "a seven-year-old, recently arrived from Mexico," who responded negatively to his teacher's use of Spanish with him. They advise "sensitivity" (p. 5) to "personal conflicts of identity" (p. 6). Exactly what they recommend is unclear. Is it to support this boy's language rejection through use of just English? Is it possible, for instance, that his family speaks a language other than Spanish, which careful observation would reveal?

The following steps should assist you in implementing a culturally inclusive, additive language curriculum.

Step 1: Observe your students' language use. Observe what language(s) are spoken and/or understood in children's homes, the space each occupies, the functions each serves, and the nature of these exchanges. Audio, video, and written records of spoken and written language are invaluable. This includes language use on the playground, at recess, and at home. Once you have a representative sample of each child's language, analyze it.

Step 2: Gauge children's language radar (i.e., their language awareness and attitudes). Are they able to differentiate between language varieties? How do they refer to each? How knowledgeable are they regarding DLLs' and others' language use? Do they (dis)associate themselves from a particular variety? If so, how and why? Invite reasons and discuss them in small groups or as a class. Remember, guided questioning is instructive.

Step 3: Assign bilingual and bidialectal resources. Preselect age-appropriate bi/multilingual resources (see Deedy, 2007) and invite recommendations, including stories children (co-)author and music from their home countries. Monitor and invite children's reactions to these. Children can view (assigned) videos online and see (e.g., words in) different languages. Music adds excitement to the classroom, bridges home and school, and puts anxious and reserved children at ease. Provide the lyrics or invite children to transcribe them, so they can practice spelling and see which language units are married. Discuss the outcomes.

Step 4: Invite children to bilingualize and/or translate resources. Engaging children in hands-on code-mixing, comparison, substitution, and translation helps them pay (closer) attention to language, problem solve (through experimentation), enrich their language and cultural experiences, and eliminate language insecurities. Children learn by doing and come away with the following insights:

1. Languages vary and reflect cultural differences
2. Each variety serves important functions and has rules (i.e., grammar)
3. The more communicative avenues we have access to, the more we learn and the more creative we are

Linguistically diverse music and media enhance language and cultural awareness more than monolingual ones. Bilingualize lyrics (e.g., "Hello, hello! How are you today?" and "Just call me Ed") by inserting sounds, words, and verses from other varieties. This way, children exercise their creativity, make the lyrics more culturally relevant, and are more attentive to language. Show movie clips (e.g., *Waking Ned Devine*, set in Ireland) and invite translations for sections (e.g., "I'd treat me friends"). Children could identify and replace segments and discuss reasons for the language variation. They could role-play scenarios and modify the language and storyline. Children are also more likely to value and share the language dances in which they engage (i.e., outside class). The result is an inclusive and hands-on learning experience for all.

Step 5: Discuss the role of diverse varieties and apply to children's lives. Discuss the use of different language varieties in literature and other resources. Share your own language(s). Invite children to record and reflect on their (and family members') out-of-class language and to share examples (e.g., address and other language forms). Compare their language use and language attitudes with Rodriquez's. Discuss why some artists (e.g., Doc Watson, Lil Wayne, and Supa Star) use specific dialects in their lyrics and (band) names, yielding increased sensitivity to sounds, words, varied sentences, musical instruments, identity, and voice. "My southern dialect has improved through my Kindergarten and first graders," observes 2nd-grade teacher Pat Tessner, who was raised in Canada and who enjoys switching accents. "They are phonetic spellers. The word *naət*, pronounced with 2 syllables is 'night,'" she continues. "We have learned to appreciate how each other speaks and laugh when we misunderstand each other, recognizing it is just a different way." Nurture bilingualism and positive language attitudes in the formative years through these and other strategies (see Chapters 6 and 7).

SUMMARY AND APPLICATIONS

This chapter attempted to raise sociolinguistic awareness. As demonstrated, by promoting additive language practices (e.g., code-mixing, language comparison and substitution), we develop children's interpersonal and academic skills, and make them appreciate language diversity. What better way to embrace a child than to take an interest in his or her language? When we bring a smile to a child's face through a familiar greeting or other expression in a heritage language or simply by referring to it by its correct name (e.g., Hindi and Urdu, not Indian and Pakistani, respectively), we show that we care, and we have an easier time facilitating learning.

Minimal or no mention of language variation in the PreK–3 classroom encourages exclusion and stereotyping (e.g., language biases and heritage language loss). Linguistic dexterity, on the other hand, is community- and rapport-building, so we must actively promote it. As noted, language tolerance is necessary for inclusion, making familiarity with sociolinguistics essential for educators.

CHAPTER 6

Food for Thought

Vocabulary, Social Studies, and Health Literacy in PreK–3

I do not like green eggs and ham.

—Dr. Seuss, *Green Eggs and Ham*

The leprechauns feasted on warm soda bread . . .
A fine feed before them of cabbage and bacon.

—Blazek, 2002

Mama, is there duck in duck sauce?

—Sahara, 4

When teacher Vicki Nevick invited her 1st-graders to dictate their favorite food recipes while she wrote them down, 6-year-old Billy offered a recipe for squirrel dumpling. "His Gran(d)pa was a hunter. They lived out in the country, so you could tell what experiences they'd had through the foods they ate," she observed. Sampling and sharing foods "teaches children new words like *dressing*, the southern term for stuffing, history (family and regional), and respect for other ways of life." She once shared a story about kneading dough and 6-year-old Jason, who commented, "Kids don't always need dough; they might have what they need." "We ended up baking bread," she said, "and the kids learned about another kind of dough and a whole lot mo(r)e." An easy and fun way to expand children's content area vocabulary and understanding of diverse cultures is through food-related activities. This chapter whets children's appetites for knowledge through enriching food words and activities that fill them up literally and figuratively.

It demonstrates how to creatively teach PreK–3 vocabulary and content—including health literacy—through a focus on food. Why food? First, food is essential to our survival and we all appreciate good food. Second, it's easy to tie food to math, media, music, PE/movement, science, and more. Children are very likely to interact and learn language and core content over food (i.e., while preparing and sharing foods), without realizing they are learning. Exploring the language, art, science, social significance, and health benefits (and risks) of foods early on is both engaging and instructive. Miss Nevick, as her children politely address her, therefore centers many lessons around food. How about you?

We've all heard that childhood obesity is on the rise, with negative outcomes for learning and social-mental health. The lure of fast food and tech gadgets—which could potentially make children less physically active—requires us to think of more mentally and physically engaging and health-consciousness-raising activities in PreK–3.

Diary of a Wimpy Kid (2007) opens with a picture of a child playing video games and eating chips. "The way I like to spend my summer vacation is in front of the TV, playing video games," observes the narrator (p. 1). We owe it to our children to help them lead healthy lives. The central premise of this chapter is that the wider the array of foods we introduce children to and the healthier the choices, the more words and concepts, and health-related ones, they will acquire and the more likely they will be to make healthy food, language, and lifestyle choices. In short, familiarizing children with health-full food words would have a placebo effect—increasing their understanding of and desire for healthy living. They would begin to weigh their words[1] and calorie intake, exercise frequently, and become more globally aware (e.g., by sampling international foods). Since language is the brain behind early learning, sharing with children—and eliciting—how foods reflect cultural differences (i.e., social studies) teaches them to look for clues in words, a valuable skill in reading comprehension, math, and more.

ZESTY VOCABULARY

Vocabulary is, in fact, the most important learning tool in PreK–3. Roughly 25% of K–12 vocabulary is food related (Marzano, 2010). Examples include food and eating, entertainment, measurement, size, quantity, color, shape, comparison, contrast (math terms, too), texture and consistency, importance and goodness, animals, trees and plants (edibles), emotions and attitudes, popularity, and familiarity. As this chapter demonstrates, it's fairly easy to use terms from these clusters to describe foods from around the world and to teach curricular content.

Research shows that children familiar with content area vocabulary are more likely to succeed academically (August et al., 2009; Wessels, 2008), so building PreK–3 children's vocabulary is the first step. It is essential to continued learning inside and outside the classroom. A child with a large(r) vocabulary has an easier time communicating with peers and others, and learns more. Foods (nouns) and multisensory measure words (adjectives and adverbs) cut across content areas and learning environments (e.g., school and home), so themed vocabulary instruction (e.g., food-related) is highly effective (Marzano, 2010).

Through a carefully planned, multiskills focus on food(s), you could quickly enrich young children's vocabulary in multiple areas, including science (e.g., mirror climate change), and promote agency, critical thinking, and intercultural understanding.

EEW! WHAT'S THAT?

"They said 'Eew!!' They hated my goulash and I cried all day!" reported a teary-eyed, 8-year-old who had taken her favorite dish to school to share. Many children (especially DLLs) are traumatized by the (negative) reactions of classmates to foods they bring to school. I recall how my Kindergartner's lunches came home uneaten the first week because she felt embarrassed about showing her un-American-looking food. "I want pizza—like the other kids!" she insisted. Somehow I doubt every Kindergartner had pizza. I couldn't believe this was the same child that asked me to pack her favorite parathas and mango jam for her first day of school.

We must transform children's disgust for (the smell, look, and taste of) unfamiliar foods to appreciation. This is especially important for newcomer DLLs who might be unfamiliar with U.S. snacks and lunches. Their feelings could be hurt and they could go hungry if their classmates scrunch their noses. Sharing the names and flavors of unfamiliar foods with children develops more than their vocabulary.

Successful instruction starts with getting to know your students. What better way to do so than through the foods they enjoy? Knowledge of children's food habits is instructive and makes us more effective teachers. Through children's food preferences and dietary restrictions, we learn much about other cultures (Peregoy & Boyle, 2001), languages, routines, and literacy practices. When we draw children's attention to foods from other cultures, they are more likely to take an interest in other languages, many of which have flavored present-day English (see Chapter 3).

Making variable culinary and literary traditions more accessible at school and sharing the composition, flavors, and significance of varied foods with peers and staff is an excellent way to ease cultural adjustment for DLLs and those with different diets, while helping all children lead fuller, healthier, and richer lives. Imagine what school would be like if lunch featured healthy, yummy treats and beverages, and even melodies from around the world?

High-quality PreK–3 programs engage all children—emotionally, linguistically, and physically. Learning about foods children consume routinely (and on special occasions) could tell us a lot about their language, values, and traditions. Given the pressure DLLs face—to speak, eat, and dress like their mainstream peers—we have an obligation to validate cultural diversity early on (e.g., through an exploration of foods consumed and how). Indeed, foods enlighten us in multiple areas. One preschool teacher reported that the mother of a Chinese boy "wants him to follow the Chinese medicine method of eating, so I am learning about what foods come from the 'cold family' (cucumber, watermelon, banana . . .)." The boy drinks "warm water only." Many children from Southeast Asia are accustomed to outside-temperature water.[2] A focus on foods allows us to cater vocabulary, healthy literacy, and content area instruction to each child's taste. Sharing the varied senses diverse foods stimulate also develops children's multisensory vocabulary and related skills. Children are bound to make academic strides when we offer and welcome healthy and appetizing international foods, the key to enhanced vocabulary, content, and cultural understanding.

To teach children to lead healthy, well-rounded lives, draw on the rich resources in your classes, namely, children from diverse backgrounds and their families. As often as possible, share a meal and ensure that each child has a hand in the menu. Start by inquiring about and sharing breakfast, the most important meal of the day. Inviting family participation increases parental involvement in learning.

FROM FORTUNE COOKIES TO FORTUNE 500

I returned from New Orleans one afternoon with a desire to make beignets (from KiCongo *menkaté*). I searched for the recipe online, and 12 minutes later enjoyed a fresh batch which my 5- and 7-year-olds excitedly dusted with the sugar they'd ground in our coffee-and-spice grinder. Collectively make salads, side dishes, and/or desserts at school. You would all have a blast and learn new words, PreK–3 content, and a whole lot more. Experiment by adapting recipes (e.g., baking versus frying), and have children evaluate different ingredients and cooking experiences orally and in writing. What parent wouldn't want their child to learn how to cook?

Recipes for Hands-On Learning in PreK–3

Through recipes we share and elicit, we teach children to identify and distinguish between nouns (ingredients), verbs (actions/steps), adverbs (quantities/measure words), and adjectives (descriptors), the primary parts of speech in PreK–3 (Marzano, 2010), in a functional (task-based) setting. Children would learn that there is an art and a science to food (e.g., processes involved in cultivation, preparation, and storage). Verbs they would learn include "add," "blend"/"mix," "boil," "pat," and "cook"/"brown." Many are math and science words (see Chapter 4).

Provide a list of international festivities, their significance, and popular foods consumed. Share the recipes (see online) for these and other regional foods with children. Stimulate their sense of sound (e.g., unfamiliar consonant clusters in *knish*), smell, taste, and touch. Add a food center to your classroom, if it doesn't have one. Invite children to design it and explain what they would include and why. Observe children in this space for 2 or more weeks and use your findings to modify (the center and/or) instruction. Below is what one 8-year-old wrote when I sought her feedback on a food center.

Share fortune cookies and decide whether you could use the words in them to teach PreK–3 content. Then, with the help of children, bake your own batch containing children's couplets or words of wisdom (in one or more languages). Serve them in class, at PTA meetings, or at school events, and share what you learned from this exercise.

A Child's Voice

If I wear [sic] to make the messages in fortune cookies, I would put fun words in them and sometimes demanding letters like Jump up and down four times, and spin around 15 times. Also, I would put Spanish and Hindi rhyming words like "For shiny bal [hair], eat lots of dal" [lentil soup], and "Si, just por ti, y for me" (Spanish, *por* = for, *y* = and).

—Selena, 8

Cooking Language and Content in PreK–3

We can enhance multiple skills (e.g., art and music) through a focus on food(s). That food is quantifiable makes it directly applicable to math. Children learn PreK–3 math and language (e.g., 2 dozen, 3 bunches, 2.5 teaspoons) faster in an authentic context. Processes like cultivation and preservation (e.g., boiling, making jam) illustrate science at work. Food also has an important social studies dimension. For example, how people eat (whether all together or children first, as in rural India; with their hands or with chopsticks; from the same container (or plate made from banana or other leaf) or separate ones, on the floor or on stools conveys a lot.

A library visit and/or online search should help you locate relevant readings, visuals, and musical accompaniments to create a mouth-watering, multisensory experience year-round. Many children's stories, for instance, feature foods and food regionalisms (see Chapter 5). International Chocolate Day (September 13), for instance, is an opportunity to teach children about the cocoa pod and chocolate production, while sharing chocolate-based recipes from around the world.

With supervision, children could collaboratively prepare foods in part or whole at school. They would learn about and sample foods from unfamiliar locations and develop collaborative language. In pairs or teams, they could host breakfast, lunch, snacks, and/or desserts, and share (verbally and in writing) ingredients, textures, flavors, colors, health benefits, and more.

Learning the terms for natural and processed foods, ingredients, and preparation builds children's health awareness and vocabulary, discourse (e.g., sequencing: first . . . , then . . .), and interpersonal skills. The colors, textures, smell(s), and taste of foods make for lively discussion and writing assignments—further extending children's language (see Chapter 7). Sampling and preparing foods stimulates children's senses and helps them practice using nouns, verbs, and adjectives in context. They get to identify similarities in foods (e.g., U.S. cookies = English biscuits; U.S. biscuits = English buns) and utensils. For instance, many cultures use a griddle (i.e., a girdle in Scottish English and Scots Gaelic) to make local breads and snacks. Indian roti/chapatti and other "flatbread," for instance, is prepared on a *tava*, a shiny black griddle. Ask children if their families use a griddle at home, how, for what, and what it's called.

VOCABULARY-BUILDING GAMES

In language arts or during recess, you could play a simple vocabulary-building game called "Fruits, Flowers, and Vegetables." Up to five players or teams could play this game. The object is to grow children's vocabulary, and knowledge of culturally diverse "things," encourage creativity, and classification. Players must first agree on categories. They could, for instance, select four to six of the following or propose their own: name, animal, country or city, language, food item (appetizer, snack, side or main dish, dessert), fruit, flower, or vegetable, musical instrument, and/or thing. The game starts after someone says the alphabet out loud or silently until asked to "stop." If they stopped at 'i,' for instance, all players have to think of words in the selected categories that begin with 'i,' as illustrated below:

> Indra (a name), *impundu* (a central African fruit that looks like a small
>   red potato), Indonesia, Iris, Iroquoian (languages), *idli* (steamed rice
>   and lentils, a South Indian dish eaten with coconut chutney and/or a
>   vegetable-lentil soup called *sambar*), and *igloo* (thing).

The game stops and points are allotted once the person who is the first to fill in the blanks raises his/her hand or says "done." At this point, everyone else has to stop writing. Single instances of words could earn five to ten points (for a total of 50 to 100 points per round). If more than one person listed the same word in a particular category, that entry scores zero points. Children will hear new words (e.g., "parsley," which will likely earn more points than the more common "pumpkin"). You could modify the game by adding verbs (e.g., harvesting and food preparation words) and adjectives. Winners or losers could propose new word categories and/or eliminate existing ones.

All About Me and Let's Celebrate

Share food, vocabulary, and more through the activities "All About Me" and "Let's Celebrate [name of celebration]." In the former, invite children to talk/write about their eating routines and the foods and beverages they consume. Each child shares information, and you lead a discussion on (sub)cultural differences in diet, science, math, and/or and health education. Words children use will give listeners a flavor for language varieties and cultures, and increase their functional bilingual skills.

Culture maps are another engaging way to involve and get to know your students. Invite children to create a language-culture map identifying the varied linguistic and cultural influences in their lives. Food, music, languages, and words for family are examples of categories they could identify. They could use a cultural symbol that best represents their unique experiences, such as the peace sign, sun, or a star.

One student used the branch of the ackee tree, native to her home country Jamaica, to chart primary cultural influences in her life. She noted that the berries are consumed for breakfast. Another used the image of a fish to capture her life, and yet another literally started from the ground up, using the parts of a shoe to lace together the multiple influences he embraced. Invite children to share and explain their visual aid (thereby enhancing their spoken and written language skills). Pair up DLLs with more-proficient English users (not necessarily predominantly monolingual English speakers) and invite them to extend their maps. They could write out what they typically have for breakfast, lunch, snacks, and dinner. Peer interactions would accelerate their language and content acquisition (see Chapter 7).

Collectively explore and sample foods from different places. Sharing a meal builds trust and understanding. Host an international food fair to celebrate cultures, cuisine, and family. Discuss ingredients, geographic and cultural roots, preparation, serving sizes, food groups and calories, consumption and storage modes and processes, temperatures, soil variations, and so on. This is a first step toward healthy and meaningful international education. After children experience different foods, they could share their thoughts and/or (co-)create a book of their favorite recipes.

Salsa-ed Stories

Children could co-create (i.e., write and illustrate) bilingual stories featuring international foods and/or recipes. These would connect students, families, and communities, and teach children vocabulary and health literacy. Children's technology skills would improve as well, through word processing, monitored online searches, and more. Encourage children to use more than one dialect/language.

Tasks could be as involved as researching and sharing the history of a term, its cultural significance, taste, texture, smell(s), and emotions it evokes, or as basic as locating and annotating (e-)visuals.

Locate Food

Many children have neither seen nor tasted guavas, mangoes, persimmons, *nance* (yellow Central American fruits like cherries), figs, or other "foreign" fruits and vegetables. Introduce children to the source (i.e., berry shrubs, fruit trees), geography, taste, and uses. Inviting children to research the root word (*parsiman*) and sharing its other name ("Korean mango"), and its high protein content, should interest many. Children could identify on a map where the fruit grows (e.g., Brazil, Spain, Israel, Korea, China, and Indiana, home to an annual persimmon festival). They could research and share its many uses (e.g., as fresh and dried fruit, laxative, jam) and read regional literature that mentions it (e.g., *Why Epossumundas Has No Hair on His Tail*), alongside other southern hospitality specialties like sweet tea. This way, a single word feeds children health, social studies, language, and more.

Showing children how the languages in persimmon-growing locations are written and how they sound is helpful, too. Invite those who speak these languages at your school to share additional information about the fruit, culture, and/or language. This is an opportunity for children who have lived in other locations to offer their expertise, increasing participants' self-confidence and strengthening their peer relations (see Pandey, 2008).

Taste and Smell

Invite children to share culturally significant beverages and foods believed to be good for them. Welcome family participation. Everyone would enjoy a freshly made snack/item (e.g., French *crêpes* and Indian *papad*, or *samosa*), thereby avoiding processed foods. Invite children to bring specific items to class, and use a portable stove, if necessary. Children could take turns counting and writing out the names of ingredients and outlining the benefits, preparation time, and/or steps—practicing math, spelling, and social skills in the process.

Compare and Contrast

During math, science, and/or social studies, invite children to pay attention to food labels (e.g., on produce) and to use these and their own words to compare foods (color, texture, etc.). Children are likely to develop a taste for healthier foods, including some consumed elsewhere, and we would divert them from unhealthy foods and poor eating habits (e.g., "all-you-can-eat"). After all, children learn best through example.

Food Field Trips

Organize field trips to regional (e.g., Latin markets/mercados) and international food stores that feature natural foods and beverages (e.g., Whole Foods, Trader Joe's). Visits involving some walking are advisable, prompting observation and interaction (i.e., additional opportunities for language and multiskills enhancement).

SUMMARY AND APPLICATIONS

This chapter offers a recipe for vocabulary-building and health literacy. It proposes activities that ensure inclusive instruction in multiple senses. The result is a feast that aims to provide children a global education. As demonstrated, it's relatively easy to teach PreK–3 vocabulary—in English and other languages—through a focus on food and associated content. Children learn unusual sounds, core content and handy words and expressions. Even the most rigid curriculum could be diversified this way, and different languages and personalities invited to the table.

The activities proposed aimed to

- Expand children's multicultural and multisensory vocabulary
- Familiarize them with healthy and diverse foods
- Develop an appreciation for different foods and languages
- Teach core content creatively

Health-related vocabulary is likely to spark children's interest in healthy foods. Some say, "You are what you eat." By mentioning healthy foods and making them readily available at school, we increase children's vocabulary, agency, awareness of self, geography, science, and more. Discussions of food(s) could prompt positive lifestyle changes, while bringing children (and families) closer and teaching them key words and expressions in other languages (e.g., of politeness).

The activities and resources proposed here will enhance multiple PreK–3 skills. Through a focus on words associated with proper nutrition; their cultural significance; health benefits; the science involved in their preparation and/or storage; and the art of serving and consuming specific foods, vocabulary learning and global understanding will follow.

Serving up a delightful menu in PreK–3 and satisfying children's appetites (and linguistic curiosity) is key to learning. Through the activities proposed, children, like us, would acquire a taste for different foods, languages, and cultures, and would grow in mind and body.

CHAPTER 7

Strategies for Dual Language Acquisition

There are so many THINKS (bilinguals) "can think"!

—adapted Dr. Seussism

If somwon speaks my language, I would feel special and we could also say things in seakret.

—Selena, 7

Mama, there are 2 kinds of 'e.' One is the Spanish y for and, and the other is the English 'e.'

—Sahara, 5

Those who know nothing of foreign languages know nothing of their own.

—J. W. Von Goethe

Mama, when you be[1] a baby again, and lose your teeth and can't walk, don't worry. I'll feed you and carry you—in the big-people stroller.

—Sahara, 5

As a child, like many dual language learners,[2] elementary school teacher Yoshiko Uchida "didn't appreciate her Japanese heritage and didn't want to learn to read and write in Japanese" (Chin-Lee, 2005) because what she read and heard made no mention of other languages. Children are very impressionable, so when we fail to mention or use languages other than English in the classroom, we send the message that (linguistic) diversity is unimportant and potentially problematic. In other words, what we do not say speaks volumes and is just as important as what we do say. If Helen Keller could master Braille in five languages (Chin-Lee, 2005), the least we can do is provide children the opportunity to develop a basic understanding of at least one other language. Simply acknowledging and commending children by saying *oui* and *si* (yes in French and Spanish, respectively), for instance, goes a long way toward interesting children in other languages and in preventing *heritage language loss* and attendant *identity crises*.

Unfortunately, when some DLLs appear to take longer to speak and/or read and write, some assume they are experiencing a language delay and/or that they are confused. In short, bilingualism and bilingual education are viewed by many as avoidable (obstacles). Some professionals still advise parents to use just English at home (Rodriguez, 1982). Some are dissuaded from using DLLs' languages when, in fact, their use could ease English mastery—for English monolinguals, as well. In schools not designated as bilingual, many teachers are afraid to use other languages in their classrooms, lest they interfere with English acquisition and/or garner criticism from their peers or administrators. They wrongly assume that their school must be English-only, particularly since curricular mandates rarely recommend use of other languages. Such views are unfounded and misguided (Casteel & Ballantyne, 2010).

As the opening quotes suggest, learning other languages, or even learning about another language, increases our understanding of our primary language. Bilinguals also have an easier time conjuring novel ideas. Bilingualism, as this volume demonstrates, is one of the most valuable skills of our time. YouTube gives us the example of Ravi, an Indian boy who sells peacock fans in many languages.[3] Three years later, his interviewer tracks him down and asks whether Ravi attends school. "No, Sir," Ravi responds. That this polite child never attended school, yet speaks multiple languages evidences children's unique language-acquisition skills.

Any discussion of *early bilingualism* or *dual language* and literacy acquisition (not just for DLLs) has to begin with first language (L1) acquisition. Indeed, we look to children for answers (Pandey, 2010; Pinker, 1994). This chapter outlines:

> The benefits of early bilingualism
> Key concepts and theories pertaining to first and "second" or subsequent language acquisition (SLA)
> *How* children acquire one or more languages
> *Strategies* to promote English language mastery and early bilingualism

INCLUSION THROUGH FUNCTIONAL BILINGUALISM

"I'm the most differentest [sic] kid in my class! I wanna be like everybody else," announced a 1st-grader to her mother one day. "Nobody else speaks Hindi in my class! Some say I speak 'Indian.'" Her words illustrate how many children are unfamiliar with the names of other languages spoken in their neighborhoods. It also illustrates the pressure children feel to assimilate in English-dominant schools, making a dual or multilingual language approach necessary early on.

Research indicates that early bilingual programs are the only ones in which all children excel (Collier & Thomas, 2004). Moreover, basic familiarity with other languages, or *functional bilingualism*, as this skill is termed in this chapter, fosters cultural understanding. *Bilinguality* (Hamers & Blanc, 2000), another term for functional bilingualism, is essential to success in our global world. A child that is *functionally bilingual* appreciates multilingual media (e.g., music). He or she can greet and thank in more than one language, differentiate between and mix language varieties, and identify at least one other writing system besides English.

The U.S. Census Bureau projects that by 2050, language minorities will constitute 50% of America's population, with Latinos in the lead (KewalRamani et al., 2007). Over 60% of preschoolers are Latino and, by 2030, roughly 40% of all school-aged children will be DLLs (Thomas & Collier, 2002). The implications of these statistics for PreK–3 instruction and nation-building cannot be overstated. *Language inclusion/cultural responsiveness* (Lim et al., 2009) should be a priority and a shared responsibility. Since DLLs make up a sizeable percentage of America's PreK–3 population and many are bicultural and bilingual, we have the unique opportunity to help all children develop functional bilingualism. DLLs already have a foundation in at least one language. All we have to do is reinforce their primary language and simultaneously promote English acquisition. As demonstrated, these are attainable and interconnected goals.

WHY LEARN ABOUT LANGUAGE ACQUISITION?

Shortly after Yahoo posted a story about China opening the Jiaozhou bridge, one post read: "I hope your kids are learning Mandarin,"[4] evidencing public recognition of the value of multilingualism. Research shows that the average monolingual English-using 3rd-grader has a vocabulary of roughly 5,000 words (Marzano, 2010). In contrast, most DLLs have a smaller English vocabulary and require 3 to 5 years to master academic English. Eventually, with individualized instruction (see Chapter 9), DLLs come out ahead (Collier & Thomas, 2004), given their larger combined vocabulary and advanced cognitive and interpersonal skills (Orellana, 2009, 2001; Pandey, 2010). Most DLLs know more-complex words than their monolingual counterparts. Moreover, the word-extension capabilities and broader functionality (i.e., applicability across content areas) of DLLs' base vocabulary are noteworthy and arguably more decisive in the long run than size alone (see Chapter 2). For example, it's easier for a child who knows Spanish to decode (i.e., learn) the words "vent," "ventilator," and "ventilation" since she already knows shared-root words like *ventana* (window) and *ventilation* (pronounced /ven*thilasion*/). Similarly, Spanish/Latin *culpa* is a natural predecessor to *culpable*, unlike the English equivalent "fault." The jump from Spanish *aeropuerto* (airport) to related English terms (e.g., *aeronautics* and *Puerto Rico*/rich port) is easier, too, when we use cognates as supportive bridges. Even the words "vocal" and "vocabulary" make more sense when you know the Spanish word *voca*, as you visualize words springing from the mouth. After reading this chapter, you will be better equipped to assist both DLLs and monolingual English speakers attain similar levels of competency.

Learning how children acquire language helps us understand how they learn what they learn (i.e., language and content). Before we misdiagnose, dismiss, or misread a child's speech and literacy skills, we must understand how it is that children come to speak, read, and write in one or more languages. We can then more effectively enhance and assess their skills. It may be that the language employed is complex and not that the child is a poor reader.

BENEFITS OF EARLY BILINGUALISM

Children exposed to other languages blossom. They enter a whole new world—of social studies and more. Knowledge of another language variety, however basic, colors children's exchanges and expands their social circle (see Chapter 5). Initiatives like the U.S. Foreign Language Assistance Program reflect this. When you learn even a smattering of another variety, it's easier to think outside the box. You begin to appreciate concepts for which your language has no words, including expressions of respect for older siblings (as in Chinese).

Functional bilingualism strengthens children's interpersonal and academic skills, and their understanding of peoples and customs. In *The Child Language Teacher* (2010), for instance, the author found that familiarity with more than one language enhances children's academic and problem-solving skills, and helps them maintain healthy, confidence-boosting ties with at least two communities. Children then have an easier time establishing relationships with diverse groups (e.g., through code-mixing). They demonstrate advanced cognitive and linguistic skills, develop "agency" earlier, and are more successful academically and socially (Beach et al., 2010; Knörr, 2008). Schecter and Cummins (2003) observe of ESL 1st-graders that their "creativity, inquiry, and problem solving represent the kind of rigorous cognitive engagement we might expect among *university graduate students*" (p. 51).

Indeed, young DLLs employ sophisticated mediation skills associated with adults (see Orellana, 2001), illustrating their enhanced understanding of language. That translation comes naturally to most bilingual children evidences their ability to intuitively decode language and their suitability for language-literacy facilitation (see Pandey, 2010).

That bilingual children from low-income households whose parents' level of education is substantially lower outperform English-speaking Kindergartners in problem solving, evidences the benefits of bilingualism (Carlson & Metzoff, 2008; CREDE, 2003). Bilingual children also demonstrate earlier vocabulary development and segmentation skills. That they often code-mix, for instance, mirrors their advanced phonemic awareness. Early exposure to phonemic diversity and expanded opportunities for (phonemic) experimentation undoubtedly help. Code-mixing also reflects bilinguals' intuitive understanding of word composition (i.e., morphology). Bilingual children also demonstrate better cross-cultural communication skills and earlier mastery of meaning, including cultural nuances (Bialystok, 2001).

Code-mixing, a valuable *communication strategy* (see Chapter 5), reflects children's *cultural hybridity or biculturalism* (Colby, 2002). It takes talent and skill, and bilingual children are more likely to code-mix, so the benefits of early bilingualism cannot be overemphasized.

Children code-mix en route to bilingualism, and/or because of the distinct meanings each language conveys. Bilingual children as young as 2 mix language varieties in culturally appropriate ways (see Harding & Riley, 1999; Pandey, 2010), reflecting advanced linguistic and cognitive skills. "My dolly is blocked from na-jar," remarked an 8-year-old to her sister. She used the Hindi word *najar* (i.e., the evil eye from which many Greeks, Turks, and others seek protection) to convey a culture-specific message, since English lacks an equivalent.

Another example of a code-mixed word a bilingual preschooler was observed using is *likhing*. "Didi is likhing," she said. *Likh* is the word for write in Hindi/Urdu (/kh/; aspirated /k/ is a distinct phoneme). This 3-year-old was aware of this, and added -ing to it, yielding a salsa-ed form for writing, half in Hindi/Urdu and half in English. This example and many others demonstrate her awareness that -ing is meaningful (i.e., communicates ongoing action). That this preschooler successfully combines parts from two languages evidences her early morphological awareness and word segmentation skills. In addition, she addresses her older sister using the culturally appropriate term *Didi*, illustrating her *dual identity*.

Note that language proficiency declines with non-use. When code-mixing is encouraged in the early years, bilingualism flourishes. Because learning essentially is recalling and applying, and bilingual children's working memory is visibly enhanced (Alloway, Gathercole, & Willis, 2004; Bialystok, 2001), we can conclude that exposing children to more than one phonological system yields positive outcomes. We should therefore attempt to similarly advantage all children; hence, the *functional bilingualism* or *functional dual language* pedagogy proposed. Sharing instructional time between languages is one option. Integrating other languages at appropriate points, including after hours (e.g., through take-home assignments), is another. This latter approach (not limited to two languages) is recommended here.

Given the research findings, we should expose children to other languages early on, when it is easiest and most beneficial to master the nuances of language/culture and utilize their skills in community engagement (Pandey, 2010). According to the U.S. Department of Education, "Early language learning is essential to increasing the number of Americans able to communicate in foreign languages at advanced levels."

As the next section demonstrates, a focus on English-only legislature helps put U.S. language policies into perspective and highlights the political face of language (identity).

U.S. BILINGUAL EDUCATION

Early bilingual education was quite successful in 19th-century America but was quickly eliminated through "English-only assimilation," which obscured "the diversity of cultures that flourished in North America" and "efforts to preserve them, among both immigrants and indigenous minorities" (Crawford, 1999, p. 21). From the 1800s through early 1917, bilingual schools were popular in most states. They reported very positive educational outcomes. By the mid-1800s, German-English schooling was offered in several cities, including Baltimore, Milwaukee, and St. Louis. In 1839, Ohio passed a law authorizing instruction in German, English, or both, depending on parents' preference. In 1847, Louisiana "adopted the identical statute," substituting French for German (p. 23). A year later, New Mexico "authorized Spanish-English bilingual education" (p. 25). In fact, more than 12 states passed laws legislating bilingual education. Even in those that did not, local school boards provided classes in multiple languages, including Czech, Dutch, and Swedish. In short, linguistic inclusion was practiced, and educators, parents, and lawmakers believed that all children would learn better with bilingual schooling.

The late 19th century saw the rise of "Americanization" and "language restrictionism" (Crawford, 1999, p. 27). In 1906, "Congress passed the first federal language law, an English-speaking requirement for naturalization" (Crawford, 1999, p. 26). In April 1917, when the United States entered World War I, anti-German sentiments led to the passing of state laws and decrees "banning German speech . . . even on the telephone" (p. 28). English suddenly became synonymous with patriotism. In Ohio, individuals were fined $25 for speaking German. Subsequently, a bill was passed banning German and other "foreign" languages in elementary schools. By 1921, "at least 18,000 persons were charged" (p. 28) with violating English-only mandates in the Midwest. Other minority languages were also discouraged. By the end of World War I, some 15 states had English-only laws in place and "minority tongues were devalued in the eyes of the younger generation" (p. 29).

At the end of the Spanish-American War, "the U.S. imposed English as the medium of instruction in its new colonies of Puerto Rico, Hawaii, and the Philippines" (Crawford, 1999, p. 27), prompting what Crawford termed "an educational disaster" (p. 27). A study by Teachers College showed "84% of Puerto Rican children dropping out by the 3rd grade" (p. 28), linking educational failure to linguistic exclusion. On the mainland, President Franklin Roosevelt discouraged use of languages other than English. By the end of World War II, English was the only publicly tolerated language in the United States.

Native American students were punished for speaking their languages. English was used to "civilize" Indian children in the United States (Crawford, 1999), Canada, New Zealand, and Australia (see the movie *Rabbit Proof Fence*). Thousands were forced to attend English-only boarding schools where their languages and cultures were eradicated. According to Senator Ben Nighthorse Campbell of the Cheyenne tribe: "One of the first English words Indian students learned was "soap," because their mouths were constantly being washed out for using their native language" (Crawford, 1999, p. 31). Even the Cherokees' printing press was "confiscated." By 1969, "40% of Cherokee adults in eastern Oklahoma were functionally illiterate" and "up to 75% of their children were dropouts" (p. 31). Today, over half of the American languages in use in 1492 have vanished. As of 2001, while many Navajos still spoke Diné, 7 of the 154 surviving languages (e.g., Coos, Eyak, and Serrano) had just one surviving speaker (Reyhner, 2001).

Even after the Bilingual Education Act was passed in 1968, schools were not required to use another language. The law was intended merely to speed up DLLs' "transition to English" (Crawford, 1999, p. 40), a remediation (versus enrichment) perspective. U.S. bilingual education failed for a number of reasons. First, there was no genuine interest in other languages and cultures. No funds were earmarked for "teacher training and professional development" (p. 47). During this period, only programs that transitioned children to English were funded. By 1974, bilingual instruction was offered to "only about 6% of eligible children" (p. 47). It was subtractive (i.e., not additive) and like sheltered ESL instruction; DLLs were initially taught in their home languages in content areas. The goal was to use the L1 as a bridge to English mastery, given research findings that DLLs need time to master academic language. The goal was not to make all children bilingual. Once DLLs demonstrated sufficient proficiency in English, the other language(s) no longer mattered. Acquainting children with other languages was never the objective. Temporary, transitional bilingualism—primarily for DLLs—was all that was permitted in the name of assimilation (Reyhner, 2001).

Students were expected to be English dominant (i.e., to demonstrate stronger English skills) within 3 years, despite research findings that mastering academic language takes approximately 5 years (Peregoy & Boyle, 2001). When DLLs were unable to meet this unreasonable timeline, "bilingual education," which was bilingual in theory but not in practice, was readily dismissed and promptly outvoted. ESL instruction, essentially immersion, was the "alternative" advocated in the 1980s. The president of "English Plus," a campaign launched in 1985, argued, "But English is not enough. . . . This nation was founded on a diversity of language and culture" (quoted in Crawford, 1999, p 77). Nevertheless, in 1986, Proposition 63 was passed in California, "giving legislative form to a backlash against bilingual education" (p. 63).

Today, while the United States does not have a designated official language, several states have English-only laws in place (e.g., Arizona) and misconceptions about bilingual education persist. However, "although the media often suggest otherwise, conflicts involving language are not really about language, but about fundamental inequalities between people who happen to speak different languages" (Ritchie & Bhatia, 2004, p. 403). Unfortunately, language becomes the scapegoat (Reyhner, 2001).

CANADA'S BILINGUAL EDUCATION

Bilingual education has been quite successful in Canada (Schecter & Cummins, 2003) because of the additive and sustained implementation, demonstrating the positive effects of "knowledge-transfer" (Krashen, 2000) or how fluency in one's primary language eases mastery of the second, and vice versa. Canada's Official Languages Act of 1969 made English and French, the colonizers' languages, official languages. A group of English-speaking parents in St. Lambert, Quebec, paved the way for bilingual education by offering a bilingual Kindergarten class. They taught both European languages, so that children could appreciate cultural diversity.

The Canadian Charter of Rights and Freedoms requires all provinces to offer public education in both languages. Approximately 7% of students attend French immersion schools. Early immersion, beginning in Kindergarten, is the most popular, followed by total immersion.[5] Various results have been found in student achievement for immersion and regular students.

The next section discusses key concepts in language acquisition.

KEY CONCEPTS IN LANGUAGE ACQUISITION

Language acquisition is facilitated by *comprehensible input (CI),* that is, easy-to-understand language. Input fosters *interaction* or *meaning negotiation*, which, in turn, enables *scaffolding* (see Soderman et al., 2005). Scaffolding can take different forms, including provision of an example or template children could use, direct or indirect feedback (e.g., "Say /y/, not /j/" and "Again!"), and positive skills reinforcement (e.g., *Bravo! Muy bien!*). The result is language acquisition or learning.

Comprehensible Input, Interaction, and Scaffolding

Note that CI alone is insufficient for language acquisition. In *The Child Language Teacher* (2010), for instance, the author found that many children receive substantial input in at least one other language, yet fail to learn it unless they *use* it. When individuals interact using a language, however rudimentary their usage (e.g., code-mixing), they are more likely to infer its component parts and patterns and receive feedback that helps them make necessary modifications (i.e., extending their proficiency).

Legend has it that King Akbar, who commissioned the Taj Mahal as a tribute to his beloved wife Mumtaz ("Mumtaj" in Hindi), hence the name Taj Mahal (Taj Palace), was convinced that infants who did not hear language would not acquire language. Apparently, he had a house built for newborns on the palace grounds. For 4 years, the babies were cared for, but nobody spoke to them or around them. By age 4, they were unable to speak. The case of Genie, a 13-year-old girl who was isolated and denied language, speaks to the importance of continued comprehensible input, interaction, and feedback in language acquisition. This story and the behaviorist studies conducted after Genie was "discovered" (alongside other "wild children") are available online.

Acquiring versus Learning Language

The relatively unconscious manner in which most children acquire their primary language, as opposed to the conscious process that characterizes much of classroom-based (language) *learning*, has prompted the distinction between *acquisition* and *learning* (Krashen, 1982). *Collaboration* is a necessary ingredient for both. Most infants and young children interact with their caregivers and others, although their level of interaction varies, depending on variables such as the *age* of the person interacting with them and *child-raising practices*. The language adults use with infants and young children (i.e., whether interactive or directive), and the nature of the responses they expect, vary. Some babies and toddlers are coaxed to respond through repetition, questions, and imperatives (e.g., "Who's my pretty girl?" "Sing!"),[6] while others are encouraged to listen and respond nonverbally (e.g., *"Baila, Papi! Baila!"*/"Dance, Papi! Dance!").

Conceptions of language acquisition are shaped by culture. Many believe that parents are children's first and/or only language teacher, and use behaviorist tools like repetition (*phir se*, Hindi for "once more") and positive reinforcement (e.g., *Si, mi amor*, Spanish for "Yes, my love") to teach children language. Yet, these strategies alone neither engender nor fully account for language acquisition. In the case of Creoles and other child-created languages, children's proficiency exceeds their parents', making peers the likeliest source of language acquisition (Calvin & Bickerton, 2000; Pinker, 1994). In the homes of recent immigrants, for instance, children generally employ the dominant language faster. In fact, many bilingual children are the primary voice of their families (Pandey, 2010).

LANGUAGE-ACQUISITION THEORIES AND RESEARCH APPROACHES

The ease with which children acquire and use language is so fascinating and insightful that they are, in fact, the starting point of language-acquisition research (see Tharp, 1997; Vogt, Jordan, & Tharp, 1987). That children potentially can acquire any number of languages further evidences their linguistic forté. *Infant bilingualism*, "the most common and successful" (Harding & Riley, 1999, p. 40), is a case in point.

Several studies have examined how the first language is acquired (Brown, 2000; Pinker, 1994) and report that for children to be vocal by age 3 they must hear language. They could hear more than one and eventually pick up at least one and sometimes more than one. The more languages an infant hears and the more consistently the more likely (s)he will be bilingual. Regardless of how many languages a child hears spoken *to* them or around them, they will acquire at least one.

Three major theories have been advanced to account for language acquisition, namely, *behaviorism*, *nativism*, and *functionalism*. They reflect varied definitions of language.

Behaviorism

Behaviorists believe that language is *imitated behavior* (Skinner, 1957) and that competent language users teach language through conditioning—specifically, modeling, repetition, and reinforcement, or rewarding acceptable language use. Repetition is believed to help children develop desired language habits—through imitation and positive reinforcement. However, behaviorists are unable to explain why children often say things they have never heard before, and how they suddenly go from zero to thousands of words in a couple of years, without drastic changes in the input they receive.

Nativism

Nativists contend that we are born with the capacity to acquire language and that, except in rare instances, this process cannot be disrupted. Much like our need and desire to communicate, language acquisition is a human instinct (see Pinker, 1994). According to linguist Noam Chomsky, we are born with a language-acquisition device that sets itself in the direction of one or more languages the moment it is stimulated (i.e., exposed to input/speech). The human brain, like a computer program, quickly identifies patterns in the language it hears or sees (e.g., sign language), prompting children to generate more words and other language units. Spoken and/or visual *language input* is then the catalyst, a necessary ingredient in language acquisition, first and subsequent. It predisposes the brain toward a specific language, helping identify patterns through mechanisms like sound and affix substitution. For instance, a preschooler might say "surpisinger," based on her recollection of comparative forms like *faster*. This trigger is termed comprehensible input. Languages heard or seen in print, sign, or online constitute *input* because they generate more of the same.

Nativists believe that we are biologically predisposed to language and that there are similarities across languages as regards the stages involved and the content and structures acquired. Why else would children follow a similar path? Another name for nativists is *generative grammarians* since they believe languages share commonalities at some deeper, semantic level (termed *universal grammar*). That children, regardless of surface-level differences in their language, quickly infer a finite number of grammar rules operant in their language, and generate an unlimited number of sentences, lends support to nativisim. Nativists believe children infer the rules of their language and put them to use, quickly doubling, tripling, and/or more than quadrupling their vocabulary and other language units. Why else would they say things they never heard before? Pinker (1994) marvels at 3-year-olds' "grammatical genius" (p. 32) and their "extraordinary acts of creation" (p. 39). So do Calvin and Bickerton (2000).

Nativists emphasize children's creativity, drawing attention to their ongoing language analysis and assembly. They contend that language acquisition is triggered by comprehensible input provided by adults and children, through interaction and negotiation of meaning or scaffolding (Brown, 2000). Unlike adults, children "aren't taught rules; . . . they *create* and *apply*" them (Bickerton, 2000, p. 32). Children are born linguists; they infer exceptions and rules, so nativists view their linguistic success as evidence of the innateness of language.

Functionalism

While nativists focus primarily on the abstract and generative (i.e., reduplicative) properties of language, *functionalists* focus on "the functional levels of meaning constructed from social interaction" (Brown, 2000, p. 27). They contend that language serves multiple functions and that a child's need to communicate prompts language acquisition (i.e., necessity is the mother of invention). In this account, *language function* or meaning drives acquisition. Most infants are quickly socialized into conversation and promptly realize that language is meaningful. Peregoy and Boyle (2001) observe that children "learn through their talking" (p. 144). Children use language to communicate their needs, collaborate, control, demonstrate, discover, invite, inquire, request, respond, and so on, so language development and communicative function go hand in hand. Language is a vital and expressive learning tool for children. In the course of communicating, young children learn how to mean (i.e., signal what they mean) and extend language (see Halliday, 1975).

Some linguists have researched, recorded, and shared their children's language-acquisition experiences. Their stories and research by other language specialists point at noteworthy similarities in the process of first language acquisition across languages, as well as in the units of language acquired. These biographical stories and supplemental research illustrate that, for young children, language acquisition and function(ality) are one and the same.

In *Learning How to Mean*, linguist Michael Halliday, for instance, shares how his son Nigel acquired language and identifies key functions of Nigel's speech, namely, informative, personal, imaginative, interactional, heuristic, regulatory, and demonstrative. You might find that this list is not exhaustive. For example, children are not immune to insulting (e.g., "I hate you!" "You're the stupid(o)est!"). What functions do insults serve? Also, some functions overlap, including personal, interactional, informative, heuristic, and interactional. Thus, identifying the function(s) a child's language serves could be challenging; some utterances might serve more than one. Ask yourself: "In imaginative play, what function(s) does thanking serve?" Interactional? Imaginative? Or both? It might help to distinguish between *primary* and *secondary functions*. Examples of a 4-year-old's utterances, organized by primary function, follow:

Examples of Children's Functional Language

Informative and demonstrative

Complaining/soliciting praise: *You hate my painting!*
Disagreeing/retaliating: *I'm not going to paint anything! ___ is forcing me to
. . .*
Announcing/stipulating: *You have to see this!*
Demonstrating: *You're opposed* [sic] *to do this* (teaching an adult how to hula
    hoop). *Like this. Here. Watch me.*
Explaining/rationalizing (inferring/problem solving through clue
    identification): *I just knew it because you don't use __.*
Assuring: *Pinky promise!*

Heuristic

Discovery verification: *Is that correct, Mama?*
Inquiring: *How do you write, "I love you"? What does* fabuloso *mean?*
Hypothesizing/accosting and verifying: *When you say, "I'm sure," that means,
    "No, that's not true."* (i.e., sarcasm)

Personal and interactional

Complimenting/evaluating: *You're the best Mama in the world, even though
    you're also sometimes the yelliest.*
Seeking consolation: (Mama) *I messed up!*

Regulatory

Consoling: *That's okay. . . .*
Facilitating: *It's easy. Hold this.*
Directing: *Shh! I'm seeing a movie in my head.*

You might find that some children use more heuristic language than others or more overtly instrumental language (e.g., "I want eggs!"), and yet others less aggressive language (e.g., "Could I please have . . . ?"), depending on the context, their age, frame of mind, (sub)culture, biological position in the family, and socialization (individualistic versus interdependent), among other factors worth investigating.

Regardless of the specific functions you identify in children's language (e.g., in different venues), the fact remains that it is purposeful. As such, PreK–3 instruction is likely to be most successful when we highlight language structure and function.

SECOND-LANGUAGE-ACQUISITION THEORIES

Children also have an advantage when it comes to mastering a second, third, or fifth language (Piatteli-Palmarini & Berwick, forthcoming; Bialystok, 2001; Marshall, 2000; Tabors, 1997). Their brains are flexible, so they have an easier time learning language and content. Unlike adults, in just 1 to 2 years, very young children are fluent in the new language. Research shows that the closer one gets to puberty, the more difficult it is to master another language. Some term this cutoff period the *critical period* (Birdsong, 1999). Others call it the *sensitive period* (Flege, 1991), suggesting that the window of opportunity closes more gradually for some areas, such as vocabulary and discourse, than for grammar and pronunciation (Sereno & Wang, 2007).

As with L1 acquisition, research on SLA goes back to the 1950s, with similar theories proposed (primarily *nativist* and *functionalist*). The key difference between L1 and second language (L2) acquisition (SLA) is that for SLA, language and literacy mastery is more conscious (Kroll, 2003), and several factors impact the outcome, including age, motivation, personality, affect or psychological state, language commonalities and differences, and learning strategies. There is no set formula for SLA success. As with L1 acquisition, a steady stream of comprehensible language, and multiple opportunities for negotiation and scaffolding help, alongside a motivated personality that is not afraid to make mistakes (see Brown, 2000; Tokuhama-Espinosa, 2001). Given their more forgiving personalities, young children quickly and effortlessly decode the rules of their primary language and of one or more languages that they hear.

SECOND DIALECT ACQUISITION

Second dialect acquisition resembles SLA. For many African American children and other minorities, including many southerners and Latinos, Standard English is not their *primary language* (see Pandey, 2000, 2008). One reason these families continue to be disadvantaged is because their language needs are improperly met.

Familiarity with the process of language acquisition enables us to help these children and their families to:

1. Acquire Standard English most effectively
2. Maintain their home language, since the L1 facilitates SLA

By drawing children's attention to language (peculiarities and differences) and engaging them in periodic analysis and comparison, we can create strong spellers, regardless of primary dialect (see Patton-Terry, 2004; Pandey, 2000). In short, language awareness is key to literacy.

Use of children's primary languages is essential. In addition to flavoring lessons, they are a vital bridge to classroom language/the L2. Examples of successful initiatives that validate home dialects include Jamaica's Bilingual Education Project (www.uwimona.edu.jm/dllp/jlu/), the San Andrés Trilingual Pilot Program, and the Belize Kriol Project.

STAGES OF LANGUAGE ACQUISITION

Children's rapidly expanding language skills are systematic, reflecting a linear order and increasingly complex cognitive skills. Children acquire language units incrementally, usually based on size, ease of production, and frequency. Most master (easier) phonemes first, then free morphemes, simple words (for L1 English speakers, generally single-syllable) and phrases, short, simple sentences, and so on. Research indicates that children acquire some bound morphemes like the -ing verb ending and plural -s before others (e.g., the -s possessive and the 3rd-person singular verb form). This observed order of acquisition is termed the *natural order hypothesis* (Krashen, 1982).

Children usually acquire sounds first, starting with easier ones (e.g., voiceless plosives like /m/ and /p/). Sounds like /sh/ and /th/ are generally harder to produce, even for Kindergartners and 1st-graders, especially when they don't hear them. This explains why some use /s/ in place of /sh/ (e.g., in *shoulder*), or don't produce /th/ when it's inaudible, even after their attention is drawn to it. "It's almost the *100 day* of school!" observed my 6-year-old. Here, the word-final positioning, and the fact that a voiced or relatively louder sound (/d/) follows, likely contribute to the difficulty she experiences with articulation.

Periodic phoneme confusion or vacillation in sounds, morphemes, and grammatical structures is not uncommon. Even 8- and 9-year-olds sometimes mispronounce or mix sounds, as do many younger children. There is no set timeline by which a child should have acquired specific sounds and/or larger language units. Many L1 Spanish speakers, for instance, conflate /b/ and /v/ because a mix of both best resembles the Spanish phoneme /v/ (e.g., in *vaca* and *voca*; cow and mouth, respectively). This is an example of *L1 transfer* (i.e., *crossovers* from the first language).[7] The stages of language acquisition are outlined below.

Prelinguistic

In the first 6 months, babies all over the world make similar sounds, suggesting that they are biologically programmed similarly. Their responses generally consist of coos and cries that express their specific needs and their awareness of language and communication. Note their responsiveness to voices. Research suggests that infant crying—specifically the *intonation*—is a rudimentary form of communication. Most caregivers can identify patterns and meanings in infants' cries. In the first month and sometimes even earlier, based on the language(s) they hear or see, babies begin to identify and differentiate between sounds (i.e., phonemes) and their meaning (Ashworth & Wakefield, 1994). "At six months, a Japanese infant can still hear the difference between the English /l/ and /r/" (Calvin & Bickerton, 2000, p. 32), even though most adult Japanese speakers conflate them. In short, infants have exceptional phonetic skills and can hear and distinguish between many more phonemes than those used in their primary language.

One- to Two-Word Stage

Around 12 months of age or shortly after that, most babies begin to produce the sounds of the language they hear most frequently and to utter one or two high-frequency words. *Ma(ma)* is said most often, followed by *Da(da)*. While some contend that this has to do with the mother being the primary care provider, research shows that /m/ requires a baby simply to smack its lips and is easier to produce than /d/.

Two- to Three-Word Sentences

Most babies acquire at least a word a month. Once they know about 50 words, they quickly begin to use two-word and three-word sentences. These (1) have a distinctive sound, and (2) mean something to the child, although not all listeners understand them. Intonation generally clarifies the intent. For example, a baby could say "Mama" to acknowledge or call out to its mother or to ask for something.

Toddler Stage

When children start asking questions, around age 3—and toddlers are "notorious" for this—their vocabulary evidences gargantuan growth. Their speech production skills are still developing, so some incorrectly pronounce certain sounds and/or conflate others on occasion or often (e.g., saying *imbite* for *invite*, since /m/ and /b/ are easier to produce than /n/ and /v/; or replacing /v/ with /b/ in speech and writing, as in *enbelope*). This does not necessarily mean that they cannot hear the sounds they have trouble producing.

At this stage, children discover that words are like the golden goose. They reproduce, rapidly expanding children's language and world view. In the course of learning to talk, scribble, and read, children create and use more words. Incorrect past tense forms like "teached" and "drinked" are common. They suggest that children have correctly identified (i.e., decoded) individual language units and associated meanings, such as the (*regular*) past tense English [-ed] morpheme, and overextend them. Other frequently overextended forms include the suffixes -er and -est, as well as the comparison signals "more" and "most," as in "I was more boreder" and "It's the most boringest." Overextension of language forms is termed *hypercorrection* in linguistics and is related to their *frequency of use*. Incorrect quantifiers (for implied nouns) and tense and aspect indicators, and longer sentences (e.g., "I ate as most as I can"), are also common at this stage, evidencing more intense language exploration and the interplay of form and function, alongside an increased desire to participate/interact (i.e., share one's thoughts).

Words become a vital means to an end. For most toddlers, the sudden jump from 50 words to thousands and to complex sentences and complex discourse units (e.g., sophisticated demonstrations of empathy) is mind-boggling, yet hard to calendarize.

Adult Competence Stage

Most children demonstrate "adult competence in a language" (Brown, 2000, p. 21). Language is their primary content-acquisition vehicle. In the process, they learn more words, idioms, and increasingly complex sentences. Phonological, lexical, and grammatical errors are not uncommon at this stage, as are misspellings. They include incorrect affixes, beyond the frequently overextended -ed form (e.g., *unpolite, unappropriate, ummimportant, drinken,* and *dranken*), incorrect comparative forms or phrases (e.g., "most likelier"), cropped or clipped phrasal verbs (e.g., *come* vs. *come over*), and even misused words. The word "until," for instance, is misused in the following 8-year-old's speech: "They haven't come until a long time." The present and past participle are also problematic for many 3rd- and 4th-graders (e.g., "I've oready drunken [sic] my juice"; and "My teacher had stucked it up"). Passive voice is still hard for many 8- and 9-year-olds. Words like "broughted," "sawed," and "stucked" demonstrate recognition of irregular base forms and continued overextension of the past tense -ed morpheme out of sheer habit. The same goes for irregular superlative adjectives, less frequent yet relatively harder forms acquired later. Even 3rd-graders overextend -est (e.g., "You can eat as muchest as you want").

Seven- to nine-year-olds tend to *self-correct* more than younger children, and usually right after uttering an incorrect form (e.g., "How can people survive when they get *shoot, shooted, shot?*"). That they do so, and frequently use *repetition* or variable forms to arrive at what they consider correct, suggests (1) that they are paying closer attention to *language form* (unlike younger children who prioritize function), (2) that they seek patterns, and (3) that they store, access, play with, and extend language. For instance, an 8-year-old's recollection of "blown" yielded "sawn." Oral language therefore facilitates grammar and literacy (see Chapter 9). Observe how children like to hear language (out loud), prompting repetition, iterations, and revision.

Remember that neither the L1 nor the L2 proceeds in perfectly linear mode. Children's language changes; one day they might use a word or other language unit correctly, only to "regress" the next day—or sometimes on the same day!

CLASSROOM APPLICATIONS

The novelty of children's language and their language-facilitative skills (Pandey, 2010) strongly support nativist and functionalist theories of language acquisition. However, you might find that children respond differently to different instructional approaches. Elements of more than one theory might best explain how each child learns language. Some children, for instance, regurgitate bits or chunks of language (e.g., mannerisms) that those around them frequently employ. Such imitative language use suggests that behaviorism also might play a small part. This should come as no surprise since much of PreK–3 instruction emphasizes modeling and repetition. For instance, many children are expected to memorize word lists. Yet many things children say and write can be explained only by nativism and/or functionalism (e.g., "There's a hair in my milk!"). Therefore, an eclectic account of language acquisition (i.e., integrative) might appeal to you.

Remember that learning a language means:

1. *Understanding it* (i.e., sounds, intonation, morphemes, phrases, sentences, varieties, and cultural meanings),
2. *Speaking it* (i.e., clearly and in a culturally appropriate manner),
3. *Demonstrating grade-level content competency,* and
4. *Reading* and *writing appropriately* (i.e., using accepted spelling and sequencing).

Get to Know Each Child

First, get to know each child. Invite children to share their routines or what "normally" happens outside class (Ryan & Grieshaber, 2004) to get a better sense of their language skills and practices. Observe DLLs and give them time to observe and learn from their peers and you. You might find that some understand and/or speak a language that has not been written or that they do not write. Some might be able to write just their names. Invite them to share this. Many experience culture shock. They might need time to adjust to the colors of your classroom, the multiple displays[8] and resources, classroom routines, and protocols. Remember that increased anxiety is detrimental to emotional well-being and learning. Give children time; draw them in gradually and strategically. Many children have an easier time learning from their peers (see Pandey, 2010), so provide multiple opportunities for interaction/scaffolding with others.

Play! Engage and Empower

Songs, drama, show and tell, choral reading, and children's "reading" of word(less) books are effective ways to expand children's language and literacy (Peregoy & Boyle, 2001, p. 111). Use free and guided play to engage and empower each child so he or she excels, linguistically and otherwise. Play enhances language (Goouch, 2008; Hanline, 2009; Zigler & Bishop-Josef, 2009), social studies, and math skills (see Edo, Planas, & Badillo, 2009; Ginsburg & Ertle, 2008; Park, Chae, & Boyd, 2008; Ramani & Siegler, 2008). Even children with special needs demonstrate enhanced competencies through freeplay (Bray & Cooper, 2007; Gregory, 2009; Hanline, 2009) and dramatic play (Gupta, 2009; Morrow & Schickedanz, 2006; Neeley et al., 2001). The authentic and sustained input, interaction and scaffolding help (Katz, 2008; Miller & Almon, 2009; Tassoni & Hucker, 2005; Youngquist, 2004). When children play, they hear and use language to negotiate, modify, and build—sand castles, words, ideas, and relationships. Their vocabulary and interpersonal skills are advanced in the process. Enhance the instructional value of play by making writing and art supplies, and technology tools readily accessible (e.g., during recess and at center time). Observing Children Learning from Each Other illustrates the value of play in preschoolers' language and literacy development. This piece and the stories these preschoolers created illustrate:

- The value of play and peer collaboration in language and multiskills development in the early years.
- That the language-literacy examples, environments, and prompts educators provide do influence vocabulary, critical literacy, and global skills development in young children.

Children develop enhanced phonemic (and music) awareness, and discourse-pragmatic skills such as compassion and sharing through play. They also imbibe culture-specific rules of engagement (e.g., what counts at school) much faster than through adult input alone. That Jacob wrote a story similar to Satya's and Sienna followed suit, in chain-reaction mode, is eye-opening. Sienna couldn't wait to share hers; she wrote it over dinner—on a dinner napkin. That's how excited about writing and reading her peers got her. So all we have to do is provide a stimulating environment and children will do the rest (i.e., build from and upon it). We must learn to step back and unleash the magic in each child. After all, facilitating means observing (overseeing) and supporting, not micro-managing or policing everything a child does, says, reads, and/or writes. The learning opportunities we present make all the difference PreK–3. The kinds of resources and learning centers or environments (e.g., relaxing peer exchange venues) we provide, including the language and literacy resources and prompts, musical instruments, foods and beverages, and the learning environment(s) we provide (e.g., multidirectional, collaborative, child-centered, and egalitarian) ultimately determine what children learn and how they learn. Interestingly, while we might assume that children will gravitate toward resources we select for them (e.g., books authored by adults), as this piece illustrates, children take great pride in their own (co)creations, so we should encourage them to continuously share their stories and lives. In so doing, we teach them to teach us how they learn, and best of all, we all learn! Indeed, to teach and to learn, we must play (along).

With proper instruction, children's out-of-class translations quickly lead to improved test scores (Dorner, Orellana, & Li-Grining, 2007). Encourage peer and intergenerational collaboration, so children receive a steady stream of feedback and draw on their out-of-class language-literacy experiences to expand theirs and their peers' academic literacy and agency (Eksner & Orellana, forthcoming). Children also learn intercultural skills faster through interactions with their peers, even in monolingual-instructor classrooms (Moon & Reifel, 2008; Sutterby, 2002). When DLLs use words and expressions from their heritage languages, they introduce their peers and instructors to culturally diverse thinking and impart concepts for which equivalents are unavailable in English. Generating peers' interest in other languages fosters creativity, dialog, and accelerated learning mirrored in children's enhanced recall skills, sharper language awareness, and mutual respect. Therefore, invite children to collaborate on diverse tasks (e.g., art, drama, and writing). Interactive (e-)writing activities are especially instructive (Carbone & Orellana, 2010).

Observe and facilitate children's engagement at all times, with parents as partners. Modify collaboration by, for instance, inviting children to share something about another language (e.g., information they obtain from a peer) and to participate in cross-age literacy encounters. Everyone will learn something new.

Children are invaluable resources. Soliciting their assistance boosts their confidence and agency (Beach et al., 2010; Knörr, 2008) and enhances theirs and others' knowledge. This approach also benefits children who use American Sign Language.

Partner with Families

Invite family members, as well as struggling and/or more-eager writers, to share and (co-)author stories, so these practices are extended at home and everyone learns. With the help of DLLs, integrate relevant words and expressions from other languages. Invite children to investigate (through friends, family, and resources) how to write their name in one or more languages and display these in your classroom. This way, everyone learns. Play language games like Scrabble™ in two languages (i.e., romanize other scripts). If children do not know how to write their home languages, encourage them to use phonetic spellings (e.g., like pidgins).

My 7-year-old suggested that I send "surprise notes" in her lunch box. When I used a mix of languages in my messages to her (e.g., "Have a great *din y mitha* meal. *Te amo!*"/"Have a great day and delicious meal. I love you!"), I noticed she was more excited about using Hindi and Spanish with her friends and inviting them to share their language(s). "At first I thought *din* was *dinner!*" she reported with a laugh. "Sria knows Telugu and also Hindi! Please write more tomorrow, Mama!" she pleaded, and her sister followed suit. Invite caregivers to send notes to children in their lunch boxes or backpacks. They could Romanize the script and children would have fun decoding the words. Periodically invite families to e-mail or text messages for you to share with children. This way, both children and caregivers recognize the value of print, enhance their (e-)literacy skills, and get in the habit of using print-based communication with one another.

Adopt a Family and Study "Abroad" Locally

Encourage participation in heritage language programs. If none are accessible, help start one (see Kipp, 2000). PTA members might be able to lend a hand. Partner with local senior centers. Help children adopt a "grandparent" who understands, speaks, and/or reads and writes another language of interest to them. Children also could study "abroad" locally. Help families befriend other-language-using families. Invite children to periodically share what they learned from this.

Teach Functional Language

At school, children learn the academic functions language serves. This includes themed science vocabulary like *seed(ling)*, *plant*, and *soil*, and associated functions (e.g., tracking plant growth) or processes (e.g., photosynthesis, pollination, and flowering). The larger a child's vocabulary, the easier it is for her to read and master core content on her own (i.e., reading as a learning tool). Therefore, emphasize task-based/functional vocabulary. Acquaint young children—including DLLs—with as many high-frequency words as possible in PreK–3, so they learn to read and read to learn. Record children's language in multiple locations (see Chapter 11). Then identify functions they express, and periodically evaluate their language-literacy skills, needs (e.g., phonemic, vocabulary), and progress. Use your findings to individualize instruction.

Explicitly teach children discovery-oriented language (e.g., What's . . . ?), so they continually learn, even when you're not around. Examples include words like *what, why, how many/much, but*, and *another way/example*; expressions like *(Let me) try again*; and handy cause-effect clauses like *if . . ., then . . . .* Questioning is especially instructive. Encourage questions. Remember that the more you ask, the more likely children are to replicate such behaviors.

Match children's developing language skills with suitable resources. Remember that judging a book by its cover or on the basis of the visuals alone is hasty. Carefully consider *linguistic complexity* (see Chapter 9). Closely match children's language competence with that of instructional resources. Understanding the process of language acquisition is essential for appropriate resource selection.

Actively Demonstrate Language Analysis and Comparison

Awareness of similarities and differences between the L1 and L2 is essential for successful SLA. Consider children's base vocabulary, for instance. By engaging in *contrastive analysis*, you not only facilitate SLA but also help children recall (i.e., maintain) their primary language.

Highlight similarities and differences. For Spanish speakers, for instance, *cognate categories* like the following might help: (1) words with the same spelling and meaning but different pronunciations (e.g., *radio*), (2) those with the same spelling but different pronunciation and/or meaning (e.g., *molest* = disturb in Spanish), (3) those spelled and pronounced slightly differently (e.g., *piloto* versus *pilot*), and (4) distinct words (e.g., *tostado* versus *tan*). Comparison is highly instructive.[9] When DLLs see equivalents, they are likely to master both form and meaning faster.

Note that not all children find the same words easy or challenging. The relative ease or difficulty of language units depends, in part, on the primary language (not necessarily the first acquired). For example, "dot" is easier than *point* for L1-English-speaking children (see Chapter 4) and "belly button" is easier than "umbilical cord," but the reverse is true for Romance language speakers. In Spanish, for instance, the equivalents are *punto* and *ombligo*, respectively. It might help to introduce DLLs to seemingly harder words first and to use these (e.g., *aggregate* from *agregar* vs. *plus*) to introduce the more frequent synonyms we consider easier in English.

Words for unfamiliar concepts could be learned relatively easily by virtue of their distinctiveness. In short, both language similarities and differences are instructive. Focusing on variable meanings of similar terms in different languages (e.g., *pasta* means toothpaste in Spanish, not noodles), as well as language-specific terms, also increases children's vocabulary and intercultural understanding. Inviting children to locate homophones across languages (e.g., /si/ = yes in Spanish; and *see* and *sea* in English) is another way to develop *phonemic awareness, vocabulary*, and *functional bilingualism*.

Focus on Multilingual Vocabulary

Keeping in mind that children should know around 5,000 words by 3rd grade, emphasize vocabulary. Integrating other languages is sure to ignite children's interest in words. Encourage children to keep a word log and to add to it daily or weekly, constructing and segmenting words—in more than just English—and using them in sentences. Cognates are especially instructive—for all children. Words that look familiar (i.e., English-like), even if they don't mean the same thing as in English also extend one's vocabulary. They also help children master skills like differentiation, classification, and counting (i.e., critical thinking). When, for instance, non-Spanish-speaking instructors and children learn that in Spanish, the word for "manners" is *educación,* they better understand the cultural regard for interpersonal skills (i.e., polite language) which, not surprisingly, is just as high as for written literacy, if not higher, since oral literacy drives the latter. This explains why, in many homes, verbal communication is emphasized—sometimes over and above—book learning or classroom education.

Learning words in Spanish, and/or other Romance languages has added advantages (see Chapters 3, 4, and 10). In addition to being widely spoken worldwide (a bonus when children join the workforce), Spanish closely resembles Latin. Key words in Spanish would help children decode math and science vocabulary in particular. For example, in Spanish, *escaler* means climb (high), so children familiar with this word will easily understand related English science terms (e.g., *escalate* and *escalator*). Similarly, the jump from *avion*, the Spanish word for plane, to science terms like *avionics* and *aviation* is easier, so Spanish facilitates mastery of math and science.[10]

Invite *language show and tell*. Children, and adults, are bound to be excited when they see how their name is written in another language. DLLs who are able to write in another language could write classmates' names in their languages.

Age-appropriate international movies would quickly acquaint children with the sounds of other languages. Turn on the closed captions and have children read along. Engage children in collaborative activities such as bilingual word journals, comic strips, art, jewelry, math, PE, and science projects that employ other languages. Inviting DLLs to share through drawings or code-mixed re-tellings, or to demo how math and science are presented in other languages is instructive for all (Schecter & Cummins, 2003). An example follows.

Use Language Trivia

Language trivia helps children pay close attention to components of their own and other languages. Ask questions like the following (e.g., in class or at school events):

What does ___ mean? In which language?
What other language does ___ speak?
Who speaks/writes another language? Where is it spoken?
What language is on that (e.g., cup or item of clothing)? What does it say?
How do you say "hello" in Arabic and Hebrew?
Why doesn't ___ have a word for "goodbye"?
Share 3 words from another language (e.g., a greeting, a word of thanks, and goodbye).

Invite children to create multilingual art, games, and resources (e.g., a letter girl/boy using different languages for facial features and body parts). In *musical languages*, a game like musical chairs my children excitedly invented, children would have to promptly supply the correct number in a sequence of 10 to 20 from another language—and older children could require each number to be in a different language. Children would have to guess the languages used. In social studies, show children a map of the world, or of a region. Provide country names in languages used in different areas and invite children to identify places and languages. Children will extend their memory and learn geography and language(s).

Other language-literacy-instructive activities include creating personalized jewelry (e.g., garlands/necklaces that string letters from two or more languages), language tattoos (e.g., Made in X, and children would have to guess language X and what it says), and t-shirts with bilingual and/or code-mixed names and sayings (e.g., *Everybody Bonjours!* by L. Kimmelman).

SUMMARY AND APPLICATIONS

This chapter surveyed L1 and L2 acquisition and how it informs instructional best practices in PreK–3. As discussed, knowledge of language acquisition enables us to more effectively assess children's *linguistic skills* or learning readiness. It helps us identify *which language units* to *focus on*, *how*, and *how best* to evaluate performance and resources.

Language-acquisition theories were surveyed. In both nativist and functionalist accounts, young children constantly analyze language and seek and identify patterns. Infants are neither blank slates, unlike what behaviorists contend, nor preprogrammed grammarians. They draw on "learning strategies . . . thought to be too complex for infants" (Kuhl et al., 2006, p. 17). In the words of Kuhl et al. (2006), "Language is . . . innately discoverable" (p. 18), and it does not take children long to discover it. As demonstrated, language is scientific—easily segmentable—and much is gained in the process, socially, academically, and otherwise. In fact, as this book demonstrates, *the heart of PreK–3 learning is language discovery* (see the movie *The Miracle Worker*).

The chapter ends by offering strategies for enhancing children's language and literacy skills. As recommended, educators can ease English acquisition for DLLs and develop monolingual children's intercultural skills early on through meaningful interaction in more than one language. To this end, *functional bilingualism* was proposed, and its benefits outlined. While it is impossible to include every language variety, when we integrate at least two, we draw children's attention to language (i.e., its scientific structure) and the diversity of expressions available. Since learning is awareness, by involving children in the process of discovery (i.e., language acquisition/learning as discovery of form and function, and their interconnectedness), we facilitate learning in PreK–3. Children then have an easier time making sense of what they hear and see and are more eager to contribute (new) meanings through their own speech and writing.

CHAPTER 8

Language for Children in Need of Special Education

Why fit in when you were born to stand out?

> —Dr. Seuss, *How to Tell a Klotz from a Glotz*

Well, the Glotz, you will notice,
has lots of black spots.
The Klotz is quite different
with lots of black dots.

> —Dr. Seuss, *How to Tell a Klotz from a Glotz*

But Daddy, a spot is a dot!

> —Sahara, 4

I'm on the right track. I was born this way

> —Lady Gaga, "Born This Way"

This chapter demonstrates that special needs coincide with specific language features, and linguistics is essential for working effectively with children with special needs.[1] Learning objectives include:

- Identifying different "special needs" (i.e., distinctive features)
- Illustrating the central role language plays in each
- Outlining a comprehensive linguistic approach to identifying, assessing, and managing special needs

ACCESS AND CHALLENGES

UNESCO estimates that "150 million children worldwide" have disabilities. In many developed countries, accommodations are made for children with special needs. U.S. law, for instance, requires *exceptional children* to be placed in the least restrictive environment. This means they should have as much access to the general education classroom as possible (Hallahan, Kauffman, & Pullen, 2009). Such a classroom would include an individualized education program (IEP) developed in consultation with professionals like special educators, occupational therapists, physical therapists, and speech-language specialists.[2] An IEP identifies a child's performance level and accommodations that will facilitate learning (i.e., which assessments work best and how to maximize learning). An IEP might recommend that a child receive specialized services (e.g., speech or occupational therapy) in a *resource room*, alongside mainstream offerings (e.g., reading). IEPs are updated periodically.

Inclusion is believed to promote academic and social success (Bowe, 2004; Purdue, Ballard, & MacArthur, 2001; UNESCO).[3] However, some children perform better in separate classrooms and/or schools. The mother of a 7-year-old with a central auditory processing disorder (CAPD) observed, "We noticed considerable improvement when we moved Jamie out of her classroom in a county school. She got more one-on-one attention and seeing other kids with challenges motivated her" (CC, personal communication).

In most developed nations, educators are required to include all children in general education classes by varying instruction and diversifying learning environments (Pepper, 2007) through, for instance, *technology integration* (see Chapter 10). In Waber's (2010) view, the "learning disabilities construct" is the most "well developed . . . in the United States" (p. 39). The Individuals with Disabilities Education Act (IDEA, revised 2004) requires that all students with disabilities be included in performance measures. Also, states must provide accommodations to enable all children to access the general curriculum. However, IDEA does not outline "the criteria for deciding which students require accommodations" (Pepper, 2007, p. 36). Since the 1980s, more *exceptional children* have been included in mainstream schools.[4] However, the implementation of inclusion clauses has not been as successful.

Recent hikes in the number of children needing special education services have been attributed to the relative newness of the field, and increased awareness that children have unique talents and that individualized services would help them attain their full potential. Social risk factors (e.g., poverty and substance abuse) have added to the numbers. So has misidentification.

Labels and Stigmas

The field is inundated with labels, including *special needs, language delayed, exceptional,* and *gifted and talented.* Responses to the labels vary. Some caregivers fear that the labels prompt teachers to lower their expectations (Lane & Pullen, 2004). In some cultures, stigmas associated with special needs prevent caregivers from seeking testing and individualized instruction early on for children with special needs. This lack-of-acceptance attitude is not uncommon even in families that reside in areas where special needs are prioritized. "We need to get beyond the fear of the label defining our children and see the label as an avenue for finding better tools to help our students," advises special educator Pat Tessner.

While research interest in special needs is at an all-time high, the field is relatively new (Mercer & Pullen, 2009). Grey areas remain, particularly as regards labels (Nussbaum, 2004), diagnoses, causes, manifestations, assessment, and responses to specific needs.

In the United Kingdom, observes Waber (2010), the term *dyslexia* is widely used for "a severe reading problem" (p. 38). "Other cognitive issues that could interfere with school adaptation are less frequently accorded official recognition" (p. 38). She continues, "The term *learning disabled* is reserved for children whom Americans would consider to have borderline intellectual functioning" (p. 39). The term *learning disabilities* (LDs) has more positive associations in the United States.

De-stigmatization of labels like *special education* and *learning disabled* has facilitated research and practice, including "communication among stakeholders" (Mercer & Pullen, 2009, p. 30). Parents and professionals have become more knowledgeable about special needs, and technology has been an invaluable resource. However, increased risk factors, such as poverty, language differences, and low self-esteem, have "weakened the support network that many students need to succeed in school" (p. 28).

WHY LINGUISTICS FOR SPECIAL EDUCATORS?

As illustrated, language and special needs, like language and culture, are inextricably intertwined. It is difficult to say which comes first. Yin yang-like, both are subject to change over time and in different (e.g., sociopsychological) contexts. Research in special education highlights the seminal role language plays in basic interpersonal skills (Schetcher & Cummins, 2003) and in illustrating the specificity and gravity of special needs. In short, language is the litmus test.

Waber (2010) emphasizes the developmental nature of special needs and the role neuropsychology plays. While she does not (directly) discuss the interconnections between neuropsychology and language or how language mirrors individual special needs, she highlights the value of language analysis—linguistics, essentially—for children with special needs (and PreK–3 practitioners).

Linguistics is invaluable for special educators. For one thing, special educators knowledgeable in linguistics are less likely to misidentify special needs. They know, for instance, when overlapping turns are unavoidable (i.e., acceptable in a child's primary culture) and will not hastily dismiss children as having a language or behavioral deficit. As linguistics makes clear, children's sounds, morphemes, words, sentences, proxemics, facial expressions, posture, topic sequencing, and/or organization reflect noteworthy differences, not necessarily deficits (see Chapter 1).

LANGUAGE ACQUISITION IS A DEVELOPMENTAL PROCESS

For children to succeed academically, in addition to decoding "words on a page" and solving math problems, they must:

> (i) accurately process meaning from the language they hear in class . . . or in conversations, (ii) find the right words and assemble them into meaningful discourse to communicate their thoughts, . . . (iii) accurately interpret social cues . . . and . . . respond appropriately. (Waber, 2010, p. viii, numbering added)

In short, children first and foremost must be language analysts. They must engage in *selective listening*, determining what is (un)important. This requires segmenting language into meaningful parts (i.e., morphemes). Further, they must acquire and use words that best communicate their intent (i.e., use grammatical and culturally acceptable words, sentences, and discourse). Finally, they must pick up context cues. In other words, they must read between the lines, drawing on their knowledge of discourse-pragmatic norms.

As noted in Chapter 7, language is not an all-or-none skill. It is developmental. "Constant correction of a child's speech is usually unproductive," observes Genishi (1988, p. 21), reminding us that "as with learning to walk," learning to talk (and read and write) takes time. Accordingly, while most PreK–3 children have acquired more or less the same or similar language features, you can expect their language to vary—even in the same child. Early childhood is, therefore, not the most reliable time to gauge specific language deficits (Benasich et al., 2006). We might want to reconsider how and when we test young children (http://www.npr.org/templates/rundowns/rundown.php?prgId=46&prgDate=5-24-2012).[5]

One also must consider the primary language the child hears or speaks outside school. It might have a different phonological, morphological, syntactic, or discourse structure. If it is a stigmatized dialect, the standard language would indeed be much like a second "language" (Pandey, 2000) and would explain the "delay."

Misidentification is not uncommon. Statements such as the following suggest that special needs educators would benefit from knowledge of the process of first and second language (and literacy) acquisition: "Older elementary and middle school students who are delayed in morphology may lack more advanced morphemes of irregular past tense or irregular plurals" (Mercer & Pullen, 2009, p.

213). Research on language disorders tends to present language acquisition as an age-controlled process when, in fact, it is not as definitive and time-driven. Often, language deficits are presented in vague terms, such as the following: "Disorders in form or morphology also include difficulties learning the language code and linking it to what already is known about the environment" (Mercer & Pullen, 2009, p. 213). It would help to know the "code" referenced and its linkage to "the environment"?

The following observation could prompt teachers to assume a child has a morphological deficit: "An elementary school student may not use the third-person -s on verbs (e.g., "He walk") or may not use -s on nouns and pronouns to show possession . . . or may not use -er on adjectives" (Mercer & Pullen, 2009, p. 213). This observation overlooks the facts:

1. Morphological forms such as the third-person -s, possessive -s, and comparative adjectives are acquired much later (see Chapter 7).
2. Vacillating language is, in fact, part of language acquisition (i.e., to be expected and not necessarily reflective of a disability).
3. Some language varieties (e.g., Hindi) do not use overt plurals. Plurality is implied or indicated through number specifiers (e.g., 50 cent in BEV).

To avoid misidentification, educators must familiarize themselves with the process of language acquisition and observe children in multiple contexts to identify contextual factors that might trigger observable changes or specific challenges.

Special educators unfamiliar with the mechanics of language acquisition are more likely to face identification and assessment challenges (Hallahan, Kauffman, & Pullen, 2009; Kirk, 2002). Most struggle with identifying whether language is the cause or the effect of a specific disability. A child identified with a language disability might have another (causative) problem that is reflected in his or her speech/language, prompting the question, "How much of the disability is linguistic (and how much neuronal)?" Information retrieval (cognitive) processes might interfere with children's language-acquisition (e.g., auditory processing or language-production) capabilities (Joanisse & Seidenberg, 1997). Regardless of the cause(s) of language delays and/or impairments, early speech and writing are some of the best indicators of reading and other challenges children are likely to encounter (Harlaar et al., 2008; Puolakanaho et al., 2007).

Like irregular verbs (which 3- to 7-year-olds might use with -ed endings or in their base form; e.g., "If you be mean"), phrasal verbs are acquired much later and are problematic even for 8-year-olds (e.g., "I'm going bathroom").

So are comparative (i.e., "more + -er" overextension in utterances like, ". . . is more nicer") and present and past participle forms (in that order). The latter generally are acquired alongside a more complex sentence type, namely, the passive, and the present and past perfect, respectively. Past participles are acquired much later, and passive sentences containing them are more complex than active ones, so many 8-year-olds use these forms incorrectly. Yet, many self-correct. Children's ability and desire to self-correct mirrors their metacognitive skills. An 8-year-old who says, "I've already drinken → dranken → drunken it," or, "I'd eatened, eated it . . . ," reflects a clear understanding of event sequencing. That (s)he *identifies* and *self-corrects* evidences strong metacognitive skills and emergent morphosemantic rules. Even 3rd-graders occasionally affix the -ed suffix to irregular verbs, yielding incorrect forms like "holded." This does not necessarily mean that they are slow or learning disabled.

As demonstrated in Chapter 7, language (and even literacy) acquisition is not so much timed as it is sequential or ordered. Research indicates that language units are acquired incrementally, from smaller to larger, and more semantically complex units, in an observed (linguistic) order termed the *natural order hypothesis* (Krashen, 1982). In short, even within the broad linguistic units (e.g., phonemes, morphemes, etc.), certain sounds, morphemes, words, and sentence structures are acquired before others. Children take variable amounts of time to acquire specific units, depending on a host of factors. Their language use also changes. They might, for instance, use a word correctly in one context only to use it incorrectly in another. It is for this reason (i.e., to de-emphasize the role of time in this developmental process) that the term *sensitive period* (Flege, 1991) was proposed instead of *critical period* (Calvin & Bickerton, 2000).[6]

Additional questions come to mind regarding assessment. Since phonological awareness is so closely tied to reading, how are "deficits" in phonological awareness identified and could these be dialectal (i.e., "differences")? Mercer and Pullen (2009) observe that "syntactic awareness may play an important role in reading achievement" (p. 214). They note that "little evidence is available in the literature" (p. 214). Hence, linguistics has much to offer. For instance, the (un)familiarity and/or (in)frequency of a word in everyday speech, as well as sentence structure and complexity, could make discourse relatively easier or more difficult for a child to process and produce (see Chapter 9).

DISTINCTIVE LINGUISTIC FEATURES OF SPECIAL NEEDS

Special needs run the gamut, from delayed speech and Asperger's syndrome to dyslexia, each with associated language challenges (see Hallahan, Kauffman, & Pullen, 2009; Lane & Pullen, 2004; Mercer & Pullen, 2009). Since each child is unique, even children with the same type of special needs exhibit differences, so case studies are especially insightful. PreK–3 special needs include the following:

Learning disabilities (LDs)
Intellectual and developmental disabilities (Meltzer, 2007)

Communication disorders like auditory dysfunction, and dyslexia (Cortiella, 2007)

Attention deficit hyperactivity disorder (ADHD; higher incidence observed in males, http://www.studentneeds.info/)

Emotional/behavioral disabilities

Autism (Pellicano & Stears, 2011; Taylor, 2011)

Blindness or low vision

Deafness

Physical challenges

Special gifts and talents

Some of these overlap. Children with LDs, for instance, usually experience multiple challenges.

Central Auditory Processing Disorder

Seven-year-old Becky was diagnosed recently with an auditory dysfunction, central auditory processing disorder (Masters, Stecker, & Katz, 1998). CAPD affects 3% of children and "often co-exists with other disabilities," including "speech and language disorders or delays, learning disabilities" (dyslexia, attention deficit disorders), and "social and/or emotional problems" (Schminky & Baran, 2000). Children with CAPD usually have difficulty "understanding conversations in noisy environments." They have trouble understanding "complex directions and difficulty learning new words." These "can affect their ability to develop normal language skills, succeed academically, or communicate effectively." Misdiagnosis of CAPD is common. The "auditory" aspect often is left unaddressed. Becky's condition prompts her to substitute sounds like /s/ and /f/, and /ch/ and /fr/. Her mother shared the following examples: "Maya's wearing a fantastic (i.e., St. Patrick's) day shirt" and "Can I have another *fr*eakin (i.e., chicken) nugget?"

I first met Becky outside the public school her younger sister attended. I mentioned how excited I was to meet and learn from her. She listened intently, then said, "Wait wait! Slow down if you want me to remember." She then proposed that we play a spy game. I accepted and was "chosen" to look for her. I found her behind a tree. She promptly asked: "Excuse me, please. Are you trying to make fun of me?" "What?" I asked, surprised. "Well, people are always trying to make fun of me," she replied candidly. "How do you know?" I asked. "Because they giggle and I can hear them say things about me," she continued. I assured her that I had no such intentions. Impressed with her manners and her ability to strategically interrogate me, I was reminded that one of the biggest challenges many children face is public opinion. The negative impact of anxiety on language learning—the basis of all learning—is well-established (see Chapter 7). Indeed, all children, including those with special needs, flourish in a relaxed environment, especially when they receive individualized attention (Pierangelo, 2004).

Becky's parents took her to several pediatricians and speech therapists before receiving a diagnosis that seemed to explain her speech and language. When she began falling behind academically, her parents decided to move her to a private school. "It seemed like the [public] school was not helping her keep up," observed her mother, Mimi. Increased self-esteem was the first and most visible change they observed in Becky following this transition in instruction/learning environment. Although her reading skills did not change markedly over a year, her parents noticed in Becky an increased desire to interact without prompting, as well as to write, draw, and read.

Some children are not as verbal and or literate as others. In literacy-oriented cultures, the pressure to speak and read from an early age is relatively high. Arguably, children in these locations face challenges that their peers elsewhere might not. They also are more likely to be diagnosed with an LD or other "special need."

Learning Disabilities and Language

Children with LDs are a heterogeneous group and account for 50% of those with special needs. In 2006, nearly 3 million children and youth in America had a learning disability (U.S. Department of Education, 2006). Those with speech/language impairments constituted the second largest group. When one considers the fact that most children with LDs also experience language challenges, whether in listening (attention-based or as a result of poor auditory quality), enunciation, reading, or writing, this number is much higher.

Since language is inseparable from social skills, language mirrors LDs. Key questions to ask include:

Does the child's language mirror specific LDs? How?
What can you do to enhance the language skills of children with LDs?

This section will address these questions. The social skills of children with LDs are consistently rated lower than their peers' without LDs (Mercer & Pullen, 2009), reflecting weaker language skills, specifically vocabulary, and discourse (i.e., pragmatic know-how). Educators would do well to monitor, emphasize, and assess specific language skills. Since language acquisition is an innate and developmental process that starts in infancy (in utero, some contend), it would appear that LDs account for distinctive language, and not vice versa.

Many children with LDs exhibit *metacognitive deficits* (Mercer & Pullen, 2009). Metacognition, the ability to accurately encode and decode meaning and employ meaningful politeness norms, is reflected in language, specifically vocabulary, semantics, and pragmatics. *Metacognitive skills* permit one to do the following: (1) identify exactly what language strategies and resources are needed to "perform a task effectively," and (2) self-evaluate and self-correct or modify one's language in order to successfully complete a task or meet communication goals. While seemingly cognitive in nature, these skills have a critical linguistic dimension; they involve hearing, evaluating, and modifying one's speech and nonverbal and (e-)written language. In order to learn, children must dialog, and sometimes even monolog with themselves, and modify their language accordingly. Some researchers contend that children with LDs do not have metacognitive deficits but simply "apply different strategies" (Mercer & Pullen, 2009, p. 24).

Many children with LDs have trouble recalling information. This memory deficit, termed *weak phonological memory* (Mercer & Pullen, 2009; Savage, Lavers, & Pillay, 2007), accounts for the high incidence of reading failure among children with LDs (Keeler & Swanson, 2001; Martinussen & Tannock, 2006; Siegel, 2003). Many children with LDs also have trouble focusing on "relevant classroom tasks" (Mercer & Pullen, 2009, p. 25). They are easily distracted and hypersensitive. In short, they have socioemotional and behavioral problems. They are more likely to become frustrated and act out, reflecting low self-esteem. As a consequence, some feel isolated and depressed. Their learning disabilities very likely limit their social participation. Since interaction is necessary for vocabulary development and acquisition of other-language units, some might become hypersensitive. Not surprisingly, their social skills suffer, which explains why they are rated lower than their peers (p. 24).

Practically every LD or special need involves language in some form or fashion. In fact, it is rare for a special need to not involve or manifest itself in language or interaction. The LDs identified under IDEA, for instance, have a language component, alongside academic and neurological dimensions. Arguably, academic and linguistic components are intertwined. As Mercer and Pullen (2009) observe, "Because language skills and academic functioning are closely related, it sometimes is difficult to determine the primary disability" (p. 23). Reading, a key academic skill, entails all-around language competence (Strickland & Morrow, 2000). Not only does it require familiarity with age-appropriate vocabulary, but it necessitates phonemic awareness, morpheme and sentence segmentation, language blending, and inferencing/language-analytic skills developed through (individualized) language-focused instruction, for instance.

ADHD and Cerebral Palsy

ADHD, a neurobehavioral condition, is reflected in periodic inattention or hyperactivity. Some have linked it to diet, making it important for us to watch what children consume (see Chapter 6). ADHD appears to be less prevalent or more accepted in oral cultures (e.g., African, Latino), where routines tend to be less rigid and children are expected to be vivacious. In these contexts, curricular flexibility generally is prioritized over and above structure. For instance, children do not need to know a peer to interact with him or her. In short, the concept of being introduced is still foreign. Overlapping turns, which often are construed as symptomatic of ADHD, are also common (e.g., in Nepali, Pakistani, and Latin cultures). Awareness of discourse practices is, therefore, crucial for instruction and assessment.

Some children stutter. Many have cerebral palsy (CP), a congenital muscular disorder. *Cerebral* refers to the brain, and *palsy* to the weakness the person experiences controlling body movement. The frequency varies. Some children with CP have severely distorted speech or are unable to speak. Phonemic strategies such as skipping problem syllables have helped some (Reese, personal communication). Many find e-mail and text messaging to be less intimidating.

Asperger's, Dyslexia, and Language-Learning Disabilities

Language is the common thread between Asperger's, dyslexia, and other special needs. Hard-of-hearing children, for instance, have trouble processing oral language (see Chapter 7). Some children have an expressive language disability. Albert Einstein apparently developed speech late, but that didn't stop him from expressing his "nobel" ideas (pun intended). Some researchers have termed this speech delay the *Einstein syndrome* (Sowell, 2001). For blind children, visualizing language is problematic. Others struggle with reading and writing (Kirk, 2002). Whether one reads vocally or silently, reading is all-encompassing, requiring strong speaking, listening, vocabulary, and problem-solving skills.

Mercer and Pullen (2009) list characteristics of children with language-learning disabilities (see p. 216). These are divisible by linguistic area (e.g., phonology, morphology, syntax, and discourse). The first, "poor peer relations," for instance, is commonly associated with Asperger's and has a lot to do with discourse. However, even children and adults with normally developing language experience some of the challenges mentioned (e.g., "impulsive behavior"), suggesting that language is symptomatic of (neuronal) difference.

Some *autistic children* use *mannerisms* that mean specific things. They might, for instance, speak and/or read with unusual pronunciations, stress, or intonation. As with unfamiliar accents, their language might take some getting used to. From a language standpoint, Asperger's is primarily a communication or discourse disability most evident in interaction. It is not so much that autistic children do not use meaningful sounds, words, and sentences (most do so) as that their turn-taking, politeness, and other pragmatic skills are relatively underdeveloped. Children with Asperger's might use conventional discourse features like eye contact, head nods, and/or discourse markers (meaningful sounds like *uhuh* that indicate following) minimally or not at all. Some use them more in their comfort zones or with certain individuals (e.g., family members), yet even these children would benefit from (individualized) communication strategies. Technology, for example, has helped eliminate barriers for many autistic children (http://thedianerehm-show.org/shows/2012-05-23/touch-screen-devices-and-very-young-children).

Hoopmann (2006) observes that "everyone is different . . . and there is a little bit of Asperger in us all" (p. 61). She highlights the creativity, language skills, and uniqueness of children with Asperger's using an analogy (pictures and qualities of cats) to share their heartwarming and awe-inspiring peculiarities. One picture shows a cat in a purse. The caption reads, "I haven't let the cat out of the bag!" Like most PreK–3 children, many interpret idioms literally. Another picture shows a cat eyeing a computer mouse and pondering, "That doesn't look like a mouse!" Misunderstanding "what people say" (p. 31) is common for children with Asperger's.

Hoopman notes that children with Asperger's are pretty organized and respond well to routines. Not surprisingly, many employ repetitive sounds, words, and expressions. Repetition appears to be a compensatory strategy for many children with Asperger's, helping them fill in the blanks and/or recall words. Repetitive language includes catch phrases, termed "canned utterances" in research on language strategies (see Pandey, 2010) and aphasia studies (where word-finding difficulty is common). In addition, children with Asperger's rarely sugar-coat their words (Johar, 2010). In short, they might come across as curt because their pragmatic skills are underdeveloped. Despite these eccentricities, Hoopmann (2006) reminds us that this person's thinking is "far ahead of his peers" (p. 37).

Expect momentary tantrums or meltdowns "when things get too much" (Hoopmann, 2006, p. 27). As regards nonverbal language, eye contact is relatively infrequent, yet, as we know, in some cultures making eye contact with older or empowered persons is disrespectful. Like cats, who love attention, children with Asperger's have a heightened sense of hearing, touch, and smell. Accordingly, "loud sounds and sudden movements may scare them" (p. 9). Vocabulary-wise, many use big words (e.g., *catastrophic*). Their vocabulary "may be very advanced" (p. 29), yet they sometimes get "little words all mixed up" (p. 30, e.g., homonyms), understandably so.

Many special needs children have dyslexia, a reading disorder (Davis, 2000). Symptoms include difficulty differentiating between left and right (or east and west), incorrect spellings based on visual memory (e.g., *dose* for *does*), difficulty with math (especially with number sequences), and writing numbers or letters backwards. These difficulties are not uncommon initially, even for children with normally developing language. So a child who misspells or writes some numbers and letters backwards is not necessarily struggling.

MISIDENTIFYING SPEAKERS OF NONSTANDARD DIALECTS AND DLLS

Children from low-income families are "at increased risk of reading failure and of being identified for special education services" (Losen & Orfield, 2002, p. 1). Many hear and speak non-Standard English or another language outside class. "Standard English," the preferred medium of instruction, is like another language to these children (Ladson-Billings, 1997; Pandey, 2000; Patton-Terry, 2004). Unfortunately, many DLLs are misidentified as "special needs." Differentiating between *Standard-English-needs* and *neurological* or neurolinguistic *challenges* is essential. The two are often conflated, prompting misconceptions and misdiagnoses involving second language users, bilingualism, and special needs.

DLLs and special needs, for instance, are frequently discussed side-by-side, leading some to believe they overlap. However, learning another language is *neither* a special need nor an LD, and should not be treated as such. On the contrary, knowledge of another language and culture makes children more proficient (Utley & Obiakor, 2001). Advising parents of "special needs" children to use just English at home is, quite simply, poor advice. It is unsubstantiated and damaging. Many DLLs take some time before they speak in the second language. This does not necessarily mean that they have a language or learning disability. On the contrary, since speech is a production skill and far more involved than listening (i.e., a passive skill), it is natural for speech to take longer.

Example

Four-year-old Suresh speaks Telugu at home and frequently uses /d/ instead of /r/ when /r/ appears in the middle of an English word (e.g., *are*). Even after 6 months of speech services, his parents observe no difference. Does he have a speech problem? Is he developmentally delayed or merely transferring a Telugu sound (/d/) that frequently is used in certain (word) environments to English?

When you look up the IPA or phoneme charts for both languages, you will notice that both are *alveolar sounds* (i.e., produced in *the same part* of the mouth) and both are voiced (i.e., involve vocal cord vibration), so it's easy for a preschooler, still learning to make the sounds of one or more languages, to conflate them. Their *place of production is the same*. They differ slightly in their *manner of production* in that /d/ is a voiced stop and /r/ is a voiced liquid. To produce /d/, the tip of the tongue brushes against the alveolar ridge and the vocal cords vibrate at the same time to produce voicing, yielding /d/. For /r/, the tip of the tongue curls or flips over backwards, in the direction of the alveolar ridge in back flip mode (without touching the alveolar ridge). It's termed a *flap*, given its hit-and-go production. As with /d/, the vocal cords vibrate, yielding /r/. Only when teachers know how these sounds are produced can they assist children (and parents) in differentiating between similar sounds that some children have trouble producing.

It is time to stop viewing DLLs as learning challenged and desperate for language assistance. We must employ instructional strategies to enable all children to learn basic facts about other languages and cultures. Remember that all children are language learners, irrespective of how many languages they understand, speak, sign, read, or write. They are still in the process of mastering one or more languages. By easing language decoding and comparison, exposure to another language facilitates language (and content) acquisition for both the primary language and the subsequent one.

ASSESSMENT AND MANAGEMENT OF SPECIAL NEEDS

"The first thing we have to do is understand how special needs children communicate. Otherwise, we will be unable to assist," observes special educator Pat Tessner. Since some children have more than one "need," effectively identifying and addressing each is especially challenging. For this reason, an interdisciplinary approach is advised (see Forness & Beard, 2007). Since language crosses all disciplines, and linguistics is by nature an interdisciplinary field, observations, language-segmentation-based instruction, and assessment are empirical and promising. A linguistic approach to special education identifies and enhances children's skills in different language areas—prioritizing language units that each child finds challenging. Analyses of children's individual speech and language (e.g., interpersonal skills), as advised in this section, should provide you with a reliable measure.

With a knowledge of linguistics, educators can better diagnose, instruct (by focusing on high-need language areas for each child), and measure progress in children with special needs. In the United States, discrepancy (performance variation) is frequently used to identify LDs and/or underachievement. However, states are not required to observe discrepancy to identify a need. IDEA identifies seven skills, namely: oral and written expression, listening comprehension, word recognition, reading comprehension, math calculation, and math reasoning. All require language proficiency, including the ability to process and appropriately engage in conversation, recognize and understand vocabulary, problem solve (in math and more), and read. Some contend that the IDEA criteria do not capture the range of LDs that afflict young children today.

Since language reflects how children adapt to different challenges, a focus on the speech and language of children with special needs is necessary for effective assessment, instruction, and management of individual needs (Alwell & Cobb, 2009). Waber (2010) draws attention to the constantly changing nature of many LDs as a reflection of children's differential engagement. She argues that assessment should focus on "the interaction between the child and the world within which that child must function" (p. viii). Since children interact with their world through language, by examining their spoken, written, nonverbal, and digital language, we can systematically identify and address individual needs and monitor progress.

Just as quality PreK–3 instruction prioritizes phonemes and vocabulary (Berkeley & Scruggs, 2010), assessment should examine children's functional language both inside and outside the classroom. Some children have more than one special need. Effectively diagnosing and addressing each is challenging. Observe each child in multiple contexts to identify the role of contextual factors in specific challenges and to avoid misidentification. Careful analysis of children's speech and language (including discourse skills that mirror their pragmatic skills) should provide you with an accurate measure.

Monitor Language Needs

Periodically assess children's language needs. A needs assessment is useful for assessing a child's language skills in different areas. Monitor additional behaviors such as attention span and task-completion (Pierangelo, 2004) that could impact children's language in different contexts (e.g., language arts versus PE). Observe and/or record children's (e-)exchanges as well (e.g., phone, Skype, etc.). Modify your checklist as needed and use it frequently to monitor children's language use in different settings and to ascertain progress.

You might find that a child's language needs change, depending on one or more factors. A child might be more visibly challenged in some environments than in others, at certain times of the day, or in the presence of certain individuals. Your checklist should help you identify variables. Keep in mind that vacillation in children's language and other performance indicators is to be expected (see Chapter 7).

Record observations as quickly as possible with minimal disruption to the exchange(s). Parents and family members that interact with a child on a daily basis must be partners in ongoing observation and assessment. Periodically compare notes with them. Solicit parents' cooperation in capturing video footage of children's out-of-class interactions so that children become accustomed to being recorded. Otherwise, the presence of the camera might impact their language and level of interaction.

Use your needs assessment instrument or a version of it as a classroom and out-of-class observation tool. Use your findings to plan instruction and measure progress. Your needs assessment can serve multiple purposes, including identifying instruction areas. Examine language as thoroughly as possible and capture as many variables as possible (e.g., setting, participants, time of day), to determine what affects each child's interactivity.

Use Reading and Writing Portfolios

Maintain speech, reading, and/or writing portfolios for each child. Use loggings from different contexts, time periods, and sources (i.e., perspectives) to assess a child's language-literacy needs and progress. Organizing your logs in different ways (e.g., chronologically versus contextually) could be quite revealing. Once again, parents and friends could be invaluable partners and much could be learned from intergenerational exchanges.

Remember that children with special needs are not deficient but unique, like cultured pearls. If reading continues to be a sore spot for some, emphasize other (communicative) competencies, and modify how you measure progress. If something has to give, better your assessments than the child. In short, individualize language learning and don't put all the weight on literacy. Assessment should emphasize each child's strengths. In a sense, all children have special needs. These are just more (linguistically) obvious in some, and it's our responsibility to read them well.

Teach Compensatory Strategies

Since each special need coincides with one or more linguistic area(s), teach individualized-compensatory language. Tabulate language measures that could help with one or more of the language challenges identified above. If one of these fails to secure the desired outcome, try another. By this time, you should have evidence that a child is challenged. Eventually, in one context or another, linguistic intervention should work.

Given the complexities and uniqueness of the developing brain, remember that children master different language units and associated content at their own pace. For this reason, exercise caution when using the terms *language delayed* and *language impaired*. It is best to tease out the variables that impact children's language proficiency and teach them *compensatory language* (i.e., communication strategies).

Examples include requests for clarification/rephrasing (e.g., "Wait"), repetition ("[Could you] please repeat"), and other handy and functional conversation-control devices. These would enable children to exercise control over interactions (a confidence booster) and develop their vocabulary, sentence-level, and interpersonal skills. Children with LDs have responded well to graphic organizers (see Ellis & Howard, 2007) and mnemonics (Brigham & Brigham, 2001). Music (e.g., humming or singing), extended language, and visual representations are additional *compensatory strategies* special needs children could be taught to draw upon so they can express themselves through multiple and alternate means. Indeed, a focus on communication strategies and functional/purposeful language use enables differentiated, self-directed, and self-regulated instruction, in line with research findings, and teaches children to engage, think, and problem solve (Bender, 2008; Brady, 2008). This type of instruction allows the learner to be in control of his or her learning, as in the case of computer-mediated instruction.

Since communication is a two-way street (i.e., the onus rests on listeners and readers), teach children to elicit information by asking questions, involving their partner, and modifying their language accordingly.

Maximize Children's Social Involvement

Remember that children are very socially aware, even if they might not appear so. Their participation will vary accordingly. All children enjoy feeling appreciated, loved, special, and needed. Increase children's social involvement by expanding their opportunities for spoken, nonverbal, and written language use with their peers and others. Such interchanges will lower children's anxiety and improve their self-esteem and performance. Most important, you will provide children with an invaluable tool that both enables and mirrors learning, namely, *language* (via meaningful sounds, words, etc.). Remember that language use or interaction (speech, in particular) is integral to the identification and management of special needs.

Since many children with LDs have trouble recalling information, equip them with strategies that will help them dissect and (semantically) process the language they hear and see at specific points. Periodically equipping children with LDs with phonemic language strategies (to refresh their working memory) is extremely beneficial. These strategies should include word-part identification and segmentation (e.g., recognition that -ing indicates ongoing action), as well as knowledge of source language(s). Eventually, all children, even those with LDs, should actively engage in language analysis. Repeated demonstrations by their peers, parents, and other family members may be necessary. A child who sees words like *measure* and *treasure*, which end in -sure, will learn to correctly pronounce the vowel combinations (i.e., ea = /ɛ/ and the letter 's' as /ʒ/ in these and similarly spelled words (like *leisure*, which they might hear in later grades). You might find yourself repeating information to compensate for differences in working memory (Savage, Lavers, & Pillay, 2007).

Simplify and Individualize Language Instruction

Ask yourself: "Which language area(s) does ___ have most trouble with?" Focus on these particular areas. Observe which language forms a child uses most frequently. With children with Asperger's, use simple (short and frequent) and easy-to-segment words, since idioms and demonstratives such as "these" and "those" are morphologically complex. Use easier-to-decode forms like *the* strawberries (i.e., definitive). While idioms, especially sports idioms, are used frequently in American English, avoid them. Try this with all children, not simply those with special needs, as even 8- and 9-year-olds have trouble with idioms. (A few, like *piece of cake*, might be easy for even 4-year-olds, if they have heard them previously.)

Use plain English and repetition to teach frequently used courtesies (i.e., discourse units) and select or (co-)create readings that use familiar language. Also, dissect words in readings (e.g., these = this + more than one; those = that + plural) and try rephrasing speech and writing.

Many special needs children are mathematically gifted. What they appear to lack in conventional language skills is usually more than adequately compensated for by their numerical intelligence—their ability to recall, parse, and compute numbers. Autistic and other special needs children therefore are likely to enjoy and benefit from a calculated approach to sounds and spelling (i.e., language math proposed in Chapter 4).

Use and encourage the use of multisensory expression, as each child is unique. You might find that many children with special needs respond better to oral, visual, and/or digital language, or even to lowercase letters. While we might think that lowercase is harder for children, research shows that the lines and curves on capital letters make them harder to process (time-wise), so some children might read or write lowercase faster.[7]

Use Linguistically Diverse Resources

Use linguistically diverse resources (see Chapter 5) to help children with special needs think outside the box. Research on early bilingualism is particularly valuable for instruction and assessment of special needs. Recall how bilingual children, even those from low-income families, consistently demonstrate a cognitive advantage (see Chapter 7). That speakers of languages like Chinese have larger *phonological* (i.e., working) memories, given the relative compactness and more explicitly meaningful spoken and written representations (see Chapters 4 and 5), is also noteworthy. Given the similarity between PreK–3 French and Spanish vocabulary and (Latinate) English words, explore the Latin in English through them. Use cognates to build vocabulary and invite children for examples. Many are fairly complex yet, you might find, relatively easy for children with special needs and, of course, DLLs who speak closely related languages.[8] PreK–3 Romance language vocabulary also might enrich special needs children's vocabulary in the arts and social studies, and jumpstart them for (decoding) multidisciplinary vocabulary emphasized in later grades.

Children fluent in oral cultures (e.g., African, African American, and Hispanic) are usually bidialectal and/or bilingual and privy to a rich folklore and musical tradition. These skills reflect their larger phonological and lexical or working memories and their metacognitive advantage. Not surprisingly, these children generally have a relatively easy time recalling and spinning engaging oral stories and/or musical compositions (Labov, 1979). Note that rapping is essentially rhyming, and many BEV speakers pick up and demonstrate rhyme skills early.

Oral storytelling and bilingual resources and activities (e.g., storyboarding) could be just the linguistic sparkplugs children with LDs need to jumpstart learning (i.e., interactivity-dependent) and overcome the challenges they face.

SUMMARY AND APPLICATIONS

As this chapter demonstrates, linguistics provides more effective identification, management, and assessment of language, literacy, and other core PreK–3 skills for children with special needs. Once again, an approach that integrates other languages is recommended, given research findings on the cognitive and linguistic advantages of early bilingualism even for children with learning disabilities. As noted in Chapter 7, children who learn another language have enhanced communication skills (i.e., more to talk about and more communication tools at their disposal), develop cross-cultural awareness faster, and are assured of a brighter future in our global world. In Walton's (2007) words, "Not only is learning a foreign language easier for children . . . , but children who are exposed to other languages also do better in school, score higher on standardized tests, are better problem solvers and more open to diversity."

CHAPTER 9

WIDA/ESL Standards Infusion and Approaches to Reading

And Horton called back to the Mayor of the town,
"You're safe now. . . . I won't let you down."

—Dr. Seuss, *Horton Hears a Who!*

Mama, *carne* makes more sense than meat. Carnivores eat *carne*! They both have car!

—Sarika, 8

As the opening quotes remind us, we have a moral obligation to include and support all children, including DLLs. The National Center for Children in Poverty reports that child poverty rates are the highest for Black, Latino, and American Indian children and that "the achievement gap for low-income young children starts early and is difficult to reverse." Ninety-seven percent of children "with foreign-born parents" are from "working families" that face economic hardship and are misunderstood. Misconceptions about Latinos and other minorities negatively impact the children, perpetuating the stereotype of DLLs as "at-risk" and high-needs linguistically. The barriers many face are more often than not sociopolitical; "How teachers, schools, and our society view differences (in race, immigrant status, social class, and language) may jeopardize children even more" (Nieto, 2012, p. 48). We simply cannot afford to let down any child. Our future rests in the hands of DLLs (Cauthen & Dinan, 2006). Their diverse experiences make them some of our most valuable assets. Ironically, we risk losing more when we overlook their wealth of experiences and life skills (even those "at risk"). Many serve as family and community translators, technology aides, and more, and enhance multiple skills in the process (see Chapter 7). As Schmidt (2011) reports, "It falls to bilingual kids to pick up the slack," when it comes to bridging intergenerational technology and language divides. Their many out-of-class literacy engagements make young DLLs even more resourceful. Research shows that "a more hostile climate post-9/11" has exacerbated many DLLs' "reluctance to seek assistance," so early childhood educators must make every effort to understand and include these marginalized children and their families. To this end, this chapter:

Examines DLLs' unique vocabulary (skills)

Familiarizes readers with the WIDA/PreK–3 English Language Proficiency (ELP) standards

Demonstrates how to integrate the standards and how to align ELP and content standards

Discusses how to comprehensively infuse key linguistic concepts in ECE training

Proposes instructional strategies and resources for use with (varied-proficiency) DLLs

STOP COMPARING APPLES TO ORANGES

"One farm winter in the high plains of Colorado where I was born and raised," shares Eugene García in his essay *El Árbol,* "my father pointed to an árbol—a cottonwood tree as I recall—near our home." His father simply asked "*Porque puede vivir ese arbol en el frio del invierno y en el calor del verano?*"[1] (How can that tree survive the bitter cold of winter and the harsh heat of summer?)" After Eugene had exhausted multiple explanations, his father "kindly provided a different perspective" through "a common Spanish *dicho* (proverb): *El árbol fuerté tiene raices maduras* (A strong tree has mature strong roots)." The tree represents the DLL, and her primary language(s), the roots that must be watered in order for her to grow tall and strong (i.e., excel). Quality PreK–3 instruction means including every child. Through programs like Head Start, many a DLL has had the opportunity to excel. As Eugene observes, his father "made very clear that without strong roots, strong trees are impossible, even though we don't see the roots." Eugene continues:

> For me as an individual with a set of cultural and linguistic roots, if my roots were to die and I was to be stripped of the integrity that lies in those roots, then I would also disappear along with all that is important to me. For many limited English proficient students in this nation, their roots have been either ignored or stripped away in the name of growing strong. Many have been directed to stop speaking the languages of their homes, to perceive their culture as one less that what it should be, and to assimilate as quickly as possible, . . . in American society. And, unfortunately many have suffered that fate of the rootless tree—they have fallen socially, economically, academically, and culturally. (García, Fradd, & Lee, 1998)

As noted earlier, for too long, DLLs' needs have been presented alongside those of "special populations." Such coverage gives the false impression that both groups are challenged (linguistically and/or otherwise). To present those who use languages other than the dominant one as handicapped represents a misconception of the value of minority languages (and cultures) in general, and of DLLs in particular. We all stand to gain when we champion the linguistic rights of DLLs and recognize the wealth of experience and cultural capital DLLs add to our schools and communities (García, 2005; García & Frede, 2010). In short, we are very fortunate to have DLLs in our midst and must do our best to make each child feel at home. We have much to learn from DLLs, in particular.

Many know more complicated words than monolingual children, yet word-for-word comparisons rarely reveal these. An example is *significa*, the Spanish word for mean(s), and the root of "significance," "signify," and "signification," terms used primarily by adults. The relatedness of many complex English words to roots and stems in many DLLs' primary languages also gives these children a lexical advantage if teachers highlight relatedness (through cognates).

A child who speaks Spanish, for instance, will have an easier time understanding (i.e., learning) the science concept and term *lunar* (e.g., eclipse) than a monolingual-English-speaking child. Most 2-year-old Spanish speakers know that *luna* means moon. Similarly, the psycholinguistic transition from *luna* to *lunar* is easier than from "moon" to "lunar." The same goes for *auto(mobile)*, the Spanish word for car, and related words (e.g., *automatic(ally)*, *mobile*, *mobility*).

So while some Romance-language-speaking children might be unfamiliar with many words (mostly Anglo-Saxon) they are required to know, like "selfish," "share," and "head," they are usually familiar with many more complex words like *egoista*, *compartir*, and *cerebro* (the Spanish equivalents). Incidentally, these are the roots of many more complex English words that adults typically use (e.g., *ego(istic)*, *compartment(alize)*, *cerebellum*, and *cerebral*). Spanish equivalents make it easier for children who speak visibly Latinate languages to quickly learn many more words and skills, including reading—when children's attention is drawn to cognates.

Many DLLs already know words English-speaking peers typically learn much later (e.g., *alta* [high] and *altitude*; as well as *domestic(ated)*, since pets are *animales domesticas* in Spanish). So instead of comparing apples to oranges by adding up the number of words monolinguals and bilinguals know—a misguided approach that almost always puts the DLL last—we should examine the structure (i.e., morphology) and semantic complexity (e.g., age or grade-wise) of the terms and other language units children know and use this as the starting point of instruction.

Quantity alone fails to give us a full picture of the complexity and/or range of words DLLs know in reality (i.e., these children's cognitive sophistication). For instance, while an English-speaking child might know three words (*grade, degree,* and *Fahrenheit*), where a Spanish-speaking child might know just one, namely, *grado*, this single word is *multifunctional*.[2] *Grado* captures the essence of all three English words and more (i.e., it's a multiword synonym).[3] Its meaningfulness or semantic potency should not be underestimated. The concept of gradation or variation inherent in the word *grado* makes it immediately applicable to grades and measurement (i.e., level-based), temperature (i.e., degreed), and employment. In the metric system, the 100-point specification inherent in the word "centigrade," with an even more transparent Spanish equivalent, namely *(centi)grado*,[4] makes the concept of temperature and degrees more meaningful to children than the non-numbers-related and minimally meaningful term "Fahrenheit."[5] Note, too, that the first part of the word "centigrade" refers to 100 (just like *cent* means 1/100, and percent = part of 100); from the Latin word for 100 (centum), closer to the Spanish word *cien* than "hundred." So in the end, the single word *grado* (like *cien*) brings key math and science words to life much more visibly than the more remote English equivalents. Arguably, science is easier for children familiar with the many Latin roots of their primary languages and the metric system. So, DLLs who on the surface know fewer English words are not necessarily lacking (linguistically and cognitively). More often than not, they are familiar with many more concepts[6] for which they seemingly lack words. Indeed, bilingualism/ bidialectalism is far more complex than superficial word-for-word comparisons reveal.

Research demonstrates that reading is the next challenging skill for all children, regardless of their social standing (Shapiro, 2011). Children who can segment words into meaningful parts will have an easier time piecing reading (and writing) in both their primary and subsequent languages, as discussed next.

COMMON CORE AND WIDA/PREK–12 ENGLISH LANGUAGE PROFICIENCY STANDARDS

The federal PreK–12 English Language Proficiency (ELP) Standards were designed to ensure quality in PreK–3 instruction by providing educators with an easily applicable framework. Like the Common Core State Standards, they reflect the importance of language in schooling and in interpersonal communication. Collaboratively developed by ESL teachers, administrators, researchers, and linguists in 2006, these standards are available on the TESOL website. They "complement discipline-specific standards" developed by accrediting bodies like the National Council of Teachers of English (NCTE) and NAEYC. Yet exactly how these different standards intersect is unclear to many PreK–3 educators, hence this chapter.

The ELP standards started out as the World-Class Instructional Design and Assessment Consortium (WIDA) standards, aimed at assessing and standardizing English language proficiency. Initiated in 2002 by nine U.S. states WIDA, the standards-based movement, was developed in response to outcomes-oriented educational models (Richards & Rogers, 2003). The central goal still remains providing equal access to education to all students by closing the achievement gaps between and among subgroups (hence the No Child Left Behind Act of 2001). The ELP standards aimed to bring "the historically marginalized but fastest growing sector of school-aged children" (i.e., DLLs) "closer to the educational mainstream" (TESOL) by providing educators with an easy-to-understand-and-apply rubric to assess individual DLLs' English proficiency.

The ELP standards are based on the following assumptions:

1. That language is the primary means through which children learn (content)
2. That children's language, learning style, and instruction and assessment needs vary
3. That DLLs' "native languages and cultures" constitute the foundation and "bridge to academic language proficiency"
4. That all children must use language for social interaction in order to master academic content and functions (i.e., first comes speech)

To correctly use these standards, educators must be familiar with:

1. Grade-level clusters
2. Language domains
3. Language proficiency levels
4. Specific skills assessed (i.e., standards)

Two grade-level clusters (PreK–K and 1–3) apply to PreK–3 children. DLLs' English skills are assessed in four language domains, namely: listening, speaking, reading, and writing. Five proficiency levels or performance ratings are identified within each: starting, emerging, developing, expanding, and bridging. The first is level 1 (basic), and the last and highest is level 5. Within each grade-level cluster, five standards (essentially content areas) are assessed. They measure both social and academic language that children use inside and outside class. These are listed below, alongside associated language and content skills assessed:

Standard 1: DLLs successfully use language for "social, intercultural, and instructional purposes"
Standard 2: DLLs successfully communicate "information, ideas, and concepts" in language arts, and
Standard 3: "in mathematics"
Standard 4: "in science"
Standard 5: "in social studies"

Using these standards, educators should be able to systematically facilitate English acquisition and rate DLLs' English proficiency in key language domains and key content areas.

APPLYING THE WIDA/ELP STANDARDS

The challenge for PreK–3 teachers lies in (1) identifying the specific language DLLs must know (i.e., hear, understand, speak, read, and write) to satisfy each standard, and (2) tying the standards to their curriculum, including daily lesson plans (i.e., teacher talk, one-on-one and group facilitation, instructional resources, and assessments).

Since language is a scientific construct and best analyzed as individual building blocks, as outlined in Chapter 1 and throughout this book (i.e., starting with phonemes and ending with discourse units), PreK–3 teachers familiar with linguistics will have an easier time applying these standards.

For example, to demonstrate *strong social behavior* skills, a curricular objective and topic area under Standard 1, DLLs must understand (Level 1) and correctly use (levels 2–5) polite language. In short, they must be able to differentiate between politeness and impoliteness and acknowledge or employ polite forms in speech and writing (e.g., say "You're welcome," as is considered polite in America and many other locations). At each proficiency level, they must reflect certain competencies, as outlined below.

> *Level 1*: Demonstrate understanding of polite requests and displays of
>   gratitude (e.g., smiles to acknowledge understanding and appreciation
>   and/or uses basic vocabulary like "You're welcome.")
> *Level 2*: When prompted, use polite language to apologize, request, and
>   thank.
> *Level 3*: Role play exchanges using polite language
> *Level 4*: Use polite forms on their own in small-group settings
> *Level 5*: Successfully accommodate multicultural audiences (e.g., through
>   code-mixing)

DLLs have to understand and use increasingly challenging language at each subsequent (i.e., higher) level, as summarized below.

> Signal comprehension (through repetition and acknowledgment; Level
>   1) → produce appropriate language forms with guidance (generally
>   first with classmates and/or teacher, then others; Level 2) → role-play
>   conversations with adults (Level 3)→ use polite forms on their own in
>   unmonitored exchanges (Level 4) → and adjust speech for audiences in
>   diverse settings (Level 5).

As advised for math concepts (see Chapter 4), teachers first must identify the language associated with specific themes. Expressions of politeness vary across language and culture (i.e., sounds, words, etc.) (see Chapters 1 and 5). Some apologize using sarcasm. Step 1, therefore, requires differentiating between (culture-specific) politeness concepts and possible ways to express them (i.e., linguistics). Presenting dialect variations in politeness and other discourse structures, and inviting DLLs to share their politeness conventions (i.e., language units) is mutually beneficial. Students in Levels 2 through 5 should be able to share such information, and Level 1 students will very likely understand differences pinpointed, even if they are unable to demonstrate their understanding orally and/or writing. This way, you go beyond the ELP standards.

Use curricular content to determine which language forms to emphasize and/ or elicit from DLLs of varied proficiencies. Also:

> Use the most appropriate language (based on individual DLLs' context- and domain-specific competencies).
> Make your language use and requirements *more challenging* for DLLs at "higher" levels.

In the piece that follows, one educator offers a field-tested grid for easy classroom application of the ELP standards and alignment with content standards.

A Teacher's Voice: Integrating the National WIDA/TESOL Standards: The CRUST Model of Alignment

As a linguist charged with professional development of PreK–3 ESOL professionals, a core component of our training (TARGET, 2011) has to do with aligning the national ELP standards with PreK–3 content standards. Standards alignment for PreK–3 teachers is much easier than for middle and high school since all students, not just DLLs are learning academic language at this stage. However, like middle/ high school teachers, PreK–3 teachers will encounter DLLs of varied proficiency levels, so they must be knowledgeable in successfully synthesizing content standards with language objectives for multi-proficient learners while maintaining academic rigor.

Alignment of standards should ensure that there is "genuine learning" (Shepard et al., 2009, p. 3) taking place in real classrooms, and not just "perfectly" aligned standards presented on paper. Literature on the standards-based movement acknowledges the current reality of mixed operationalizations including, on the one hand, "vague general goal statements" and, on the other, "overly-full, encyclopedic standards" (Shepard et al., 2003). Current TESOL standards fall into the former category. While the debate between these two realizations is beyond the scope of this piece, a central question remains: How can teachers ensure that their alignments are not just "outlines of similar topics" but, rather, alignments that "address deeper issues of conceptual congruence between national-/ state-mandated goals and curricular content on the one hand and actual student learning (content and language) on the other?

Standards alignment is tedious but necessary. Alignment of standards should be approached in a piece-meal fashion using a building-blocks approach in which the standards—and specific language units—are clearly differentiated across grade levels and cumulative in focus. Conformity to these standards in the early years is relatively easy, as you are still building children's knowledge base.

The CRUST model provides a visual template to ensure that alignments are clear, specific, rigorous, and realizable, and work from the CRUST down. Consequently, alignments should be:

Coherent	i.e., should ensure a careful marriage of content and language outcomes
Rigorous	i.e., spotlight academic language objectives to ensure the immediate success of DLLs (Abedi, 2007)
Uniform	i.e., should strive for uniform outcomes for all children, no matter their linguistic proficiency levels
Specific	i.e., should translate content objectives into clear, understandable linguistic objectives. All lessons should clearly indicate the language demands embedded in tasks for multi-proficient learners and should clearly outline *both* the language needed FOR the task (known language) and the language IN the task (new language to be learned as a result) (Folse, 2009).
Teachable	i.e., alignments should translate into real learning for multi-leveled learners.

Observe an "at a glance" standards-alignment grid for a 3rd grade class was first developed (version 1: pre-training), and subsequently refined (version 2: post-training) by a team of elementary school teachers. A comparison of versions I and 2 reveals how all five components of the CRUST template yield uniform lesson design for all proficiency levels. This framework provides clear linguistic scaffolding to realize content objectives across proficiency levels. Indeed, training models that prompt teachers to think carefully about both content objectives and language objectives result in all children achieving the same outcomes. The CRUST model has at its foundation "curricular coherence" (Shepard et al., 2009, p. 4) in that standards and assessments work in tandem. Only then can DLLs make necessary progress in both content and language (Anjali Pandey, 2004).

INTEGRATING LINGUISTICS IN ECE OFFERINGS

For PreK–3 classrooms to be truly inclusive, all ECE coursework and professional development must be (sociolinguistically) inclusive. While more and more ECE administrators recognize the importance of linguistics (e.g., SLA theory) in teacher preparation and instructional success, more educators would benefit from a survey course or workshop in linguistics. In fact, given the value of linguistics for qualitative PreK–3 instruction/learning, all ECE training should incorporate essential linguistics. This way, we move beyond token attempts at inclusion through, for instance, a single or a couple of units on diversity (e.g., multicultural literature as the primary venue for cultural diversity).

Review all ECE service offerings with an eye to diversifying content and delivery. Linguistic infusion (e.g., ELP standards integration) is the most effective mechanism for revamping ECE offerings and ensuring inclusive education, as outlined here. Integrating linguistics at every step is fairly easy.

Start by infusing relevant linguistic strands into syllabi and assessments for coursework and other ECE offerings. Questions to guide you include:

1. Does the course content include DLLs?
2. Are DLLs viewed as a homogenous group or varying in proficiency?
3. Do the resources, activities, and assessments consistently feature linguistic diversity (i.e., appeal to different language groups) and/or integrate core linguistic concepts, theories, and pedagogy?

Examine whether diverse populations and language varieties other than Standard English are mentioned in syllabi, resources, and assessments, and whether linguistic inclusion is consistent. Remember that it's not enough to devote a small percentage of class time (e.g., a single week or unit) to DLLs (and special needs). Such token representations do not do justice to our increasingly diverse population or monolinguals, for that matter. For representative coverage, ensure that each and every unit carefully considers DLLs. Use activities and assessments that cater to varied-proficiency DLLs.

Using the guidelines outlined earlier, a Theory and Practices in Early Childhood course[7] was made more (linguistically) inclusive for a funded ECE program (see Pandey, 2008). For instance, ELP standards were added to the unit on professional standards. Weekly readings and activities integrated linguistically diverse resources, and students were invited to recommend others. For each unit, classroom discussions consistently applied key concepts to DLLs, as did the activities and (pre- and post-) assessments. Collaborative assignments requiring students to apply key concepts, theories, and pedagogical principles to multilevel DLLs were added to each unit.

As demonstrated, practically any ECE training module could be created and/or revamped to include ELP standards and other essential linguistic content. For example, in a children's literature course (required of most early childhood/special educators), in addition to including bilingual/bidialectal resources, examine language strategies employed (e.g., code-mixing) and the role-specific language varieties play in identity construction (see Chapter 5).

Welcome and Examine Bilingualism

We have a tendency to assume that DLLs are (the ones) on the border(line) and forget that it's time to include monolinguals in a global world where linguistic borders are shifting. The large number of DLLs therefore present a wonderful learning opportunity for professionals and children alike—if we tap DLLs' linguistic skills.

We stand to learn much from each child, including DLLs. Many are familiar with and can conceptualize (e.g., visually) many more concepts (some fairly abstract) than their monolingual peers. For example, the bilingual 4-year-old who reminds her "*Didi*" (respectful Hindi term for older sister) that "it's *paap* to step on books," is saying that it's distasteful, irreverent, shameful, and inadvisable to touch books with one's feet. She has imbibed the (cultural) belief that sustenance (i.e., food and knowledge, which nourish the body and mind, respectively) should be respected and elevated—literally and figuratively—and, as such, handled with the utmost respect and care—not with the lowest and potentially unclean body part, namely, the feet. Her ability to convey an abstract philosophical construct for which English has no translation equivalents reflects her cognitive and linguistic skill. So just because a DLL uses an un-English word (i.e., code mixes) does not mean that she is limited-English-proficient. In short, the language—not the child—might be lacking or insufficient for the purposes for which a child attempts to use it—necessitating language modification. Demonstrating to children how a single language variety is often unsuitable for the broad(er) range of functions language serves is essential. Apart from clarifying the value of bilingualism, it helps children to focus on language structure.

Inquiring about the names for numbers in DLLs' primary languages and integrating them in a math lesson or in any collaborative exercise where you assign or call out groups (e.g., *cinq* = 5 in French) is highly advisable. Integrating other languages throughout the day expands children's memory, introduces them to key words in other languages and in a meaningful context that facilitates recall, and sends the message that code-mixing and (functional) bilingualism are welcome and exciting. Cross-language activities have additional benefits. When, for instance, we use more-meaningful names of math symbols like *mas* (the Spanish word for more and a more natural bridge to *mass* than the English word *weight*) instead of "plus" (+), all children learn math and science faster (see Chapter 4), given their greater communic-ability. The more widespread use of these words in many languages prompts children to use them outside math class as well (e.g., at lunch time: "I need *mas agua*"). Use of other languages also adds excitement to the classroom, facilitates recall, and builds community, as children develop *a salsaed language* that differentiates them.

Knowledge of other writing systems could help us ease literacy for all children regardless of whether they read another language. In addition to the physical appearance of writing, the closer the match between sound and spelling, the easier children find reading. Notice, for instance, how the names of the letters and the sounds they make coincide in Spanish (i.e., 'A' is consistently /a/, 'B' is /bɛ/, 'Y' is /jei/).[8] In Hindi, letters are literally strung together with a line across the top to signal words created by combining sounds. When one hears just a hint of a sound, one slices the sound-letter in half, yielding half a /b/, /s/, and /n/ sound, for example. As in Arabic, many words with short (i.e., barely audible) vowel sounds are spelled with just consonants (e.g., pr /pər/ = but). What better way to represent sound-letter blending? Some languages provide additional reading hints. In Spanish, for instance, questions are indicated in writing through the inverted question mark at the start and not just at the end. When Spanish-speaking children see this symbol, they automatically know to expect a question and promptly use question intonation. When they approach written English, they do not see similar cues (which mirror the orality of written Spanish). We should, therefore, consider using such reading-assistive devices. Their use in English could facilitate (reading) comprehension, even for non-DLLs.

Indeed, the more phonetic a language, the easier it is to read and write. Observe how young children spell like they hear words (e.g., *Mary* for *merry*). When children (including DLLs) don't hear English vowels, for instance, they omit them (e.g., *evry*), suggesting that writing is an extension of speech. In a pilot study conducted by the author, four out of five 2nd-graders whose primary language was English were correctly able to read and write 94% to 96% of Spanish sentences dictated to them ("*Hola. Mi nobre es Dora. Tengo cinco años. Me gusta frutas. Donde es tu libro?*"). Many of the letters they misspelled coincided with sounds absent in English (underlined above). That they successfully wrote and read (part 2 of the survey) a language barely known to them is very telling and suggests that children seek speech (sounds) in writing. Therefore, (i) focus on building DLLs' fluency first (by growing vocabulary), since familiarity with sounds and words is prerequisite for both accessing and contributing to *secondary literacy* (Snow et al., 2005), and (ii) make written English more readable and writable.

Cater to DLLs

Make every effort to cater assignments and assessments to DLLs. When resources make little to no mention of DLLs, think of creative ways to consistently include diverse populations. One way to accommodate and welcome DLLs is to invite them and/or their families to translate stories you (co-)select and read in class.

Through this intergenerational and translinguistic reading activity, educators successfully cater to both DLLs and monolinguals, with families as partners. Predominantly monolingual children also learn key words and expressions in other languages, and all participants' interpersonal and intercultural skills are enhanced.

When books are unavailable in DLLs' heritage languages, families could translate what they read (ahead of time and/or extemporaneously). Such activities motivate children and adults alike. Invite families to share tales, poems, and/or writing samples. Listening to another language enhances children's phonetic skills and strengthens home–school partnerships. As a follow-up assignment, group children by primary language and invite them to retell stories in bilingual mode.

If adult family members are unable to lead (e.g., read English and/or their language), invite them to team up with children and/or young adults in their families and communities. This way, families embrace and collaboratively grow their primary language skills (Pandey, 2010).

Use Easy English and Evaluate Readability: Handy Reading Strategies

Another way to ease English acquisition for DLLs is by making it more readable. Research shows that reading, the broader context within which PreK–3 phonics and vocabulary instruction is generally reinforced, poses the biggest challenge for young children, including DLLs and children of college graduates, who presumably acquired early and good literacy habits (Shapiro, 2011).

Don't rush reading. As with speech (see Chapter 7), reading is easier when it involves interaction, continuous feedback, and opportunities for revision. Remember that children are not pressured to read by a certain age (e.g., 8 years) in all parts of the globe, so rushing reading could contribute to reading difficulties. Key questions to consider include: By what age have children mastered the phonemes of their language? How about the primary morphemes (e.g., plural, past tense)? Once this is assured, reading instruction can begin in their primary language and/or English. If some children have trouble reading even familiar words, read to them and/or use buddy reading and reading technologies, so they enhance their phonemic and vocabulary skills and develop an interest in reading.

Second, segment language every step of the way. Step-by-step language analysis facilitates fluency, literacy, and other skills, even for DLLs. Two competing views of reading, top-down and bottom-up, both require language analysis (i.e., processing) at different levels (and in opposite directions; e.g., sounds-to-discourse or vice versa). Owens (2005) proposes a third account involving interaction across language levels. When you teach young children to dissect language into (blended) phonemes, syllables, and word parts, in order of increasing size, they *routinize* this skill (i.e., imbibe it as a practice). They are then more likely to apply it to reading and writing, and to exhibit the *automaticity* or speed associated with good readers.

What's missing in reading research? While research emphasizes phonemic awareness (Ritchey & Speece, 2006), segmenting and processing larger language units, including words, sentences, and discourse (i.e., the key to cultural meanings) ,receives minimal attention. Therefore, emphasize these, too, using games like Word Up™ (see Chapter 2). With some help, most 4-year-olds should be able to identify four parts in *snowy day*, namely: *Elsina's Clouds*, namely, Elsina + s + Cloud + s.

Before you label a child as a struggling reader, evaluate the readability or linguistic complexity of the (e)reading in question. In "The Problem Princess" (Sneller, 2001), for instance, much of the vocabulary and even many sentences (e.g., "She could even order to have Elizabeth put to death" [emphasis added] are fairly complex for the target age group (see Chapter 7). The following reading comprehension question and many of the choices provided require an understanding of complex language and historical and cultural content.

Example

Circle what you think was Elizabeth's main problem.
a. She wanted her mother's name cleared.
b. She did not want Mary to have her beheaded.

Few 3rd-graders, much less DLLs, will be familiar will the schema/content and the language used in this indirect question. Items (a) and (b) are not merely passives but embedded passives. Passives are relatively complex for 3rd-graders. Few 8- and even 9-year-olds use passives frequently (see Chapter 7), much less embedded ones (i.e., incorporated into another clause and with parts like to be and by . . . merely implied). According to one 9-year-old who was invited to comment on the passive sentences in this reading, "I think I understand them but I don't use them." "So how did you answer these questions?" "I just tried to guess the answers," she responded.

Replacing passive sentences with simpler (active) forms should ease comprehension for DLLs and even monolingual English users. Use culturally familiar and age-appropriate words (e.g., "She thought people thought bad things about her mother and wanted to change their mind"). You could also add the missing words "by . . . ." When invited to rephrase the passive sentences, the 3rd grader who was interviewed was unable to provide active equivalents. However, when these simpler forms were provided, she promptly observed "Oh! So why didn't they just ask it like that?" In short, the language of readings and the questions we ask to determine children's comprehension should be familiar from both a structural and a cultural standpoint. It should also be bias-free. So before you dismiss a child's reading skills, take a hard look at the language of the readings and ask "Is the language suitable?"

Just because a book is classified as a children's book does not mean that children in the target age group will find it readable. Vary spoken and written language for DLLs and remember that shorter isn't always better (e.g., most will find *make late* easier than *delay*). Replace difficult and unfamiliar words in readings using sticky notes which children (including DLLs) could lift up to learn more difficult synonyms (when they're ready). Whenever possible, invite children to propose synonyms. For instance, since *sometimes* is more frequent than occasionally, replace "occasionally" in the following sentence from the book *Dotty*: "Dotty occasionally poked people with her horns" (Perl, 2010, p. 4). You are likely to find that it's not that Alex *can't read* but that (s)he has trouble decoding relatively complex language.

Bridge Languages and Cultures

Many words DLLs know (e.g., *mil* and *sal*) are more compact and close(r) in meaning to the words we expect them to know (e.g., *million* or *millipede*, and *salt*, respectively), making them potentially more meaningful to DLLs whose primary languages contain these cognates. Given the many similarities between Romance languages and Latin, on the one hand, and English and Latin, on the other, with individualized instruction that draws attention to the distinctive features of each language through a focus on similarities and differences across language units (see Chapter 7), DLLs should master English fairly easily and strengthen their L1 skills.

Research the concepts and words DLLs and their peers already know and use them as a bridge to the others—many more basic—they are expected to know. The result is individualized and strategic language-literacy and content instruction that comprehensively builds on their strengths. Remember that while a DLL's vocabulary might not be as large (e.g., synonym-filled), the content value of the words many know might, in fact, be just as high if not higher, so simply comparing the number of words children know does not give us an accurate picture of their knowledge base. Having a larger vocabulary does not necessarily translate to knowing more.

Given the scientific base of many DLLs' primary vocabulary, bridge language and content divides by pinpointing similarities, even if you consider the English equivalents relatively complex. Instead of inviting a Spanish-speaking child to "show me," try saying, *demonstra me,* and watch their faces. It's close to both the English synonym and the Spanish equivalent, and if you don't get an instant smile, modify your pronunciation. You might find that Spanish is not this child's primary language. Regardless, when children see you making the effort to learn another language, they are usually very appreciative and more motivated (see Chapter 7). Language comparisons also symbolize something larger—cultural responsiveness.

To successfully explain word-extension-based sound changes to young children, for instance, language comparison and a basic knowledge of linguistics are essential. If DLLs have teachers who know a little about their languages or who take time to research their languages using a handy linguistic approach that quickly reveals the kinds of difficulties they (are likely to) encounter, they can draw on what they know to learn what they don't. They would learn important details early on instead of struggling and hopefully (but not necessarily) stumbling upon the answer someday. While contrastive analysis has not worked as well for the predictive purposes for which it was proposed (i.e., error analysis), it is a valuable instructional tool since children learn much through comparison. The novelty of examples is often just as instructive.

With the help of DLLs, create comparable listings of sounds, words, and so on (organized functionally, thematically, or by source language), pinpointing commonalities and differences. Remember that when children are involved (e.g., in content creation), they usually learn more. Include variations in sentences such as subject-less or implied-subject sentences in Spanish (e.g., *Am Juan* versus *I am Juan*) and underline differences. Do the same for speech acts and paragraph organization, and other distinctive discourse features, so you systematically prepare DLLs for success in PreK–3 and beyond. Similarly, use children's spellings as a bridge to conventional spelling.

Use Comics and Other Visuals

Keep language/reading(s) real, multisensory, and fun! Try using comics. In Cary's (2004) experience, they engage and relax students. One ESL teacher recommends giving students "cut-out comic strip panels without text" (Cary, 2004, p. 82) and inviting them to create their own dialog. Like cartoons, comics add a visual dimension that appeals to all children, especially visual learners. Use existing comics (e.g., *Ziggy* and *Garfield Has a Field Day*) and/or invite children to (co-)create their own. When children write and illustrate text, they learn more. Post-reading discussions and dramatizations are advisable. Invite children to share if they identify with any characters, for instance, and to explain why. You could even invite them to rewrite stereotypic depictions (e.g., Zena and Ursula in Bazooka Joe, www.bazookajoe.com). Children could even comic-strip prose stories they read.

For every lesson, (co-)compile a list of individualized resources your DLLs could use to supplement class discussions. With the help of children, assemble content kits that DLLs of varied proficiency could use inside and outside class. First create a matrix or rubric integrating the WIDA/ELP and content standards.[8] This will help you determine what to include. Periodically invite and adopt or adapt child creations and/or selections. In a pilot study involving PreK–8 teachers in rural Maryland, all six PreK–3 teachers reported great success with ESL Content Kits. The ones they co-created were very well received in their respective schools (see Pandey, 2011a).

SUMMARY AND APPLICATIONS

This chapter outlined the PreK–3 ELP standards and illustrated how to use them as a guidepost and successfully align both WIDA/ELP and content standards to provide effective instruction to each DLL. It also discussed how to infuse these and other essential linguistic concepts into teacher preparation and professional development. As demonstrated, knowledge of linguistics helps educators better understand and instruct DLLs (i.e., seamlessly integrate designated standards in instruction and assessment). It also ensures more qualitative and diversified instruction, yielding *inclusivity*, an essential element.

PreK–3 educators can aid DLLs, first, by familiarizing themselves with the WIDA/PreK–3 ELP proficiency standards and, second, by integrating these in lessons and assessment and aligning them with content standards, so that no child is left behind. The linguistic CRUST model was proposed and its applicability and relatively easy alignment with content standards demonstrated.

Handy resources aimed at facilitating autonomous language learning and reading (interconnected) for DLLs of varied proficiency were also identified, including ESL Content Kits tied to national standards.

By including DLLs in every sense of the word, through the linguistic give-and-take recommended, we ease learning for DLLs and, in turn, learn much of value. I recall the afternoon I picked up my 5-year-old and, before I could ask her about her day and what she had learned, she excitedly announced, "Mama, Mr. Kilbert knows Hindi! He said, 'Table ek, Table ðo, Table theen,' and I was so surprised and the game became so cool!!" Then she turned to her sister and repeated the story in a louder voice ("Didi, did you know that . . . ?"). When her father returned home, he also heard this first.

Like all children, DLLs have much to offer and should not be underestimated. Critical thinking, mediation, and problem solving, for instance, are skills bilinguals imbibe much faster. Not surprisingly, DLLs generally outperform monolinguals (see Chapter 7), so we should not merely seek input from DLLs but actively partner with them to enhance instruction for all. Remember that linguistic novelty is appealing and promotes success. This includes the newness of another *lengua* (i.e., tongue in Spanish). Just think about the word *lengua* for a moment. Language is literally what the tongue says (i.e., the sounds it makes). So while Spanish-speaking children think of the tongue as both a language and an organ and understand the connection between the two from the start, most English-speaking children think of the tongue solely as an organ. Few are familiar with the term *mother tongue*.

As reiterated throughout this book, a focus on language (diversity) in PreK–3 is one way to ensure that children develop respect for differences early on. National initiatives like Promoting Social Inclusion and Respect for Diversity, and Head Start's National Center on Cultural and Linguistic Responsiveness emphasize the need for early childhood educators to be more responsive to diversity. Until we consistently diversify theory and "progressive practices" (Nager & Shapiro, 2000), we simply will be paying lip service to diversity.

It's virtually impossible to be culturally responsive without being linguistically responsive. One of the questions we should be asking is, "Who should be accommodating to whom?" For too long, our discourse (e.g., "accommodating" and "including DLLs") has been sending the message that English speakers have the right and obligation to call the shots (see Chapter 7). Often, this message is sent in the absence of legislative backing, as though we are doing DLLs a favor by, for instance, permitting them to use their languages when, in fact, we usually do so only because we consider those languages easy bridges to the dominant one we are fortunate to speak, namely, English. The reality today and in the near future is that we are at the mercy of those proficient in diverse languages and cultures, including children. Inviting DLLs to the ECE table is and should be as much about what monolingual English speakers stand to gain from intercultural exchange as about making DLLs feel at home.

CHAPTER 10

Language and Literacy in the Digital Age

Of course the world didn't stand still. [It] grew. In a couple of years, the new highway came through.

—Dr. Seuss, *The Sneetches and Other Stories*

U got my hw a lil late

—text message (hw = homework)

Mama, what does humongous mean? (pause) Giant! I learned it from PBSKids.org.

—Shlok, 4

Yahoo's streaming of the Clinton Foundation gala concert on October 15, 2011, evidenced the power of technology—a medium with international reach. In Chinese, the word "computer" translates to "electric brain," reflecting the power and volatility of technology. Indeed, technology has been driving innovation in instruction and other areas. Even popular music and literature echo its impact.[1] Most of us cannot imagine life without e-mail, text messaging, and other communication technology. Technology has transformed the way we communicate and even how we "write." As this chapter demonstrates, technology enhances PreK–3 instruction and learning. Learning objectives include:

1. Outlining the benefits of technology in the early years
2. Discussing technology's impact on PreK–3 language and content learning, as well as on linguistics
3. Recommending technologies for independent and classroom use
4. Offering guidelines for successful technology integration PreK–3

THE PREK-3 APPEAL OF TECHNOLOGY

Today's technology includes a broad range of instructional/learning tools. These include computer technology (e.g., laptops, tablets, PDAs), smartphones, digital recorders, software applications like multimedia authoring tools (e.g., Power-Point), and others that allow you to (re-)create interactive e-communities with avatars (e.g., Second Life). From assistive technologies for those with special needs to (e-)tools that facilitate language acquisition (e.g., interactive programs), technology is a powerful language with virtually undisputed potential (Nussbaum-Beach, 2008; Richardson, 2009; Clements & Sarama, 2005) and more benefits than negatives. Mobile learning through handheld devices (e.g., e-readers) exemplifies technology's value. That many tech tools are student-owned is an added plus (i.e., reducing cost).

Technology transports many a child to a whole new world. When the narrator of *Diary of a Wimpy Kid* joins the Jeffersons on their vacation, he is disappointed that their cabin has "no TV or computer or ANYTHING with a screen" (p. 163). Three days later, cabin-fevered and tech-deprived, he gets on Mr. Jefferson's work laptop and sends "an e-mail to Mom" (p. 171) because "I've never gone this long without TV or computers or videogames" (p. 170). Like most Web 2.0-generationers, he is not merely tech-savvy, but addicted to technology.

Most children are more responsive to technology than to humans. My 4-year-old was enamored by the computer by age 2 and has been glued to it since then. She looks for any and every opportunity to hop on the iPhone or computer and promptly accesses her favorite sites and programs. Interestingly, she could enter the password to my laptop and a few URLs long before she could write her name. Like many children, she is more excited about "reading" and typing on the computer than reading paper-based books and handwritten materials. "Better a computer geek than a TV addict!" says my neighbor.

Not surprisingly, many young children are more knowledgeable about technology than adults are. In this sense, they are "digital natives" while most adults are "digital immigrants" (Bennett, Maton, & Kervin, 2008). Schmidt (2011) reports that in many Latino homes, the children are the primary technology users. Given (1) their greater English proficiency and (2) their translation and tech skills, many conduct online searches for their parents. Until their parents "can use those devices the same way English speakers can," DLL children will be closing the language divide—and the digital divide, too." Since English occupies the lion's share of the Internet and other technology tools (e.g., gaming applications), "it falls to bilingual kids to pick up the slack."[2] Children find technology exciting, so it makes the most sense to reach them using this medium.

One of the attractions of today's technology is its *multimodality* (multisensory capabilities), which (1) appeals to multiple learning styles, (2) promotes inquiry and problem solving (i.e., learning), (3) enables interactivity, and (4) facilitates acquisition of multidisciplinary vocabulary and content in context. Since technology is exciting and inviting, it looks more like fun than like schoolwork, so children learn without realizing they're learning. Such task-based, integrative-skills instruction is one of the appeals of technology. Language learners, for instance, can interact with the target language at any time and from any location, without having to rely on classroom instructors.

Through streaming media, stories come to life, unlike in traditional book and paper-and-pencil formats. Technology wows children and prompts them to create and share, and to read and write more than they would in its absence. For instance, as they interact with (e-)programs (e.g., Starfall) or conduct web searches, they learn words, many subconsciously (see Chapter 7). The more written words they encounter, the more spellings they recall. They also learn correct pronunciation. Since less than half of the workday is spent in the classroom, and sustained interaction and feedback are essential for language and content learning (Pandey, 2010), tech provides us with a viable solution—expanded learning opportunities.

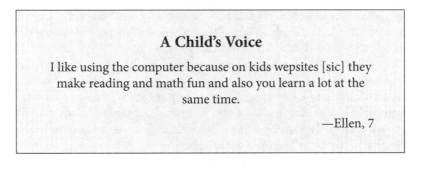

A Child's Voice

I like using the computer because on kids wepsites [sic] they
make reading and math fun and also you learn a lot at the
same time.

—Ellen, 7

One way children share what matters to them, and demonstrate their cognitive and language skills, is through their stories and/or artwork. Their literacy also reflects variations in language practices (i.e., socialization). Many children mention current technologies in their stories. In 8-year-old Anna's story "Summer Stocks," bunnies use the computer to trade stocks and "earn money."[3] In another story (by Anna), close friends communicate primarily through e-mail. Incidentally, Anna communicated with another 8-year-old, who resided in another state, using e-mail, after their initial face-to-face meeting. Their language skills were noticeably enhanced through e-mail exchanges.

Anna learned the name of another language and was excited about learning Hindi expressions, as evidenced by her responses. Her use of "Wow" and repetition of the Hindi leave-taking expression her friend supplied (evidencing learning), as well as her request for "more Hindi!" are exemplary. They suggest that bilingual children can easily interest their peers in other languages. That a child also inserts some Spanish words in her e-mail evidences her functional bilingualism, which she clearly views as relationship-enhancing. In short, her desire to share her bilingual skills evidences confidence; she would do so only if she felt linguistically secure and believed she had something valuable to share. That Anna's e-pal uses English to capture the sounds of Hindi signals her phonemic skills.

(E-)LANGUAGE AND LITERACY

Technology is at the nexus of traditional speech and writing, and a novel and distinct communication medium. Like the rim of a wheel (see Figure 1.2), technology drives instruction and learning in PreK–3, yielding a smoother ride. Technology has modified language and literacy, most visibly at the vocabulary level, followed by the sentence level and written discourse. Accordingly, it is synonymous with language innovation (see Pandey, 2005, 2009). Technology accounts for the lion's share of new vocabulary. Examples include semantic extensions (e.g., web and e-mail), new nouns and verbs (e.g., texting and Facebook's use of *friend* as a verb), novel spellings (e.g., 4U = for you), and more flexible sequencing in (e-)messages (see Pandey, 2011b). The speed with which (e-)lingo has been adopted in multiple languages reflects the impact of Englishization and specifically of technology. Not surprisingly, technology and science vocabulary in most languages consists almost entirely of English(-like) vocabulary. For instance, "computer" is *computadora* in Spanish and *computa* in Japanese, Yoruba, and many other languages. Indeed, technological advancements have accelerated the spread of English.

WHY INTEGRATE TECHNOLOGY IN PREK–3?

To compete in a global world, children must have technology skills (Kamil, Pearson, Moje, & Afflerbach, 2011). These constitute strategic literacy, so we must strive to erase the digital divide. Few DLLs and/or children eligible for free and reduced-price lunch, for instance, have after-school Internet access.

Today's technology provides what Egbert (2005) terms "a whole learning environment" (p. 2). Interactive, innovative, and multimodal by default, technology could help us meet and exceed our curricular objectives by (1) engaging every child and (2) sparking creativity, independence, and sustained learning.

As Sheffield (2007) reminds us, "The time has passed to decide if technology improves student achievement" (p. 2). Mandates like the U.S. Department of Education's Enhancing Education Through Technology Act of 2001 evidence its value. NAEYC, NCATE, TESOL, NCELA, NABA, and many other bodies also require technology integration in PreK–12.

Effective tech use ensures high-quality teaching and learning for all students (Culp, Honey, & Mandinach, 2003; Herrington & Kervin, 2007). Technology has numerous benefits. First, it provides affirming and enriching instructional/learning communities and lends itself to individual use, as well as collaboration. Same-language, mixed-language, and cross-age collaboration via e-mail, storyboarding, text messaging, IM, Skype, WebQuests, file sharing (e.g., documents, slides, and images), and more are just a few ways through which technology:

1. Expands instruction/learning time and contexts
2. Creates (global) learning communities
3. Provides and generates funds of knowledge (Moje et al., 2004)
4. Enables interaction and continued learning

Technology accommodates variable abilities and learning and teaching styles through diverse formats that benefit instructors and children alike, explaining why many autistic children are more responsive to it than to human collaborators. It improves access to information and promotes self-paced and self-directed learning in multiple contexts. Adjustable challenge levels, individualized formats, and expanded learning opportunities are additional pluses. Deaf and hard-of-hearing children, for instance, can connect with each other and with the hearing community via video relay services, and use e-reading tools. The latter illuminate text (Burke, 2001), making reading more understandable, even for struggling readers. E-readers and word processing programs offer definitions, and visual and auditory cues (sometimes in other languages). Similarly, spelling and grammar checkers provide instant feedback, so children continue to learn—even without feedback from human instructors. The novelty of technology also increases children's reading and writing engagement (e.g., through 'e-paling' and texting).

LINGUISTICS IN THE DIGITAL AGE

Even linguistics has taken on a new life in the 21st century. Technology has advanced linguistic research and made linguistics more readily accessible. Indeed, technology allows us "to share the world's linguistic heritage with a wider community of teachers and learners," and we have the opportunity to both "salvage" and "revive" languages (Burke, 2001, p. 7). *Language documentation* is one way tech has helped with both (Nicholson, 2009). Linguists can now use powerful recorders to "analyze the elements of a vowel in seconds or compare sounds across languages." E-dictionaries on mobile phones are especially promising; DLLs and monolingual children can enhance their vocabulary in English and other languages relatively quickly and on-the-go.

Which came first, technology or linguistics? It's hard to say. Communicative technologies (e.g., (e-)translators and voice recognition technologies) employ linguistics. Most use *Boolean logic* (essentially semantics and syntax) to access key words from databases constructed using linguistics. Semantic search engines, for instance, scan and access synonyms in Venn diagram mode, yielding meaningful searches. Algorithms based on the structure of individual languages drive (e-)translators (e.g., Google Translate) and web crawlers. Ontologists/knowledge engineers use (computational) linguistics to capture and categorize information,[4] further exemplifying the value of linguistics.

TECHNOLOGY FOR PREK–3 EDUCATORS

Multiple tech tools and resources provide audio examples of phonemes and other language units, including step-by-step visuals of their production, making linguistics more meaningful to educators.

The websites linguistlist.org and www.cal.org, for instance, are reputed (e-) communities for those interested in languages and linguistics. They provide a comprehensive list of resources. You also can ask questions and gain a better understanding of key concepts and their applications. Language blogs, videos (from credible websites), and wikis are additional resources. The Internet provides a vast repository of cross-language and how-to information, including:

> Examples of visual storytelling (e.g., the *aarwe-iltyinke*, a game like cat's
> cradle that the Arrernte of Australia play)
> *Oghan*, the Celts' line-based writing system
> Cuneiform, hieroglyphics, and runes
> The unique whistled speech and tones of Chiquihuitlan Mazatec
> Vowel-less words in Bella Coola/Mosan (British Columbia)
> The Rongorongo script of Easter Island
> The complex morphology of Kiwai (from Papua New Guinea)
> The click sounds of Bantu languages (e.g., Xhosa)

Today's technology helps us appreciate different cultures and linguistic diversity.

TECHNOLOGY FOR LINGUISTIC RESEARCH

Technology has made linguistic research more rigorous, accessible, and timely. It has resuscitated dead and dying languages, an area termed *language revival*. Linguist James McElvenny, for example, has helped develop software to revitalize Dharug, an indigenous Australian language.

Technology provides "information and tools to empower communities to make their languages SEEN and HEARD" (http://www.ilinative.org). These could be accessed in class. Thanks to technology, "enthusiasts are raising their children bilingually in English and Cornish"[5] (Comrie, Matthews, & Polinsky, 2003, p. 214). The success of recent language revival efforts for Hawaiian, Welsh, and even Maori, is attributable in large part to technology; interested individuals can collaborate electronically and access multiple resources. Language nests like the Punana Leo, a Hawaiian immersion program that teaches children the local traditions of song and dance, have been facilitated by technology, as has Jamaica's Bilingual Education Project.

TECHNOLOGY FOR ENHANCED PREK–3 INSTRUCTION/LEARNING

Today's technology makes it easy to integrate music and more—and not just in English—in your classroom. There is no shortage of PreK–3 instructional technologies. On the contrary, there is more than one possibly can integrate in the classroom. From e-readers like the Barnes & Noble nook and Amazon's Kindle to computer animation software, the face and focus of communication, as well as of reading, writing, learning, and instruction, have been transformed. Free animation programs (e.g., Xtranormal) are readily available and, like e-readers, ideal for young children. Many find animation more engaging than other tools (e.g., composing).

Vocabulary, Reading, and Writing Applications

Educational technology is "nudging literacy instruction beyond its oral and print-based tradition to embrace online and electronic texts as well as multimedia" (Holum & Gahala, 2011). How so? Audio books, e-books and online texts, electronic talking books, and programmed reading instruction are some of the tools currently available to support PreK–3 reading. Technology is especially beneficial in reading instruction "because of its power to keep students interested while they are engaged in meaningful literacy activities" (Hollowell, 2011). "Books bore me," observed one student at a tech school, "but not technology." Technology facilitates PreK–3 reading by making it interactive and multisensory through:

> Graphic organizers and other printables, which are readily available for individual and collaborative use and are customizable
> E-readers
> Interactive reading sites (e.g., Starfall and Internet4Classrooms)[6]

Single and multi-touch tablets and e-readers allow children to annotate readings and compile word lists while they read. To make PreK–3 language and content more enjoyable, collaborative, and multisensory, allocate some time on interactive websites where children can hear age-appropriate vocabulary and other languages, view writing, read excerpts or entire books (e.g., download them), and periodically assess their understanding. Hollowell (2011) contends that "a child's reading fluency will increase as she [or he] hears more examples of proper reading."

In Holum and Gahala's (2011) view, "The Internet is constructing global bridges for students to communicate" and "influencing how people read, write, listen, and communicate." Computers foster collaboration via e-mail, texting, and storyboarding, for instance. The result is child-facilitated and extended language and content learning (see Chapter 7). The Internet also enables children's literacy to be showcased globally, sharing PreK–3 language-literacy research and motivating young children (see Holum & Gahala, 2011).

To interact with tech tools, children have to understand what is expected of them. This usually requires some listening and/or reading (of text, visuals, etc.). These interactions and the feedback children receive undoubtedly enhance their literacy skills. Since reading and writing overlap, their reading impacts their writing (i.e., conceptualization, description, and spelling), and vice versa. While reading one's own creations does not necessarily guarantee reading success, it generates pride and literacy interest, which inevitably enhance key skills, particularly for struggling readers and writers. E-puzzles are an excellent way to expand children's vocabulary and reading skills. Pictures of coins, fruits, flags, lyrics, and more are readily available online, making technology one of the handiest and most sensory-rich tool for math, music, and social studies.

Math and Science Applications

While not all technology was designed with early childhood instruction in mind, many applications could be used in and/or adapted to PreK–3. For instance, capitalize on the relative newness of the smartphone to encourage children to add, subtract, and perform other basic math functions. One Kindergarten teacher shared how she gave each student a cell phone and asked them to dial home to ensure they knew their numbers. Have them dial other numbers (e.g., a local theater) as well, and monitor their language. Invite PreK–1 students to add up the digits in their phone numbers and make words using the letters that correspond to their phone numbers on the key pad. Split them into teams and have them compete to see which team creates the most words in a specified time period.

Interactive online resources for math, such as IXL, enhance and reinforce (through repetitive language and steps) multiple skills: language, math, and more. First, children have to understand the language through which math is presented (see Chapter 4). When children's response to a math problem is "correct" (a screen response that appears after they "submit" their answer), they quickly learn this word, particularly when the check symbol appears next to it. Children also are more likely to recall the spellings of words they encounter. Similarly, if their answer is "incorrect" (the response provided instead of the ego-bruising term "wrong"), they learn the opposite word and how to politely convey bad news. Most infer the meaning of the prefix in- so when they come across similarly patterned words (e.g., incomplete), they are likely to assign correct meanings to them. Another polite term used on IXL is "sorry." The correct answer is then presented using a complete sentence (e.g., "The correct answer is _____"). Exposure to this and other sentence types, generally through the "explanation" option that appears on the screen, inductively teaches children correct word order, handy phrases (e.g., "try again"), and sentence structure and variety (e.g., statements versus directives and questions). They also learn punctuation by example.

Many websites (e.g., IXL) also track the time children take to solve a problem through the "time elapsed" feature, so, outside class, children could prepare for timed tests, while practicing their numbers (i.e., symbolic language), word recognition, counting, and other skills.

Dual Language Learning Applications

Today's technology allows us to learn languages even outside the classroom. We can hear the sounds of endangered, lesser known, and other heritage languages, and revisit and unlock the meanings of ancient and dead languages (e.g., Sanskrit and the Mayan number system). Technology allows us to appreciate classics like *Beowulf*, and to learn Braille, sign language, and more.

Educators unfamiliar with DLLs' languages can electronically gather and share pertinent information (e.g., about sounds and politeness routines) relatively easily. Technology motivates, teaches, and empowers all. It provides opportunities for sustained interaction with visual and textual language. Children and families could take pictures (e.g., of objects and scenes) and use these to (re-)create stories. With some guidance, they could even create and upload video clips (e.g., podcasts) for their peers and others to view.

GUIDELINES FOR EFFECTIVE TECHNOLOGY
USE IN PREK–3

When technology changes at a rate faster than it can be evaluated, its value is not as apparent unless it is systematically monitored. To this end, some guidelines follow.

Using technology for the sake of technology or merely because it is required or new is inadvisable. Carefully consider which tool to use and why and how best to ensure positive outcomes. In addition to developing well-thought-out lesson plans, educators today have to adapt to rapidly changing technology and utilize it when its use is most appropriate and "not necessarily as soon as it emerges" (Kozloski, 2006, p. 5). Provide clear guidelines (e.g., a list of resources, programs, or activities you would like children to access; instructions; and timelines). Also, track the impact of specific technologies on each child (i.e., individual learning). Only then can technology help you reach specific milestones.

Children need to first learn basic tech terms (e.g., for hardware like *keyboard*, *keypad*, and *cursor*) and functionality (i.e., software) in order to browse the web. Their spellings will determine what kinds of returns they get, prompting them to pay closer attention to spelling. Entering and encountering words strengthens children's vocabulary. Technology might appear to increase the learning burden initially, in the sense that children have more to learn, including how to use the technology. Nevertheless, the multisensory and "authentic learning" it provides is unparalleled (Herrington & Kervin, 2007) and offsets the initial burden. So children learn more than they would in its absence.

Providing relevant examples prompts greater (e-)participation and facilitates interaction-based learning. Experiment with different technologies to determine which one(s) work with each child (see Herrington & Kervin, 2007). Also, make tech activities and examples as appealing as possible, and periodically monitor and invite feedback.

CHOOSING THE RIGHT TECHNOLOGY

The multitude of websites and tools that promise to teach children core competencies means that we must work harder to identify those that teach what they claim and those that merely entertain.

Pre-Use Evaluation

Be sure to monitor the utility of the technology every step of the way. Before recommending a website to DLLs for instance, consider the following:

Language (i.e., ease of understanding) and visual variety
Collaborative potential
Ease of use (i.e., child-friendliness) and/or cultural relevance
Currency
Instructional focus
Cost-effectiveness

Sample questions to ask at the outset include:

1. Is the language (oral/written/visual) age-appropriate?
2. What is the primary purpose and how did you determine this?
3. Could you use it to teach X or Y?
4. Is it more suitable for out-of-class use?

Create a handy checklist using these or related questions.

During- and Post-Use Impact Assessment

One of the challenges technology poses is how to determine whether children are indeed learning as a consequence of specific technology. Create a checklist to help you monitor and identify learning resulting from children's interactions with different technologies.

In the following example, a 5-year-old reacts to a rhyming word activity on the website Roy the Zebra. C refers to the child, S to her 7-year-old sister, and M to her mother, who asks questions to assess S's understanding along the way.

Example

Prompt: Select words that rhyme with "cat." ["Chap" is one of the choices]
M: "Chap" ka matlab kya hei (i.e., Hindi for "What does 'chap' mean?")
C: (silent)
S: Chap Stick?
M: No. It's like "guy" in British English. And "lad"?
C: I don't know.
S: Me neither.
M: What does "gap" mean?
C: It's a skirt!
M: It's a small space.
S: It's like a hole.
M: Good. It's also the name of a children's clothes company. "Ram"?
C: Like in Didi's school, there's one.
M: That's a ramp. This is R-A-M, like a goat (shows a picture). What's "ban"?
C: It's like these (pointing at S's bangs).
M: Try again.
C: Oh! I know. It's like when you have a party.
M: That's a band.
C: English is weird.

As this example shows, many words are unfamiliar to children either because they are regionally distinct (i.e., dialect variants like *ram*, *lad*, and *chap* versus *goat*, *boy*, and *guy/fellow*), have a different meaning than the one with which a child is familiar (e.g., *gap*), or infrequent and cognitively complex (e.g., *ban*). That this Kindergartner promptly associated *gap* with the Gap clothing company is note-worthy and confirms that children listen, read, draw and write what they know (e.g., *hao* versus *how*), so we must familiarize them with much more. Periodically assess children's understanding through questioning.

SUMMARY AND APPLICATIONS

This chapter outlined the benefits of technology for PreK–3 children and educators. As demonstrated, technology has modified childhood, learning, and instruction. It enables autonomous learning of language, literacy, and content, even for DLLs and children with special needs (also see Chapter 8). Technology also gives agency to children and allows multiple voices to be captured online. The result is a three-dimensional perspective, ideal for PreK–3 classroom use and research. The continuity in language, literacy, and multiskills development that technology enables could make all the difference, especially for struggling learners who need sustained scaffolding. Yet, tech integration poses challenges as well, and must be goal-driven, meaningful, and carefully monitored.

The professional development potential of technology also is discussed. Early childhood educators, for instance, can easily access linguistic concepts and applications through the variety of resources currently available. They can readily research children's heritage languages (e.g., through websites and blogs) to learn how to ease mastery of specific sounds, words, and more. Technology is a powerful research and instruction/learning tool and publicity vehicle. It better prepares PreK–3 teachers to meet children's individual needs and demonstrates the practical value of linguistics (e.g., its use in knowledge engineering and language revitalization). Whether its use by children has the same or greater instructional impact than classroom instruction remains to be seen. What is clear is its ability to engage and instruct by appealing to multiple senses.

CHAPTER 11

Continually Investigating Language in School and Beyond
Concluding Remarks

> There's no limit to how much you'll know, depending how far beyond zebra you go.
>
> —Dr. Seuss, *On Beyond Zebra!*

One evening, my 5-year-old and I were taking a walk when she jumped in the stroller that I took along. Just then she spotted a classmate playing outside his home and observed: "Mama, when we get there (pointing to the end of the street), I'm going to get out because I don't want him to think I'm a baby." What others (especially their peers) think of them is of critical importance to most children. Observing children's language in multiple environments allows us to understand how children construct meaning and what and who influences them, since classroom-based learning and socialization (informal learning) are mirrored in language.

This chapter illustrates how even a basic understanding of linguistics gives us a fuller picture of actual (versus assumed) power roles in interactions involving children. It also emphasizes the importance of periodic language observation and analysis, and offers strategies for continued language investigation inside and outside the classroom.

THE LANGUAGE OF AGENCY

As we seek to develop agency (i.e., independence and critical thinking) in early childhood (Beach et al., 2010; Lee & Recchia, 2008; Ryan & Grieshaber, 2005), key questions we must ask include:

How is agency manifested?
Could agency be negative?
What approaches (e.g., frameworks) are most suitable for monitoring and imparting agency?

As this section demonstrates, language is, in fact, the most tangible and reliable indicator of agency. Language reflects agency or lack of it better than any other behavior trait (which explains why conflict mediators use and emphasize positive language). The primary vehicle through which individuals obtain and sustain their power (Fairclough, 2001) is language. "My teacher is such a meany," confides one Kindergartner to another. "Mine, too. She yells a lot." These children are exercising their agency. Expressing themselves helps them feel better.

Knowledge of linguistics helps us build positive agency in early childhood. A simple conversation analysis of the kind outlined in this chapter helps us monitor children's (and others') language in diverse contexts. It also enables early childhood practitioners to detect negative agency, including abusive language and/or bullying language (see Epling, 2011; Johar, 2010) early on, when intervention is easiest. Kevin Epling, co-director of *Bully Police USA*, lost his son to bullying and stresses the importance of early identification of bullying. Analyses of children's language help teachers monitor behavior inside and outside the classroom and modify instruction and assessment accordingly (i.e., systematically). By studying the language children, resources, and teachers use, we can more effectively track (1) individual and group identity, (2) influential social variables (see Chapter 5), and (3) learning.

Powerful speech/language includes assertive and control-indicative sounds, signs, words, sentences, and discourse structures, as outlined below.

Examples: Agentive Language

Sounds: aah! huh! uhh, oooh (i.e., not quite), duh! shush! (progressively
    signaling greater disagreement), sighing (i.e., indicating disappointment
    or annoyance), angry, defiant, accusatory, and/or interrogative
    intonation
Vocabulary: negative words (e.g., *idiot*, *stupid*), question words, and
    emphatic verbs (e.g., "do")
Sentences: directives (e.g., "Stop!" "Give me . . . !"), negatives ("No!" "I'm not
    going to . . . !" "I hate you!"), questions, threats, conditionals (if/unless-
    type sentences), and ego-bruising active voice (e.g., "Jack hit Tina"
    versus the ego-shielding passive, "Tina was hit" or "Tina's [been] hit")
Discourse units: silence; mention of taboo, sexist, ageist, and other face-
    threatening themes (see Ryan & Grieshaber, 2004); (non)verbal
    displays of aggression (e.g., hitting, pushing, shoving, punching, and/
    or meltdowns); direct or unbuffered negativity; and turn-slicing moves
    that purposely challenge or divert attention

Agency is therefore synonymous with powerful language and an ideology of control. It's best demonstrated using linguistics, specifically the subfield termed *discourse analysis*. We can record language devices that mirror a child's positive agency, suppression, and/or bullying behavior in specific contexts. We could, for instance, demonstrate that the dominance of the teacher is reflected in teacher *talk*, which constitutes over 50% of class time as contrasted with the relative voicelessness of the children. We similarly could analyze peer exchanges and children's resources, and use our findings to modify instruction and make children and colleagues more attentive to language. When we are alive to language (Arndt, Harvey, & Nuttall, 2000; Thornbury, 1997/2007), we are more likely to teach children to use language strategically and can watch the sense of wonder children experience as they extend its luminescence.

Linguistics offers easy-to-use frameworks for analyzing children's language and the language adults employ with children. As demonstrated below, linguistics provides a fuller and more accurate picture of each child's power(lessness) than constructivist, developmental, and postmodern theories provide.

Research Gaps

As this section illustrates, linguistics, through discourse analysis, enables early childhood researchers to study child behavior more consistently and empirically. Behavior, unlike language, is an abstract construct. As demonstrated, language is the most effective tool for investigating and modifying human behavior. Analyses of children's language reveals their individual and in-group institutional and out-of-class behavior. However, some PreK–3 educators conceptualize language in relatively broad terms and their focus on language tends to be tangential. Analyzing language into phonemes and consecutively larger units—using a linguistic approach—is most revealing and highly advisable.

Developmental theory, while widely embraced, rarely examines language per se (i.e., reflective of and responsible for power variations), prompting some to look to postcolonial theory (Ryan & Grieshaber, 2004), which also overlooks language. Power, like behavior, is an abstract construct. Since it is asserted or realized through language, we must analyze language here.

Another research gap in ECE is the absence of analytic tools that quickly demonstrate power asymmetries in PreK–3 interactions. The most common approach in ECE is to describe an exchange or reproduce an anecdote and assume that it is self-evident (i.e., that the researcher and reader interpret it similarly). However, researchers need to systematically demonstrate how they arrived at their interpretation(s), using a data-driven approach and/or framework that either corroborates or negates their hypotheses. Merely describing an interaction is insufficient. Linguistics helps fill this need, as demonstrated.

When we attempt to evaluate behavior in the absence of language analyses of the kind proposed, our assessments could, in fact, be inaccurate, as the example that follows illustrates. Indeed, when you look past language, you can misinterpret behavior. Conjectural observations like the following, for instance, are disputable:

> "It is *obvious that Calvin openly ignored* Ira's attempt to initiate play with him."
> "*The anecdote illustrates* that Calvin *wasn't really talking about Jackie and seemed quite bothered* by the fact that the teacher pushed him to . . . "
> (Lee & Recchia, 2008, emphasis added).

The reader is entitled to ask, "How is this *obvious*?" or "What part of the anecdote illustrates this?" An excerpt from their methodology section follows:

> The researchers analyzed data collaboratively . . . bringing meaning to the data. Both read all the data several times . . . and then examined the data to identify emerging themes, recurring ideas or language, and patterns of teachers' and children's behavior through the analytic process. . . . All emerging themes were discussed and compared. (Lee & Recchia, 2008)

First, the focus is unclear.[1] No mention is made of criteria or a framework of analysis. What constitutes an "emerging theme"? How were these identified, and why are they termed "emerging"? (How) was language examined? These and other questions point at methodological gaps in many ECE studies. Reliable data analysis is essential to any scientific endeavor. Formulating research questions and collecting data is only half the work.

Words like "seemed" and "quite" reflect subjectivity. Linguistic analyses, in contrast, get anecdotes to talk. Analyses of agency are, therefore, incomplete without a systematic (and central) focus on language. Mentioning applicable theories, citing anecdotes, and/or describing them is insufficient. Linguistics, through frameworks like conversational analysis, provides data-driven, demonstrative, and verifiable analyses of interactions, as demonstrated below.

Enter Conversation Analysis!

In a *conversation analysis* (CA) account, language units, turns (type and quantity), sequence, and timing[2] are recorded and compared to determine the power each participant exercises (i.e., who secures and/or loses the floor and when; see Pandey, 2005, 2010) and their relationship (i.e., hierarchic, semi-hierarchic, egalitarian). Even pauses could signal agency (i.e., resistance), depending on their length.

First identify and number conversational turns, and label them as self-selected or speaker-selected. Self-selected turns, as the name suggests, are self-initiated. They are more powerful (i.e., agency-indicative). Some participants select others' turns, yielding speaker-selected turns. For instance, many teachers and other adults select young children's turns by asking questions and/or issuing directives that necessitate a response. In general, participants who have the most turns and the most self-selected ones, and/or who use the most negative terms and employ the most directives and/or questions, wield the most power (i.e., they have the floor).

The following analysis of an exchange involving 4-year-olds Calvin and Ira (from Lee & Recchia, 2008) is intended solely for demonstrative purposes. The actual number of turns (some might have dove-tailed) is unclear. I stands for Ira, C for Calvin, HR = Harry, and H = Hana, the TA. The text is reproduced below, and nonverbal language noted in parentheses, as is standard practice in linguistics. The turns are numbered and categorized using the description provided. Note that a conversation analysis (CA) reveals a very different picture of who has the floor.

1. I: Calvin, Calvin, Calvin. I'm talking to you, Calvin!
2. C: (responds with silence, reaches over and takes a Spiderman cup from Harry who quickly turns and looks at him)
3. C: (smiles and puts it back)
4. HR: (smiles) [speaker-selected]
5. I: Calvin, Calvin. (looks directly at Calvin, waving a large plastic bottle of juice in front of him)
6. C: (does not look up. Leans toward HR and says something. HR smiles as Calvin speaks)
7. I: Calvin! Talk to me!
8. C: (responds quietly without looking up) No.
9. I: Do you use the bathroom?
10. C: Stop it! I don't want to talk to you.
11. I: Calvin, Calvin! (waving his juice)
12. H: Calvin is not being such a good friend to you right now. Show someone else who's interested.
13. I: Calvin!
14. C: OK, OK. (looking up). I'm not talking to you.

Ira has six (40%) of the 14 turns in this exchange. Calvin has 6, as well, but 3 of them (turns 2, 3, and 6) are nonverbal and directed at Harry, whom Calvin quickly satisfies by promptly returning the cup he yanked from him. Hana has one turn. Harry's single turn is nonverbal (his smile could be interpreted as acquiescence).

Ira uses louder speech, signaled by his use of repetition, imperatives (he uses the most), and the exclamation points in the transcript. He uses six directives and one question. In contrast, Calvin employs just one imperative (see turn 10). Ira's louder voice stands in stark contrast to Calvin's (see turn 9).

Vocabulary-wise, Ira uses 22 words in contrast to the 17 Calvin uses, once again demonstrating his greater verbal control. Interestingly, Hana uses 17 words in her single turn alone (i.e., 12). Of note, too, is Calvin's negative statement in turn

10, the first time he confronts Ira as opposed to avoiding him or politely respond-ing to his question. Yet, he does not exert his power until more than halfway into the exchange, finally letting Ira know exactly how he feels, albeit momentarily. Arguably, "Stop it!" is not as abrasive as "Leave me alone!"

Unlike Ira, none of Calvin's turns are self-selected. Ira, in contrast, consis-tently attempts to select Calvin's turns for him through his use of questions and directives (Pandey, 2010), turns that require a response. That Ira doesn't only de-sire but requires a response signals his more powerful language. So while Calvin makes an attempt to exclude Ira and finally lets him know that he does not wish to talk to him, his indirect and less face-threatening approach does not dissuade Ira. He finally looks up (turn 14) and acknowledges Ira with a loud "OK, OK," his repetition and loudness of voice (see capital letters) admitting defeat. Yet, even as he verbally resists by saying "I'm not talking to you," ironically he *is* talking and it's the most he says in this exchange (i.e., using his longest utterance). In contrast, Ira's language is more aggressive, confrontational, louder, and literally in-your-face (see turns 1, 7, 9, 11, and 13).

Contrast Ira's directive "Talk to me!" with Calvin's barely audible "No." Note that Calvin responds "without looking up." Why he doesn't is open to interpre-tation and necessitates verification (i.e., follow-up dialog with Calvin). His not looking up cannot automatically be interpreted as an act of resistance. Reasons he does not look up include distraction, fear (e.g., of being badgered), or cultural reasons. Research demonstrates that in many high-context cultures, eye contact generally is avoided (Bovee & Thill, 2007) and that avoiding eye contact is a sign of respect, not an assertion of power or act of defiance as is typically assumed in the United States. Ira, in contrast, completely ignores Hana's advice, as evidenced by his assertive and repetitive language (see turn 13), reflecting confidence, control, and persistence. In the final analysis, Ira's language, both verbal and nonverbal, is more powerful, unlike what the researchers contend. In their view, Hana chose to redirect Ira "rather than requiring Calvin to respond to him." A linguistic analysis reveals that she was unsuccessful in redirecting Ira. It's unclear how the authors determined that she allowed "Calvin to choose to ignore Ira." Such adult-centric statements suggest that children's language is adult-mediated. Just because Calvin momentarily ignored Ira does not mean that his doing so was necessarily permit-ted and contingent upon adult approval. In fact, some might describe Ira's lan-guage as incorrigible, and we wonder what his next turn would have looked like had Hana not attempted to redirect him. Based on his language, we can predict that he would continue to call on Calvin, despite Calvin's relatively futile attempts to hide and/or drown him out.

Sometimes, agency is unclear, as when a participant does not respond after being asked a question or given a directive. Silence is technically a turn and, de-pending on its length and frequency, might reflect an individual's transitional or total empowerment (i.e., success at countering the control another party exercises).

Some participants' language mirrors covert power, as in the case of Calvin. Indeed, silence can be a powerful form of protest. When children refuse to respond to questions, as does Calvin, they usually are challenging the questioner's authority. The other party's response determines whether or not they succeed.

Conversation analysis is relatively easy to use and can be corroborated. Separate analyses by raters yield what in linguistics is termed greater inter-rater reliability. Dialoging with participants is a back-up field technique. This generally takes the form of post-interaction interviews. These reflection sessions probe participants' language choices (e.g., Why did you say ___? Why didn't you respond the first time?) and help verify or nullify hypotheses.

Monologues and dialogs in children's literature and media can also be analyzed using conversation analysis. For instance, writers disempower certain characters by keeping them nameless and/or lacking in voice. Anjali Pandey (2004) demonstrated that Disney movies frequently depict minority languages negatively.[3] Any wonder why many children develop language prejudices? Linguistics draws attention to *powerlessness* (i.e., we also can systematically identify not-as-obvious relations). Conversation analysis also illustrates whether a child is likely to dominate an exchange and who is able to scaffold DLLs' and/or special needs children's language (i.e., workable pairings and groupings).[4]

Systematic analysis of language is, therefore, eye-opening and essential. Knowledge of linguistics visibly enhances educators' understanding of power dynamics and more. The next section illustrates this further.

INVESTIGATING CHILD AGENCY

Since linguistics provides us with a sharper lens through which to observe, zoom in on, and analyze children's and other individuals' language and associated power, and to map their influences on childhood, ongoing analysis of the language of schooling makes ECE more navigable and revealing.

Lee and Recchia (2008) observe that "to create early childhood classroom communities that truly embrace diversity and empower all children . . . , teachers will need to . . . bring issues of power in from the shadows . . . ." Yet, educators need an easy-to-use, demonstrative, and replicable approach. As shown, linguistics provides ECE with such tools, enhancing PreK–3 instruction and learning.

As noted, linguistics offers two ways to investigate power: (1) by analyzing the language employed and (2) by observing and dialoging with the parties involved. Gauging children's language in diverse contexts is essential since language (and agency) can vary, depending on multiple variables (see Chapter 5). So while Calvin might control the floor at lunch, in Ira's presence his language and agency change. Linguistics helps us (1) identify factors that impact language (behavior) and (2) individualize instruction. Recommended linguistic techniques include:

Step 1: Unobtrusively observe children's language in multiple contexts and with different participants, and formulate a working hypothesis.

Step 2: Verify hypotheses by gathering representative samples using scientific research methods.

Step 3: Analyze language systematically, using reliable and easy-to-use frameworks (see Fairclough, 2001; van Dijk, 2009).

Step 4: Determine whether your findings corroborate your hypothesis and discuss the implications.

Step 5: Implement your findings and monitor the impact (i.e., identify loopholes and modify instruction and assessment accordingly).

These steps are discussed in greater detail next.

Observe, Analyze, and Review

OAR is a handy tool to engage in ongoing language analysis in multiple environments. OAR stands for *observe*, *analyze*, and *review*, as noted below.

Observe: watch, listen, record, and reflect on language use in speech and (e-) writing

Analyze: segment language and identify patterns that reflect power dynamics and/or other variables

Review, recreate, revise, and/or recommend most workable language practices (e.g., resources) for each child

Use OAR to monitor all language children use and encounter (e.g., teacher talk, parents' and other family members' and peers' language). Use your observations to maximize and enhance children's interactivity (i.e., expand their language-literacy skills).

Re-create and extend positive interactions (e.g., child–child; child–self or pretend friend, child–sibling; child–technology; and child–adult). Create multiple opportunities for interaction, fostering vocabulary and whole-language development, alongside content mastery (see Chapter 7).

Observing how children read, talk about, and/or nonverbally respond to readings helps us monitor and plan reading instruction (McGee & Schickedanz, 2007). In the final analysis, linguistics (e.g., through CA and OAR) offers ECE practitioners and researchers superior assessment/research tools and analyses that are immediately applicable to multiple areas (e.g., instruction, assessment, and professional development). Even with a basic knowledge of linguistics, you come out ahead.

Observe Language and Reflect. Observation and reflection are key ingredients in instruction and learning (yin yang-like). The developmental-interaction pedagogy (Nager & Shapiro, 2000), for instance, recommends observation as a prerequisite for behavior modification (i.e., learning). Ongoing observations of children's language and the language they encounter in resources and interactions inside and outside class (Hull & Schultz, 2001) make instruction and assessment more effective. Observation helps educators gauge children's language and content skills and determine how best to teach children agentive language (i.e., to gain relief from overbearing individuals and/or minimize belligerent language use).

Reflection helps us problem solve. Similarly, reflection helps children make sense of what they hear, see, and write. It helps them successfully negotiate in-class and out-of-class encounters, including tech-assisted and cross-age brokering (Pandey, 2010; Schmidt, 2011). Both observation and reflection help us identify the most suitable resources for instruction, learning, and assessment. Once again, language is the common thread and the most effective measure of learning.

Observe Children Interact. Studying children's language is the first step in understanding:

> Their evolving identities (i.e., their self-identification, sense of belonging,
>   power, and ideology)
> Their goals (age- and gender-specific, linguistic, monetary, and academic)
> Their needs and wants (i.e., reflected in discourses of inclusion and exclusion
>   they navigate)
> The intersections between these

Often, children's out-of-class language differs (sometimes drastically) from their in-class language in tone, vocabulary, syntax, sociolinguistic flavor (e.g., localisms), and even politeness.

Some children's language (i.e., behavior) is so regimented at school that they literally break loose (linguistically) after hours. Their out-of-class language might reflect greater agency, especially if they don't have to seek permission to speak. When we observe how children interpret and use language, we learn more about teaching, learning, and reaching each and every child. Yet, when we observe children, what do we seek to determine? Behavior? Language? Behavior through language or vice versa? Both? How do and should we analyze language? As demonstrated here, linguistics provides us with evidence-based frameworks for capturing and analyzing children's language.

"You can't not eat your vegetables!" a mother insisted. "Okay, I won't" responded her Kindergartner. "You won't what?" her mother asked, eyeing her angrily. "Well, you said *not*! That means *don't*," she continued, her smile admitting that the interpretation she had assigned to her mother's directive was both convenient and accurate. "That doesn't make sense: *can't* and *not*!" she insisted. Would this child feel free to openly criticize her teacher's language? Children learn by making sense of the language they *hear*, experience (e.g., nonverbally and emotionally), and read.

Children's classroom language generally is dictated by the teacher. Like parenting styles, teaching styles differ. While there are those children who might challenge a teacher's authority by, for instance, talking while the teacher is talking, most children quickly learn that they are expected to follow rules. Few PreK–3 teachers permit children to have the floor unless they raise their hands. Even then, they might be passed up. If teachers don't invite questions or input, children might go for an entire day or longer without saying much. Does this mean they don't wish to speak or merely that they don't have the go-ahead to use the language of their choosing at certain times of the day?

In the following example lesson, a teacher dominates the exchange, as evidenced by her greater number of turns (6 out of 10; 60%) and her more powerful turns (self-selected).

Example

Context: The teacher handed out a poem ("Autumn Leaves") and read it
    aloud. [T = teacher; other initials stand for students.]
1. T: So what's another word for *autumn*? Shush, Tom!
2. S: [raises her hand to answer]
3. T: [looking toward Jen] Yes, Jen.
4. J: Umm [pause: 5 seconds] Red.
5. T: Nods to indicate the answer is incorrect.
6. S: [raises her hand higher to answer]
7. T: [glancing at S] You'll get your turn. Ray?
8. A: Fall.
9. T: Good. [glancing at the clock] Story time! Come to the front—quietly—
    and [the children gather around her on the rug] Ben, *bottoms flat*!
10. [B and the other children press their behinds down and bring their legs
    in]
11. T: We're going to read . . . .

Let's analyze her language unit by unit. Phonemic indicators of her power and control include "Shush" in turn 1 and rising intonation in turns 1 and 9. She also uses the most words in this exchange (33 out of 35). Her use of the impersonal "you" (instead of the child's name) signals her power and creates a noticeable teacher–student hierarchy. Similarly, phrases like "your turn" (turn 7) and "bottoms flat" reference rules and conformity. Sentence-wise, she employs mostly questions and directives (three each). Their frequency and staccato-like timing (one after another) reinforce her control. The teacher's voice tightly clasps and consistently interlaces the length and breadth, and arguably knots (i.e., controls) these Kindergartners' language (and behavior) or, some might argue, silences them. S and B don't get a turn. In fact, the teacher arguably ignores S. *Discourse sequence* reveals the following involvement pattern:

T-(S)-T-J-T-(S)-T-A-T-(B)-T

Later that evening, S complained (to her mother) that she felt ignored. Whether the teacher chose not to call on S is an open question. Even if we add in a margin of error, we end up with a teacher-dominant exchange. (Q & A sessions typically are teacher-centered unless teachers invite input and permit free talk.)

The next section focuses on children's out-of-class language. Similar analyses are advisable. Linguistic analyses either lend support to hypotheses or negate them. By analyzing randomly selected language segments throughout the school day, and in different settings or at different times of the day (e.g., at center time), we get a fairly accurate picture of children's and teachers' learning and teaching styles, relationships, and more. Since language is open to interpretation, we must provide as much background information (e.g., contextual) as possible.

Children's classroom talk and writing give us only a partial picture of their (language-literacy) skills and their agency, which they may or may not get to exercise at school. Periodically videotape class, lunchtime, and playground interactions and analyze them. You might even witness unfamiliar cultural practices, such as removing shoes at the door (common in Indian and Japanese homes). Also, research children's out-of-class literacies (Edwards, 2004).

Self-Reflection as Observation. Did you know that successful ECE starts with you? You determine the academic language, content, and many interpersonal rules of engagement children imbibe. Since instruction is a collaborative exercise, you must be responsive to children. *Self-observation* is essential and a critical component in instruction.

Genishi, Ryan, Oschner, and Yarnall (2001) report that ECE researchers "have focused little on teachers, teaching, or its effects" (p. 1176). Self-reflection, peer observations, coaching, and mentoring are therefore necessary. Remember that you lead by example. As you are children's advocate and coach for the bulk of the work day, your language impacts children. Most children reproduce language they observe adults (e.g., teachers and parents) employ. It's therefore imperative you periodically assess your language-literacy practices.

To excel at instruction, you must understand the art and science of language. Investigate whether and why, for instance, you use more questions and directives than requests, or why you refer to yourself as *Mrs.* (versus *Ms.*). The language you use to instruct and assess should be comprehensible and collaborative. When instruction is collaborative, learning is more likely (see Chapter 7). Collaboration also enhances children's phonemic, vocabulary, grammatical, discourse-pragmatic, and multicontent development. Use child-created literature and other resources that involve and empower children, yielding collaborative, agency-facilitative, and inclusive instruction.

Use handy questions and/or a questionnaire to give you a better picture of your language practices. Peer observations and self-reflection through journaling (e.g., recordings) also help us evaluate our language use. Using CA, for instance, analyze the language you use in lessons, on student papers, and when you write. Viewing random (audio/videotaped) lessons should help you identify what you might have missed in class, including each child's (non)verbal responses to your language, how many hands went up when you asked questions and even when you didn't, questions children asked (directly or indirectly), how you responded, how they responded to your response(s), and more.

Assistive questions to ask include:

> What do you consider your primary role/responsibilities?
> Do you consider facilitation to involve research? If so, what kind(s)?
> Do you analyze language use in your classroom? *Whose language, how*, and
> *how often*?
> Do you invite input from children? On what (assignments, assessments)?
> How and how often?
> Do students and peers evaluate your (instruction/assessment) *language*, and
> have you attempted to modify it? How?

The questions you ask, and the fact that you ask questions, reflect not merely your power but also the kinds of identity (i.e., agency) you emphasize and permit. Invite children to share their assessment of your teaching. When you consider evaluating your classroom language as a core component of instruction, you are likely to provide more responsive instruction. Children's assessment of your teaching—essentially your language use—enhances delivery.

Ferris and Hedgcock (2005) recommend exposing children to our "academic literacy . . . processes and practices" (p. 12). To this end, ask yourself what you read and write, and how often, and whether your literacy habits have changed and why.

Inviting children's reactions to your language, including resources you employ, is essential. Invite students to pretend they are you, for instance. What does their role play reveal about your language? Encourage parents to try this activity at home. Role reversal, or "opposites," as my 5-year-old describes one of her favorite games, is fun and educational. It prompts you to pay closer attention to your language (as you hear how you sound to children). It also develops children's phonemic awareness as they attempt to capture the nuances of individuals' accents and other distinctive traits.

Have you ever wondered why parent–teacher conferences and PTA meetings rarely include or require the participation of children whose lives are under focus? Ironically, these meetings are more frequent and accepted than teacher–child and parent–teacher–student conferences. Even the names of such performance-enhancing endeavors suggest that when it comes to children's education, adults know what's best and children's views are relatively unimportant.

Analyze Language. Remember that teaching is Janus-like (i.e., its other face is learning). Analyzing the language of instruction, assessment, and resources you use is important. Some teachers evaluate teaching without focusing on language, the central ingredient. Language is the most effective indicator of instruction, learning, and assessment available to us. When we make teaching a learning experience, by evaluating our language, instruction and learning are prioritized.

Periodically record sounds (e.g., /sh/), words, phrases, sentences, and discourse units you employ in class. Next, identify patterns that mirror your instructional style (e.g., learner-centered language). Next, research the primary variables that determine your language choices (e.g., the curriculum, standards, subject area, time of day/school year, location, children's personalities, their primary language, parental observations, and personal factors like your psychological state—arguably nourishment- and sleep-dependent). Did you expect to find what you did? You might find that your language choices vary considerably from student to student or by time of day. Regardless, awareness of your language use is essential.

Linguistics teaches us to weigh our words, and other language devices as well, since different language units convey distinct messages and can either build or obstruct relationships. We should strive to use positive and bias-free language. Examples include friendly signs and sounds (e.g., *ahah,* which is more inviting than *shh*, *shush*, *na,* and even a throaty negative sound and/or a pout), word parts like *un-* (more polite) versus *not*, words (e.g., *tardy* versus *late*), sentences (e.g., the more collaborative "Let's stop" versus the more abrasive "Stop!"), and positive discourse (Pandey, forthcoming).

Also evaluate the languages children encounter and use outside class, including that employed in resources they access on their own. In addition, periodically review the language of the assessments you employ and the comments you write on student papers.

Example: Assessment Language

At one elementary school, of the 12 "learning behaviors" assessed (using a rating scale where 1 = outstanding, 2 = satisfactory, and 3 = needs improvement), most emphasize conformity. For example:

Follows established rules
Exercises self-control
Listens attentively
Responds appropriately to *directions*

Completes assignments
Completes homework *on time* (emphasis added)

That asking insightful questions is not on this list suggests that children learn by *conforming.* This includes *listening* and *responding* versus talking and inquiring or facilitating (presumably the teacher's charge); exercising restraint; and doing as they are told. The italicized words signal the dominant view—of children as respondents. Terms hinting at children's contributions are few in number and unclear.

Carefully review the language of assessments you use. The Stanford Achievement Test (SAT), for instance, frequently administered in 3rd grade, measures *cumulative language skills* (i.e., phonemic awareness, spelling recognition, vocabulary, grammar, and dominant discourse structures, including children's ability to identify main ideas and details). These are assessed through *reading* and *math.*

Many children perform poorly on reading. Research points to a positive correlation between language proficiency and reading, on the one hand, and language and math, on the other (see Chapters 4 and 9). Increasing the school year, reducing class size, credentialing more teachers, and/or using more resources alone will not improve outcomes. Instructional approaches and, more specifically, instructional focus need to change. Awareness of how language impacts learning and assessment makes a difference, as this volume illustrates.

Review, Revise, and Re-create Child-Centered Learning Spaces. Ironically, ECE is still an adult-dominant field. While some might argue that adults know what's best for children and that PreK–3 children are too young to make sound decisions, research consistently demonstrates children's skill in mediation and more (Pandey, 2010; Schmidt, 2011). In other words, involve children in decisions involving their futures.

REVITALIZING EARLY CHILDHOOD EDUCATION

It's time to ensure that children have a voice in Early Childhood Education (ECE). To this end, future research should gather teachers', caregivers', and children's views on inclusion. ECE practitioners knowledgeable in linguistics could revitalize the field by re-envisioning "fundamental concepts" (Nager & Shapiro, 2000, p. 14). Since language is the most visible and effective (i.e., analyze-able) signal of child development (e.g., biological and academic) and interaction, the cornerstones of developmental-interaction and other reincarnations of child development theory and practice, linguistics (1) provides a more "culturally responsive understanding of development" (p. 15) and (2) helps revamp and connect theory and practice. By magnifying and forefronting language, it enhances learning theory and practice.

As demonstrated, linguistics helps us provide verifiable insights through step-by-step analyses of language. One way forward is to invite linguists to work with early childhood professionals both inside and outside of school, for curricular and instructional planning purposes, assessment, and home–school–community partnerships. Linguistics is essential to success in ECE, and, in turn, ECE provides linguists with authentic data to test and fine-tune theory and praxis. In short, we need to put linguistics to work in ECE. The onus of educating our children in the most effective manner should be shared, as there's simply too much at stake. *Cultural competence*,[5] for instance, is essential to success in practically every field today, and language is its face and voice. When linguists, natural and social scientists, and early childhood educators join hands, we will be able to provide our children with the stronger start they need.

Linguistics is not merely applicable to ECE but essential in this day and age of increasing diversity. Knowledge of linguistics helps us provide an integrative, multiskills, globally sound, and multilingual education to PreK–3 children. Since education in the early years is essentially about mastering academic language, and we insist that children must be institutionally schooled (and that life experiences alone do not constitute education), PreK–3 is first and foremost a critical phase in language socialization. Vocabulary is the primary differentiator, and linguistics the glue that binds seemingly disparate content areas and learning environments.

CONNECTING THEORY TO PRAXIS

One of the challenges of academia is to familiarize ourselves with the different theories, analytic tools, and practices proposed in diverse fields connected to ECE. Should one ignore these multiple research approaches or attempt to make sense of them? *Language Building Blocks* proposes the latter approach. Unless we attempt to understand and wholeheartedly embrace difference (e.g., in theory and practice), we will be left behind. Since doing so requires considerable time, effort, and prior knowledge (not always readily accessible), transdisciplinary partnerships are highly advisable and should yield a more functional whole.

On close examination, different theories and pedagogies are sometimes similar. Yet they usually use different terminology or focus on variable concepts. Theoretical parallels between disciplines are noteworthy.[6] For example, linguists investigate power dynamics, as do developmental psychologists and political scientists. By merging theories and/or praxis, we strengthen teaching practice and gain a better understanding of the diverse ingredients involved in building stronger childhoods and communities.

Transdisciplinary collaborations would bring together diverse perspectives pertaining to early childhood, a shared responsibility. As Genishi, Ryan, Ochsner, and Yarnall (2008) remind us, "Together, practitioners, researchers, and theorists can construct an agenda for thought and action" (p. 1205). Given children's diverse learning experiences, developmental theory alone is insufficient (Ryan & Grieshaber, 2004). We must pull from teachers' observations and other fields (Genishi,

Ryan, Ochsner, & Yarnall, 2008), including linguistics, which could be integrated relatively easily into PreK–3.

Linguistics is the 21st-century technical knowledge that ensures a smoother and more memorable ride in PreK–3. Some of us are more knowledgeable about cars than others. We can tell, for instance, from the sounds a car makes or how it drives whether it needs new brake pads, rotors, or more. *Language Building Blocks* invites you to learn more about the engine that drives ECE (i.e., language). Indeed, linguistics familiarizes you with core language components that work together to enhance education in the formative years.

SUMMARY AND CONCLUSION

This chapter reminds us to pay close attention to language and shows us how to frequently and systematically analyze language across the board, from the classroom and playground to children's homes. As demonstrated, linguistics clarifies who exercises agency and how.

Our children's underpreparedness in reading, math, and science necessitates use of best practices that prepare them for success in a competitive global world. The solution offered in this book is *systematic language instruction and analysis* (i.e., essential linguistics).

Since language is the most effective means to and measure of PreK–3 instruction/learning (behavior), PreK–3 professionals knowledgeable in linguistics can easily segment language into distinct and universal components and analyze child behavior more effectively and scientifically.

Linguistics makes us better facilitators. We reflect on why children, the curriculum, resources, peers, and we ourselves say, read, and write what we do. We can more accurately contextualize and identify, address, and assess every child's (language) needs, using our findings to mediate learning in key areas. The result is greater success.

Language analysis is, in fact, one of the most effective instruction/learning strategies in PreK–3. Children who have a feel for the nuts and bolts of language are partners in education. They master content, reading, and writing early on and continue learning on their own. *Language Building Blocks* emphasizes the centrality of language in PreK–3. It demonstrates that language undergirds and powers all learning, connecting and enhancing key components in PreK–3 (e.g., the curriculum, instruction, learning, and assessment). By making language the primary focus in PreK–3 and continually investigating language in school and beyond, we also bridge the home and schoolhouse.

As demonstrated, integrating other languages, another way to meet core PreK–3 objectives, (1) helps children master vocabulary and content, (2) empowers DLLs (the fastest growing group), and (3) prepares all children, including monolinguals, for greater success in a global world. Even monolingual educators can successfully employ this integrative and international pedagogy (i.e., sans prerequisites).

As a popular Sanskrit saying goes, "Language is everything." The central premise of *Language Building Blocks* is that the more linguistically aware we are, the more likely we are to embrace diversity, and the more effective we are at PreK–3 (language-literacy and content) instruction. As this volume demonstrates, a working knowledge of linguistics (e.g., through coursework or workshops) is essential for ECE professionals today. It helps us close the achievement gap at-risk children face, using handy evidence-based strategies that give all children a strong start. This inclusive and individualized approach is exactly what each child needs in order to succeed. In Dr. King's (1957) words, "Language comes to our aid beautifully in giving us the real meaning and depth." This is especially true in PreK–3 education.

Notes

Chapter 1

1. Some contend that such declarations could spoil children. "I love you" is frequently employed in Bollywood movies to reflect "modern" characters. The closest equivalent in Chinese is "I like you."

2. By the same token, we would expect English learners to master English spelling and reading from exposure alone, including use of the telecaption decoder. Yet, as we know, written language, like speech, requires interest (Cary, 2004), interaction, reflection, feedback, and conducive contexts for mastery. Only then can children connect two remotely different forms (spoken and written).

3. Some Hindi speakers borrow the /z/ sound from Urdu (spoken in Pakistan and parts of India). The differences between these two languages are minimal (a few sounds, words, and the writing). However, they are considered separate languages (versus dialects) for political reasons. Urdu borrowed much from Arabic, including /z/.

Chapter 2

1. Sounds include /ð/ in Spanish *dos*/two (/ðo/ in Hindi), and /θ/ in *barato*/ cheap(ly)/ inexpensive from /baraθ/ (groom's wedding party in whose honor food and gifts are plentiful/ free-flowing). Similar-sounding words for shirt (*camisa* vs. /kəmidʒ/) and others (e.g., *diez* [the number 10] vs. /ɖəs/; *que*/what vs. *kya*) signal a shared source.

2. This is an example of consonant cluster reduction.

3. The terms *monothongs* and *diphthongs* more effectively capture the difference between single-vowel sounds and vowel pairs.

4. The IPA uses "close" and "open" (based on the jaw) versus "high" and "low."

5. E.g., the 's' in "was," which initially was pronounced the (phonetic) Germanic way.

6. Although *Daisy* and *Mayzie* differ in spelling, they are a minimal pair (i.e., /dejzi/ and /mejzi/). The single sound that differentiates them is italicized.

7. Children also would learn homophones and different categories of paired words faster (e.g., *nana-nani* = material grandma and grandpa in Hindi).

8. Phoneme-level sound variations are termed *allophones* (e.g., /w/ versus /hw/, the voiceless southern U.S. glide in *what*).

9. "Derivetion is unacceptable in English, since -tion generally follows 'a,' as in "education." The middle 'e' is therefore replaced with 'a.'

Chapter 3

1. "Sugar" is /shəkər/. *Shakar kandi* (i.e., sugar candy) is the Hindi word for sugar cane.

2. Names like Johnson are from Norse, another Nordic language. So are "sister," "husband," and "knife."

3. The Aztecs made a chocolate drink from cacao, and taught the Spanish how.

4. Normans were French and rule conscious. They implemented *administration* and the law as we know it and insisted on correctness, even in spoken language. The Alliance Français (French Alliance) has been policing the French language since the 16th century.

5 Many words from dialects of Sanskrit (Prakrits) are still used in Hindi and related languages.

6. The dot under the 'n' signals an /r/ sound.

7. How accents of American English coincide with settlement patterns should interest children.

8. "Bizarre" is from Basque (Metcalf, 1999).

9. Invite children to share how they and/or family members acquired regionalisms.

10. Produced in the hard palate.

11. "Freedom" (free + doom), which most children have heard (e.g., through the Pledge of Allegiance), was first used by King Alfred around 888 (Metcalf, 1999). Then, "doom" meant something closer to today's "deem" (i.e., considered free).

12. Also the name of the long banana consumed in many (e.g., African, Caribbean, and Latino) households.

Chapter 4

1. http://nces.ed.gov/pubsearch/pubsinfo.asp?pubid=2009001. Asian countries generally score in the 98th percentile. The United States clusters "somewhere between the 26 and 36 percentile" (Gladwell, 2008, p. 231). Gladwell also correlates culture (e.g., discipline) and performance.

2. Examples include Demi's *One Grain of Rice* and Burns and Silveria's *The Greedy Triangle*. In Nesmith and Cooper's (2010) study, both received high ratings for mathematical content and skillful visual-textual elements. The raters were math and English professors, math and literacy educators, and 3rd-grade teachers.

3. In Chinese and Korean math is more visibly mathematical (lexically and visually).

4. This suggests that some cultures are more open to diversity. In some languages, children learn opposites, synonyms, and key math and science concepts faster through frequently used paired words and measures (e.g., *chota-mota* and *lamba-chawra*, Hindi and Gujarati for short-big/tall, and long-wide, respectively). These have a sing-song musicality (many are minimal pairs) that, like their coupling, promotes early phonemic awareness and vocabulary development.

5. Also likely to interest children is Mayan writing, which evidences superior math skills. The Mayans 365-day calendar is exemplary.

6. Log = the Greek (root) for thought, word, and speech; -ic and -al = having the quality of "log."

Chapter 5

1. In Nigerian English, strangers are friends. Nigerian languages do not have a word for "stranger" in the Western sense (i.e., distrusted outsider).

2. In Yoruba culture, in particular, one's children are one's wealth. You "invite trouble" when you let others know exactly how many you have. Many African languages (e.g., Swahili) have equivalent expressions, evidencing high infant mortality in Africa.

3. Dialects have their own slang.

4. Ebonics was proposed by a group of Black psychologists to celebrate African American roots.

5. In contrast, in New England and in RP, r-less speech is considered more prestigious.

6. "Ethnicity" is used often (vs. race), for sociopolitical reasons. One individual might identify his or her ethnicity as Hispanic, another as Black, and yet another as Black Hispanic. While all three signal cultural identity, they're not comparable. For instance, while Black and African American are used in the same context, as in racial and ethnic identification forms issued by the Howard County School Board (MD), they are not synonymous. "Black" is a racial descriptor, and "African American," cultural. "Hispanic" is geographical. How about "Jewish"?

7. Some (e.g., Nyanja, Zambia) have unique sounds (e.g., /ny/). The clicks of Xhosa, another Bantu language, are bound to excite children. Some websites contain sound files (e.g., explore.ecb.org/surf/ surf_report?subject=78), so children can hear languages for which speakers are unavailable at their school.

8. "Patois" refers to French-based pidgins (e.g., in Haiti). That Jamaican pidgin is "patwa" (Anglicized spelling) speaks to the regional influence of French. Language rivalries are noteworthy (e.g., Dominican President Trujillo massacred over 20,000 when they mispronounced *perejil*/parsley).

9. In Standard English, speakers mention themselves last (i.e., "and I").

10. *Chiac* is a mix of French and English (reflecting the impact of English on Acadian French speakers).

11. *Zouk* means party or festival in French Creole.

12. This is not surprising; he was older and English has more exceptions than Spanish.

Chapter 6

1. E.g., refraining from describing a classmate as fat or overweight.

2. In most parts of India, children rarely are given cold or iced water—to prevent them from getting sick when they come indoors from the excessive heat.

3. From Armenian, it entered English through Turkish (*siskebabiu*).

Chapter 7

1. BEV uses this multipurpose form (*be*) for habitual, continuous, and future tenses. It's semantically dense.

2. DLL is preferred to English language learner since all children are technically language learners.

3. www.youtube.com/watch?v=6PrleqeCAPw&feature=related and www.youtube.com/watch?v=-URtZfIgKAU

4. news.yahoo.com/photos/china-s-jiaozhou-bay-bridge-1309439624-slideshow/

5. Children are totally immersed in the second language until 4th or 5th grade, then immersed roughly 80% of the time. They finish junior high school with 50% immersion in both languages (http://education.alberta.ca/francais/admin/immersion/handbookimm/03leadership/results.aspx).

6. Rising intonation eases understanding and its successful use confirms that very young children are highly sensitive to sounds.

7. A phrase-level example is "more better" (from Spanish *mas mejor*).

8. I recall the bare walls and concrete floors of my classroom in Nigeria. Many had leaking roofs and little to no furniture, artwork, books, and supplies. Some might argue that while most U.S. classrooms are cozy and visually appealing, the many items displayed could distract (like the many toys well-to-do children have), accounting for many children's limited attention spans.

9. E.g., focusing on distinctive affixes (e.g., English -ly = Spanish *-mente*).

10. Not surprisingly, Jamaica's Draft Language Education Policy identifies Spanish as "the preferred foreign language" (Limited English Proficiency, 2001, p. 20).

Chapter 8

1. A discussion of causes falls outside the scope of this chapter.

2. Termed *individual education plan* in Canada and the United Kingdom.

3. Inclusion is generally more time consuming. It requires more coordination,

given the team teaching, often in the same room. "You have to be willing to pull small groups to make it work." A lot depends on instructors' willingness to put in the extra effort. Some might observe that a child "doesn't belong" in that classroom, "without giving inclusion their best shot." (Pat Tessner)

4. New Zealand's Ministry of Education aims to make children with disabilities "competent and confident." However, research points toward a prevalence of exclusionary discourse (Purdue, Ballard, & MacArthur, 2001). Te Whāriki, the Maori name of the national ECE curriculum, means "a mat for all to stand on" (Carr & May, 1996).

5. We should also research the impact words like "test" have on children. How does their awareness that they will be tested affect outcomes? "I couldn't sleep last night because I was worried about my test," observed my 8-year-old. Do children need to know when and/or how they will be tested, or should we monitor their progress unobstrusively? If we ask them to prepare for a test, should we explain the value and the measures used?

6. Some contend that phonology acquisition (i.e., undetectable accent) is time sensitive.

7. While not all languages have case differences and/or cursive, English allows you to experiment with upper- and lowercase.

8. Children would learn more words (e.g., *option*, in addition to *choice*) early on.

Chapter 9

1. A migrant worker like Tomás Rivera (see the movie . . . *and the earth did not swallow him*).

2. As are many words in pidgin and creole (see Pandey, 2005).

3. For example, "graduation" (end point), "gradation," and "degradation" (i.e., a literal downgrade).

4. The first part often is omitted (i.e., implied).

5. Named after the originator, just like "Celsius," which, in many Romance languages, refers to more than temperature.

6. Multiple concepts share words, evidencing communality at work even in the lexicon.

7. Most teacher education programs require students to take this course. Contact the author for a copy of the revamped syllabus.

8. WIDA's 2012 "amplified" standards include a "complementary" strand that covers the language of additional content areas, including music, visual arts, and technology (http://wida.us/standards/eld.aspx). Level 6, Reaching, marks the end of the proficiency continuum. It's not a level per se, so some might consider it redundant.

Chapter 10

1. See *Mrs. Right* (Mindless Behavior) and *Ese yo soy* (Spanish: This is me). In Malaniña's *Havana Mambo*, the singer promises to buy a *computadora* (i.e., computer) on one condition—that the listener takes good care of him.

2. This allows them to access and translate the many more and more responsive English sites. Spanish ones are fewer in number and frequently inaccurate. Many languages have limited or no web presence. Keyboards for many writing systems remain to be developed.

3. Contact the author for a copy. Asked about the inspiration for her story, Anna mentioned "Grandpa," who "uses the computer to buy and sell stocks."

4. This area is termed *corpus analysis*. It requires creating representative databases and writing programs to access language (i.e., information).

5. A Celtic language spoken in Cornwall, UK.

6. Starfall offers games to help children with vocabulary and beginning reading. Internet4Classrooms offers activities by grade level. E-mail students' tech picks and experiences with digital language, samples of technology-mediated exchanges, and/or (co-)creations to the author.

Chapter 11

1. Examining language through a focus on "recurring ideas" is unreliable (i.e., interpretations could vary). Research must be verifiable.

2. In some parts of the world, overlapping turns indicate that participants feel comfortable with one another.

3. This includes nonverbal language (e.g., metaphors). Hyenas, for instance, operate in packs and are gangsters who speak Black English Vernacular in *The Lion King*.

4. Using CA, the author (2010) verified that children are not only successful language learners but also some of the most effective language-literacy facilitators—and not just for their peers but for adults as well.

5. Research shows that the competence of medical practitioners, and many other professionals, is as much (and increasingly) a product of their *cultural* (i.e., communication) competence as it is of their technical know-how. The two are flesh and bone.

6. Shortly after the author (2010) proposed *collaborative continuity*, highlighting intergenerational collaboration and expanded learning, she soon discovered that it was similar to *development-interaction* (Cuffaro & Nager, 2011).

References

Abedi, J. (2007). *English language proficiency assessment in the nation: Current status and future practice.* Davis: University of California, Davis Press.

Allington, R. L. & Baker, K. (2007). Best practices for struggling readers. In L. B. Gambrell, L. M. Morrow, & M. Pressley (Eds.), *Best Practices in Literacy Instruction* (pp. 83–103). New York: Guilford Press.

Alloway, T., Gathercole, S., & Willis, C. (2004). A structural analysis of working memory and related cognitive skills in young children. *Journal of Experimental Child Psychology, 87,* 85–170.

Alwell, M., & Cobb, B. (2009). Social and communicative interventions and transition outcomes for youth with disabilities. *Career Development for Exceptional Individuals, 32,* 94–107.

Arndt, V., Harvey, P., & Nuttall, J. (2000). Alive to language: Perspectives on language awareness for English language teachers. Cambridge, UK: Cambridge University Press.

Ashworth, M., & Wakefield, P. (1994). *Teaching the world's children: ESL for ages three to seven.* Toronto, Canada: Pippin.

Aud, S., Hussar, W., Planty, M., Snyder, T., Bianco, K., Fox, M., Frohlich, L., Kemp, J., and Drake, L. (2010). *The condition of education 2010* (NCES 2010-28). Washington, DC: National Center for Education Statistics.

August, D., Hakuta, K., O'Day, J., et al. (2009). The American recovery and reinvestment act: Recommendations for addressing the needs of English language learners. Retrieved from http://www.migrationinformation.org/integration/files/ELL Stimulus-Recommendations.pdf

Baron, D. (2000). Ebonics and the politics of English. *World Englishes, 19,* 5–19.

Bauer, C. (1997). *Leading kids to books through puppets.* Chicago: American Library Association.

Baugh, A. C., & Cable, T. (1993). *A history of the English language.* Englewood Cliffs, NJ: Prentice Hall.

Beach, R., Campano, G., Edmiston, B., & Borgmann, M. (Eds.). (2010). Literacy tools in the classroom: Teaching through critical inquiry, grades 5–12. New York: Teachers College Press.

Bell, A. (Writer), Smith, B. W. (Director). (2006). Happily ever after: Fairy tales for every child [*television series*]. New York: HBO.

Benasich, A., Choudhury, N., Friedman, J., Realpe-Bonilla, T., Chojnowska, C., & Gou, Z. (2006). The infant as a prelinguistic model for language learning impairments: Predicting from event-related potentials to behavior. *Neuropsychologia, 44*(3), 396–411.

Bender, W. N. (2008). Differentiating instruction for students with learning disabilities: Best teaching practices for general and special educators (2nd ed.). Thousand Oaks, CA: Corwin.

Bennett, S., Maton, K., & Kervin, L. (2008). The 'digital natives' debate: A critical review of the evidence. *British Journal of Educational Technology, 39*(5), 775–786. Retrieved from http://www.blackwellsynergy.com/doi/abs/10.1111/j.1467-8535.2007.00793.x

Berkeley, S., & Scruggs, T. E. (2010). A focus on vocabulary instruction. *Current Practice Alerts, 18.*

Bialystok, E. (2001). *Bilingualism in development: Language, literacy, and cognition.* Cambridge, UK: Cambridge University Press.

Bickerton, D. (2000). How protolanguage became language. In C. Knight, M. Studdert-Kennedy, & J. R. Hurford, (Eds.), *The evolutionary emergence of language: Social function and the origins of linguistic form.* Cambridge, UK: Cambridge University Press.

Birdsong, D. (1999). *Second language acquisition and the critical period hypothesis.* Mahwah, NJ: Lawrence Erlbaum Associates.

Blachowicz, C., & Fisher, P. (2010). *Teaching vocabulary in all classrooms.* Boston: Pearson.

Blazek, S. (1997). *A leprechaun's St. Patrick's day.* Gretna, LA: Pelican Publishing.

Bowe, F. (2004). *Making inclusion work.* Upper Saddle River, NJ: Prentice Hall.

Brady, M. (2008). *Cover the material—Or teach students to think.* Alexandria, VA: Association for Supervision and Curriculum Development.

Bray, P., & Cooper, R. (2007). The play of children with special needs in mainstream and special education settings. *Australian Journal of Early Childhood, 32*(2), 37–42.

Brigham, R., & Brigham, M. (2001). A focus on mnemonics instruction. *Current Practice Alerts, 5.* Retrieved from http://www.teachingld.org/

Bovee, C., & Thill, J. (2007). *Excellence in business communication.* New York: Pearson.

Brown, D. (2000). *Principles of language learning and teaching.* New York: Longman.

Burke, J. (2001). Illuminating texts: How to teach students to read the world. Portsmouth, NH: Heinemann.

Burnett, C. (2002). Learning Indian arithmetic in the early 13th century. *Bolétin de la Asociación Matemática Venezolana, 9*(1), 15–26.

Buurman, P. (1988). *Wayang Golek: The enchanting world of classical Javanese puppet theater.* New York: Oxford University Press.

Carr, M., & May, H. (1996). Te Whariki, making a difference for the under fives? The new national early childhood curriculum. *DELTA: Policy and practice in education, 48*(1), 101–102.

Carbone, P., & Orellana, M (2010). Developing academic identities: Persuasive writing as a tool to strengthen emergent academic identities. *Research in the Teaching of English, 44*(3), 292–316.

Calvin, W. H., & Bickerton, D. (2000). *Lingua ex machina.* Cambridge, MA: The MIT Press.

Cardona, G. (1999). *Recent research in Pāṇinian studies.* Delhi, India: Motilal Banarsidass.

Carlson, S., & Metzoff, A. (2008). Bilingual experience and executive functioning in young children. *Developmental Science, 11*(2), 282–298.

Cary, S. (2004) *Going graphic: Comics at work in the multilingual classroom.* Portsmouth, NH: Heinemann

Casteel, C., & Ballantyne, K. (2010). *Professional development in action.* Washington, DC: National Clearinghouse for English Language Acquisition.

Cauthen, N. K., & Dinan, K. A. (2006). *Immigrant children: America's future.* National Center for children in poverty. Retrieved from http://www.nccp.org/publications/pub_657.html

Chambers, J. K., Trudgill, P., & Schilling-Estes, N. (Eds.). (2002). *The handbook of language variation and change*. London, UK: Blackwell.

Charles, R. (2009). *EnVision math*. New York: Scott Foresman-Addison Wesley.

Chi, M. T. H., Bassok, M., Lewis, M. W., Reimann, P., & Glaser, R. (1989). Self-explanations: How students study and use examples in learning to solve problems. *Cognitive Science, 13*, 145–182.

Chin-Lee, C. (2005). *Amelia to Zora: Twenty-six women who changed the world*. Watertown, MA: Charlesbridge.

Chomsky, N. (1995). *The minimalist program*. Cambridge, MA: The MIT Press.

Clements, D. H., & Sarama, J. (2005). Young children and technology: What's appropriate? In W. Masalski, & P. C. Elliott (Eds.), *Technology-supported Mathematics Learning Environments: 67th Yearbook* (pp. 51–73). Reston, VA: National Council of Teachers of Mathematics.

Colby, R. (Producer). (2002, September 15). *Almost a woman* [television broadcast]. New York: PBS.

Collier, V., & Thomas, W. (2004). The astounding effectiveness of dual language education for all. *NABE Journal of Research and Practice, 2*(1), 1–20.

Common Core State Standards. (2010). Retrieved from http://www.corestandards.org/assets/CCSSI_ELA%20Standards.pdf

Comrie, B., Matthews, S., & Polinsky, M. (Eds.). (2003). *The atlas of languages*. New York: Facts on File.

Coulmas, F. (1999). *The Blackwell encyclopedia of writing systems*. London, UK: Blackwell.

Cortiella, C. (2007). *Rewards and roadblocks: How special education students are faring under No Child Left Behind*. New York: National Center for Learning Disabilities.

Crawford, J. (1999). *Bilingual education: History, politics, theory, and practice* (4th ed.). Los Angeles: Bilingual Educational Services

Center for Research on Education, Diversity, & Excellence (CREDE). (2003). A national study of school effectiveness for language minority students' long-term academic achievement. Retrieved from http://www.cal.org/resources/digest/ResBrief10.html

Crystal, D. (1997). *English as a global language*. Cambridge, UK: Cambridge University Press.

Cuffaro, H. K., & Nager, N. (2011). The developmental-interaction approach at Bank Street College of Education. In J. Roopnarine & J. Johnson (Eds.), *Approaches to early childhood education*. (5th ed.). Upper Saddle River, NJ: Prentice Hall.

Culp, K. M., Honey, M., & Mandinach, E. (2003). A retrospective on 20 years of education technology policy. Retrieved from http://www2.ed.gov/rschstat/ eval/tech/20years.pdf

Daily Spiral Review 2-2. New York: Pearson. Retrieved from http://owlsharenest.wikispaces.com/file/view/3rd+grade+topic+2.pdf

Darling-Hammond, L. (2012). Foreword. In B. Falk (Ed.), *Defending childhood: Keeping the promise of early education* (pp. vii–ix). New York: Teachers College Press.

Davis, R. (2000). *The gift of dyslexia*. New York: Perigree.

Deedy, C. (2007). *Martina, the beautiful cockroach*. Atlanta: Peachtree.

Dehaene, S. (1997). *The number sense: How the mind creates mathematics*. Oxford, UK: Oxford University Press.

Dorner, L., Orellana, M., & Li-Grining, C. (2007). "I helped my mom" and it helped me: Translating the skills of language brokers into improved standardized test scores. *American Journal of Education, 113*(3), 451–478.

Echevarria, J., & Graves, A. (2007). *Sheltered content instruction: Teaching English language learners with diverse abilities.* Boston: Allyn & Bacon.

Edo, M., Planas, N., & Badillo, E. (2009). Mathematical learning in a context of play. *European Early Childhood Education Research Journal, 17*(3), 325–341.

Edwards, P. A. (2004). *Children's literacy development: Making it happen through school, family, and community involvement.* Boston: Allyn & Bacon.

Egbert, J. (2005). *CALL essentials: Principles and practice in CALL classrooms.* Alexandria, VA: TESOL.

Eggers, T. (2010). Hands-on science for young children. *Early Childhood News.* Retrieved from www.earlychildhoodnews.com/earlychildhood/article

Ehrlich, E. (2000). *You've got ketchup on your muumuu.* New York: Henry Holt.

Ellis, A. K., & Howard, P. W. (2007). Graphic organizers: Powerful tools for teaching students with learning disabilities. *Current Practice Alerts, 13.* Retrieved from http://www.teachingld.org/pdf/alert13.pdf

Eksner, J., & Orellana, M. (forthcoming). Paraphrasing in the zone of prozimal development: Latino child translators and the co-construction of knowledge. *Ethos: Journal of Psychological Anthropology.*

Epling, K. (2011, November). Your antibullying toolset. Paper presented at the NAEYC Conference. Orlando, FL.

Ewart, F. (1998). *Let the shadows speak: Developing children's language through shadow puppetry.* London, UK: Trentham.

Fairclough, N. (2001). *Language and power.* New York: Longman.

Ferris, D., & Hedgcock, J. (2005). *Teaching ESL composition: Purpose, process, and practice* (2nd ed.). Mahwah, NJ: Lawrence Erlbaum Associates.

Flege, J. E. (1991). Age of learning affects the authenticity of voice-onset time in stop consonants produced in a second language. *Journal of the Acoustical Society of America, 89,* 395–411.

Folse, K. S. (2009). *The art of teaching speaking.* Ann Arbor: University of Michigan Press.

Forness, S. R., & Beard, K. Y. (2007). Strengthening the research base in special education: Evidence-based practice and interdisciplinary collaboration. In J. Crockett, M. Gerber, & T. Landrum (Eds.), *Achieving the radical reform of special education* (pp. 169–188). Mahwah, NJ: Lawrence Erlbaum Associates.

Fortson, B. W. (2004). *Indo-European language and culture: An introduction.* Malden, MA: Blackwell.

Furrman, L. (2000). In support of drama in early childhood education, again. *Early Childhood Education Journal, 27*(3), 173–178.

García, E. (2005). *Teaching and learning in two languages: Bilingualism and schooling in two languages.* New York: Teachers College Press.

García, E., & Frede, E. (2010). *Early education of dual language learners.* New York: Teachers College Press.

Gathercole, S. (2006). Nonword repetition and word learning: The nature of the relationship. *Applied Psycholinguistics, 27,* 513–523.

Genishi, C. (1988). Children's language: Learning words from experience. *Young Children 44*(1): 16–23.

Genishi, C., Ryan, S., Ochsner, M., & Yarnall, M. (2001). Teaching in early childhood education. In V. Richardson (Ed.), *Handbook of research on teaching* (4th ed.). Washington, DC: American Educational Research Association.

Ginsburg, H. P., & Ertle, B. (2008). Knowing the mathematics in early childhood mathematics. In O. N. Saracho & B. Spodek (Eds.). *Contemporary perspectives on mathematics in early childhood education.* (pp. 45–66). Charlotte, NC: Information Age Publishing.

Gladwell, M. (2008). *Outliers: The story of success.* New York: Little, Brown & Co.

Goouch, K. (2008). Understanding playful pedagogies, play narratives and play spaces. *Early Years: An International Journal of Research and Development, 28*(1), 93–102.

Gregory, S. (2009). Inclusion vs. exclusion: A study of play and social interactions of children with disabilities (Unpublished master's thesis). University of Arkansas, Fayetteville.

Gupta, A. (2009). Vygotskian perspectives on using dramatic play to enhance children's development and balance creativity with structure in the early childhood classroom. *Early Child Development and Care, 179*(8), 1041–1054.

Hallahan, D. P., Kauffman, J. F., & Pullen, P. (2009). *Exceptional learners: An introduction to special education* (11th ed.). Boston: Pearson.

Halliday, M. (1975). *Learning how to mean: Explorations in the development of language.* London, UK: Edward Arnold.

Hamers, J., & Blanc, M. (2000). *Bilinguality and bilingualism* (2nd ed.). Cambridge, UK: Cambridge University Press.

Hanline, M. F. (2009). The relationship between preschool block play and reading and math abilities in early elementary school: A longitudinal study of children with and without disabilities. *Early Child Development and Care, 180*(8), 1–13.

Harding, E., & Riley, P. (1999). *The bilingual family: A handbook for parents.* Cambridge, UK: Cambridge University Press.

Harlaar, N., Hayiou-Thomas, M., Dale, P., & Plomin, R. (2008). Why do preschool language abilities correlate with later reading? A twin study. *Journal of Speech, Language, and Hearing Research,* Vol. 51, 688–705.

Heath, S. B. (1983). *Ways with words: Language, life and work in communities and classrooms.* Cambridge, UK: Cambridge University Press.

Herrington, J., & Kervin, L. (2007). Authentic learning supported by technology: 10 suggestions and cases of integration in classrooms. *Educational Media International, 44*(3), 219–236.

Hollowell, K. (2011). How to improve reading using technology. Retrieved from http://www.ehow.com/how_5932291_improve-reading-using-technology.html

Holum, A., & Gahala, H. (2011). Using technology to enhance literacy instruction. Retrieved from http://www.ncrel.org/sdrs/ areas/issues/content/cntareas/reading/li300.htm

Hoopmann, K. (2006). *All cats have Asperger syndrome.* London, UK: Jessica Kingsley.

Hudley, A. H., & Mallinson, C. (2010). *Understanding English language variation in U.S. schools.* New York: Teachers College Press.

Hui, A., & Lau, S. (2006). Drama education: A touch of the creative mind and communicative-expressive ability of elementary school children in Hong Kong. *Thinking Skills and Creativity, 1*(1), 34–40.

Hull, G., & Schultz, K. (2001). *School's out! Bridging out-of-school literacies with classroom practice.* New York: Teacher College Press.

Invernizzi, M., Bear, D., Johnston, F., Templeton, S. (2012). *Words their way: Word sorts for within word pattern spellers* (5th ed.). New York: Pearson.

Joanisse, M. F., & Seidenberg, M. S. (1997). [i e a u] and sometimes [o]: Perceptual and computational constraints on vowel inventories. Proceedings of the 15th Annual Conference of the Cognitive Science Society.

Johar, K. (2010). *My name is Khan*. New Delhi, India: Dharma Productions.

Johnson, A., Moher, T., Choo, Y., Lin, Y. J., Haas, D., & Kim, J. (2002). Augmenting elementary school education with VR. *IEEE Computer Graphics and Applications*, (March/April), 6–9.

Jones, J., & Yandian, S. (2002). *Supporting the home language and promoting English acquisition within migrant and seasonal Head Start*. Washington, DC: Retrieved from http://ece.aed.org/publications/ mshs/secondlanguage/secondlang.pdf

Kachru, Y., & Smith, L. (2008). *Cultures, contexts, and world Englishes*. New York: Routledge.

Kamil, M., Pearson, D., Moje, E., & Afflerbach, P. (2011). *Handbook of reading research* (Vol. 4). New York: Routledge.

Katz, L. (2008). Review of the article 'Play and learning in early childhood settings: International perspectives.' *International Journal of Early Childhood*, 40(2), 147–149.

Keeler M. L., & Swanson, H. L. (2001). Does strategy knowledge influence working memory in children with mathematical disabilities? *Journal of Learning Disabilities*, 34(5), 418–434.

KewalRamani, A., Aud, S., & Fox, M. (2007). *Status and trends in the education of racial and ethnic minorities*. Washington, DC: National Center for Education Statistics.

Kimmelman, L. (2008). *Everybody bonjours!* New York: Knopf for Young Readers.

Kinney, J. (2007). *Diary of a wimpy kid*. New York: Amulet.

King, M. L., Jr. (1957). Loving your enemies. Retrieved from www.mlkonline.net/enemies. html

Kipp, D. (2000). *Encouragement, guidance, insights, and lessons learned for native language activists developing their own tribal language programs*. Browning, MT: Piegan Institute.

Kirk, M. (Producer). (2002, March 27). *Misunderstood minds: Searching for success in school* [television broadcast]. New York: PBS.

Kozloski, K. (2006). Principal leadership for technology integration: A study of principal technology leadership (Unpublished dissertation.) Philadelphia: Drexel University.

Krashen, S. (1982). Principles and practice in second language acquisition. Oxford, UK: Pergamon.

Krashen, S. (1996). *Under attack: The case against bilingual education*, Culver City, CA: Language Education Associates.

Krashen, S. (2000). Bilingual education, the acquisition of English, and the retention and loss of Spanish. In A. Roca (Ed.), *Research on Spanish in the U.S.: Linguistic issues and challenges*. Somerville, MA: Cascadilla Press.

Kroll, B. (Ed.). (2003). *Exploring the dynamics of second language writing*. Cambridge, UK: Cambridge University Press.

Kuhl, P., Stevens, E., Hayashi, A., Deguchi, T., Kiritani, S., & Iverson, P. (2006). Infants show facilitation for native language phonetic perception between 6 and 12 months. *Developmental Science*, 9, 13–21.

Labov, W. (1966). *The social stratification of English in New York City*. New York: Cambridge University Press.

Labov, W. (Ed.). (1979). *Language in the inner city: Studies in the Black English Vernacular*. London, UK: Blackwell.

Ladson-Billings, G. (1997). *The dreamkeepers: Successful teachers of African American children*. San Francisco: Jossey-Bass.

Lane, H. B., & Pullen, P. (2004). Phonological awareness, assessment, and instruction: A sound beginning. New York: Pearson.

Learning Horizons. (2009). 2-digit equations and big numbers, grade 1. Cleveland: Learning Horizons.

Lee, R., & Recchia, S. (2008). "Who's the boss?" Young children's power and influence in an early childhood classroom. *Early childhood Research and Practice, 10*(1). Retrieved from http://ecrp.uiuc.edu/v10n1/lee.html

Lewis, P. (2009). *Ethnologue: Languages of the world*. Dallas, TX: SIL International.

Lim, C., Maxwell, K., Able Boone, H., & Zimmer, C. R. (2009). Cultural and linguistic diversity in early childhood teacher preparation: The impact of contextual characteristics on coursework and practica. *Early Childhood Research Quarterly, 24*, 64–76.

Losen, D., & Orfield, G. (Eds.). (2002*). Racial inequality in special education* (pp. 1–14). Cambridge, MA: Harvard Education Press.

Madden, D. (2006). *A pocketful of prose: Vintage short fiction* (Vol. 2). Boston: Thomson.

Marshall, B. (2000). Is there a "child advantage" in learning foreign languages? *Education Week, 19*(22), 39–41.

Martinussen, R., & Tannock, R. (2006). Working memory impairments in children with attention-deficit hyperactivity disorder with and without comorbid language learning disorders. *Journal of Clinical and Experimental Neuropsychology, 28*(7), 1073–1094.

Marzano, R. J. (2010). *Teaching basic and advanced vocabulary: A framework for direct instruction*. Boston: Heinle.

Masters, M. G., Stecker, N. A., & Katz, J. (1998). *Central auditory processing disorders: Mostly management.* Boston: Allyn & Bacon.

McGee, L., & Schickedanz, J. (2007). Repeated interactive read alouds in preschool and Kindergarten. *The Reading Teacher, 60*, 542–551.

McGuinness, D. (2004). *Early reading instruction: What science really tells us about how to teach reading*. Cambridge, MA: The MIT Press.

Meltzer, L. (2007). *Executive function in education*. New York: Guilford Press.

Mercer, C., & Pullen, P. (2009). *Students with learning disabilities* (7th ed.). Upper Saddle River, NJ: Pearson.

Metcalf, A. (1999). The world in so many words: A country-by-country tour of words that have shaped our language. Boston: Houghton Mifflin.

Miller, E., & Almon, J. (2009). Crisis in the Kindergarten: Why children need to play in school. College Park, MD: Alliance for Childhood.

Moje, E., Ciechanowski, K., Kramer, K., Ellis, L., Carrillo, R., & Collazo, T. (2004). Working toward third space in content area literacy: An examination of everyday funds of knowledge and discourse. *Reading Research Quarterly, 39*(1), 38–70.

Moon, K., & Reifel, S. (2008). Play and literacy learning in a diverse language pre-Kindergarten classroom. *Contemporary Issues in Early Childhood, 9*(1), 49–65.

Morrow, L., & Schickedanz, J. (2006). The relationships between sociodramatic play and literacy development. In D. Dickinson & S. Neuman (Eds.), *Handbook of Early Literacy Research*, Vol. 2. New York: Guilford Press.

Nager, N., & Shapiro, E. K. (Eds.). (2000). Revisiting a progressive pedagogy: The developmental-interaction approach (SUNY Series, Early Childhood Education). Albany: State University of New York Press.

National Association for the Education of Young Children. (1996). Position statement: Technology in early childhood programs serving children from birth through age 8. Washington, DC: Author.

Neeley, P. M., Neeley, R. A., Justen, J. E., & Tipton-Sumner, C. (2001). Scripted play as a language intervention strategy for preschoolers with developmental disabilities. *Early Childhood Education Journal, 28*(4), 243–246.

Nesmith, S., & Cooper, S. (2010). Trade books in the mathematics classroom: The impact of many, varied perspectives on determination of quality. *Journal of Research in Childhood Education, 24*(4), 1–19.

Nicholson, C. (2009, July 27). Linguist's preservation kit has new digital tools. Retrieved from www.nytimes.com/2009/07/28/science/28prof.html

Nieto, S. (2012). Honoring the lives of all children: Identity, culture, and language. In B. Falk's (Ed.), *Defending childhood: Keeping the promise of early education*, (pp. 48–62). New York: Teachers College Press.

Nussbaum, D. (2004, February 8). A surge in autism, but why? *New York Times*, pp. NJ–6

Nussbaum-Beach, S. (2008). No limits. *Technology & Learning, 28*(7), 14–18. Retrieved from http://www.techlearning.com/article/8466

O'Grady, W., Archibald, J., Aronoff, M., & Rees-Miller, J. (2004). *Contemporary linguistics*. Boston: Bedford/St. Martins.

Orellana, M. (2001). The work kids do: Mexican and Central American immigrant children's contributions to households and schools in California. *Harvard Educational Review, 71*(3), 366–389.

Orellana, M. (2009). *Translating childhoods: Immigrant youth, language and culture*. New Brunswick, NJ: Rutgers University Press.

Owens, R. (2005). *Language development: an introduction* (6th ed.). New York: Pearson.

Pandey, A. (Ed.). (2000, Spring). African American language and the ebonics debate [Millennium issue]. *World Englishes, 19*(1).

Pandey, A. (2004). Disney's designs: The semiotics of animal icons in animated movies. *Sankofa: A Journal of Young Adult Literature, 3*, 50–61.

Pandey, A. (2005). Western Caribbean Creoles (entry). In P. Strazny (Ed.), *Encyclopedia of linguistics* (pp. 1172–1177). New York: Routledge.

Pandey, A. (2008, November 10). Project ABCDE: Grant presentation. Administration for Children and Families, Washington, DC.

Pandey, A. (2009, April 12). *"Who dis?" E-literacy and overt identities in HBCU students' text messages*. Paper presented at the College Language Association Convention, Easton, MD.

Pandey, A. (2010). *The child language teacher: Intergenerational language and literary enhancement*. Mysore, India: Central Institute of Indian Languages.

Pandey, A. (2011a). The content teacher's ESL kit: A handy resource for all teachers? *Language Forum, 22*(1), 15–36.

Pandey, A. (2011b). Introduction, professional communication in the age of outsourcing. *International Journal of Communication, 21*(1), 1–4.

Pandey, A. (2011c). Training and retraining grades P–12 Eastern-Shore teachers (TARGET) (Contract: T195N070327). Washington, DC: Office of English Language Acquisition, U.S. Department of Education.

Pandey, A. (forthcoming). When "second" comes first—Hindi to the eye? Sociolinguistic hybridity in professional writing. In S. Canagarajah (Ed.), *Writing as translingual practice in academic contexts: Premises, pedagogy, policy.* New York: Routledge.

Park, B., Boyd, B., & Chae J. (2008). Young children's block play and mathematical learning. *Journal of Research in Childhood Education, 23*(2), 157–162.

Patton-Terry, N. (2004). An investigation of early linguistic awareness and spelling ability among African American English and Standard American English speakers. (Unpublished dissertation.) Evanston, IL: Northwestern University.

Pellicano, E., & Stears, M. (2011). Bridging autism, science and society: Moving toward an ethically informed approach to autism research. *Autism Research, 4*(4), 271–282.

Pepper, D. (2007, September 25). Assessment for disabled students: An international comparison. Retrieved from http://www.ofqual.gov.uk/ files/ Assessment_disabled_international_briefing.pdf

Peregoy, S., & Boyle, O. (2001). Reading, writing, and learning in ESL: A resource book for K–12 teachers. New York: Longman.

Perl, E. (2010). *Dotty.* New York: Harry Abrams.

Piatteli-Palmarini, M. & Berwick, R. (Eds.). (forthcoming). *Rich languages from poor inputs.* Oxford, UK: Oxford University Press.

Pierangelo, R. (2004). *The special educator's survival guide.* San Francisco: Jossey-Bass.

Pinker, S. (1994). *The language instinct: How the mind creates language.* New York: William Morrow.

Puolakanaho, A., Ahonen, T., Aro, M., Eklund, K., Lepannen, P. H. T., Poik-keus, A. M. (2007). Very early phonological and language skills: Estimating individual risk of reading disability. *Journal of Child Psychology and Psychiatry, and Allied Disciplines, 48*(9), 923–931.

Purdue, K., Ballard, K., & MacArthur, J. (2001). Exclusion and inclusion in New Zealand early childhood education: Disability, discourses and contexts. *International Journal of Early Years Education, 9*(1), 5–15.

Pyles, T., & Algeo, J. (1993). *The origins and development of the English language.* Fort Worth, TX: Harcourt Brace Jovanovich.

Ramani, G. B., & Siegler, R. S. (2008). Promoting broad and stable improvements in low-income children's numerical knowledge through playing number board games. *Child Development, 79,* 375–394.

Reed, J., Hirsh-Pasek, K., & Golinkoff, R. (2012). A tale of two schools: The promise of playful learning. In B. Falk (Ed.), *Defending childhood: Keeping the promise of early education,* (24–47). New York: Teachers College Press.

Reyhner, J. (2001). Cultural survival vs. forced assimilation: The renewed war on diversity. Retrieved from http://www.culturalsurvival.org/ourpublications/csq/article/cultural-survival-vs-forced-assimilation-renewed-war-diversity

Richards, J., & Rodgers, T. (2003). *Approaches and methods in language teaching* (2nd ed.). Cambridge, UK: Cambridge University Press.

Richardson, W. (2009). *Blogs, wikis, podcasts, and other powerful web tools for classrooms* (2nd ed.). Thousand Oaks, CA: Corwin Press.

Richgels, D. J. (2001). Phonemic awareness. *The Reading Teacher, 55*(3), 274–278.

Ritchey, K. D., & Speece, D. L. (2006). From letter names to word reading: The nascent role of sublexical fluency. *Contemporary Educational Psychology, 31,* 301–327.

Ritchie, W., & Bhatia, T. K. (Eds.). (2004). *The handbook of bilingualism.* London, UK: Blackwell.

Rodriquez, R. (1983). *Hunger of memory: The education of Richard Rodriquez.* New York: Random House.

Ryan, S., & Grieshaber, S. (2004). It's more than child development: Critical theories, research, and teaching young children. *Young Children, 59,* 44–52.

Ryan, S., & Grieshaber, S. (2005). Shifting from developmental to postmodern practices in early childhood teacher education. *Journal of Teacher Education, 56*(1), 34–45.

Salley, C. (2009). *Epossumondas plays possum.* Boston: Houghton Mifflin.

Savage, R., Lavers, N. & Pillay, V. (2007). Working memory and reading difficulties: What we know and what we don't know about the relationship. *Educational Psychology Review, 19*(2), 185–221.

Schecter, S., & Cummins, J. (2003). *Multilingual education in practice: Using language as a resource.* Portsmouth, NH: Heinemann.

Schmidt, A. (2011). Immigrant parents rely on kids for help online. Retrieved from http://www.npr.org/2011/10/12/141232534/immigrant-parents-rely-on-kids-for-help-online

Schminky, M., & Baran, J. (2000). Central auditory processing disorders: An overview of assessment and management. Retrieved from www.tsbvi.edu/seehear/spring00/centralauditory.htm

Schmitt, N., & Marsden, R. (2006). *Why is English like that?: Historical answers to hard ELT questions.* Ann Arbor: The University of Michigan Press.

Schwartz, D. (1985). *How much is a million?* New York: Lothrop, Lee, & Shepard.

Sereno, J. A., & Wang, Y. (2007). Behavioral and cortical effects of learning a second language: The acquisition of tone. In O. Bohn & M. Munro (Eds.), *Language experience in second language speech learning: In honor of James Emil Flege* (pp. 241–258). Amsterdam, Netherlands: John Benjamins.

Siegel, L. S. (2007). Perspectives on dyslexia. *Paediatrics & Child Health, 11,* 581–588

Shapiro, E. S. (2011). *Academic Skills Problems* (4th ed.). New York: Guilford.

Shepard, L., Hannaway, J., & Baker, E. (2009). Standards, assessments, and accountability. Education policy white paper. (1-16) Washington, DC: National Academy of Education.

Shatzer, J. (2008). Picture book power: Connecting children's literature and mathematics. *The Reading Teacher, 61*(8), 649–653.

Sheffield, A. (2007). Necessary variables for effective technology integration. Retrieved from http://edtech2.boisestate.edu/sheffielda/571/sheffield_tech_use_synthesis_paper.pdf

Skinner, B. F. (1957). *Verbal behavior.* New York: Appleton-Century-Crofts.

Shepard, L., Hannaway, J., & Baker, E. (2009). Standards, assessments, and accountability. Education policy white paper. (1–16) Washington, DC: National Academy of Education.

Smitherman, G. (1999). *Talkin that talk: Language, culture and education in African America.* New York: Routledge.

Sneller, N. (2001). *Basic skills: Story elements.* Columbus, OH: Instructional Fair.

Snow, C., Griffin, P., & Burns, M. S. (Eds.). (2005). *Knowledge to support the teaching of reading: Preparing teachers for a changing world.* San Francisco: Jossey-Bass.

Soderman, A., Gregory, K., & McCarty, L. T. (2005). *Scaffolding emergent literacy: A child-centered approach for preschool through grade 5*. New York: Allyn & Bacon.

Sowell, T. (2001). *The Einstein syndrome: Bright children who talk late*. New York: Basic Books.

Sterne, T. (2002). *Animals of Africa: Sounds of the jungle, plain, and bush*. Nairobi, Kenya: High Fidelity Productions.

Strickland, D., & Morrow, L. (2000). *Beginning reading and writing*. New York: Teachers College Press.

Sutterby, J. A. (2002). *Todos somos amigos: Cross-cultural and cross-linguistic play interactions in a two-way immersion preKindergarten classroom*. (Unpublished doctoral dissertation). The University of Texas at Austin.

Tabors, P. (1997). *One child, two languages*. Baltimore, MD: Paul H. Brookes.

Tarnowska, W., & Hénaff, C. (2010). *The Arabian nights*. Cambridge, MA: Barefoot Books.

Tassoni, P., & Hucker, K. (2005). *Planning play and the early years*. Oxford, UK: Heinemann.

Taylor, P. (2011). *A beginner's guide to autism spectrum disorders*. London, UK: Jessica Kingsley.

Tharp, R. (1997). *From at-risk to excellence: Research, theory, and principle for practice*. Santa Cruz: University of California Center for Research on Education, Diversity and Excellence.

Thomas, W., & Collier, V. (2002). A national study of school effectiveness for language minority students' long-term academic achievement. Santa Cruz, CA, & Washington, DC: Center for Research on Education, Diversity & Excellence. Retrieved from http://www.cal.org/resources/digest/ResBrief10.html

Thornbury, S. (2007). *About language: Tasks for teachers of English*. Cambridge, UK: Cambridge University Press.

Tokuhama-Espinosa, T. (2001). *Raising multilingual children: Foreign language acquisition and children*. London, UK: Bergin & Garvey.

UNESCO. Retrieved from http://www.unesco.org/new/en/education/themes/strengthening-education-systems/inclusive-education/

U.S. Department of Education. (2006). 26th annual report to Congress. Retrieved from http://www2.ed.gov/about/reports/annual/osep/2004/index.html

Utley, C. A., & Obiakor, F. E. (2001). *Special education, multicultural education, and school reform: Components of quality education for learners with mild disabilities*. Springfield, IL: Charles C. Thomas.

van Dijk., T. (2009). *Society and discourse: How social contexts influence text and talk*. Cambridge, UK: Cambridge University Press.

Vogt, L., Jordan, C., & Tharp, R. (1987). *Explaining school failure, producing school success: Two cases*. Anthropology & Education Quarterly, *18*(4), 276–286.

Waber, D. (2010). *Rethinking learning disabilities: Understanding children who struggle in school*. New York: Guilford Press.

Walton, B. (2007, January 10). More children learn more than one language. *USA Today*. Retrieved from www.usatoday.com/news/education/2007-01-09-language-children_x.htm

Wessels, S. (2008). *IBA vocabulary framework: Ignite, bridge, and associate vocabulary development for culturally and linguistically diverse students* (Unpublished doctoral dissertation). Kansas State University.

White, T., Sowell, J., & Yanagihara, A. (1989). Teaching elementary students to use word-part clues. *The Reading Teacher*, *42*, 302–308.

Whorf, B. L. (1956). *Language, thought, and reality.* Cambridge, MA: MIT Press.

Wilbur, H. (2011). *F is for friendship: A quilt alphabet.* Ann Arbor, MI: Sleeping Bear Press.

Wolfram, W., Reaser, J., & Vaughn, C. (2008). Operationalizing linguistic gratuity: From principle to practice. *Language and Linguistics Compass, 2*(10), 1–26.

Wolfram, W., & Schilling-Estes, N. (2006). *American English: Dialects and variation.* London, UK: Blackwell.

Xin, Y. P., & Jitendra, A. K. (1999). The effects of instruction in solving mathematical word problems for students with learning problems: A meta-analysis. *The Journal of Special Education, 32*, 207–225.

Youngquist, J. (2004). Revisiting "play": Analyzing and articulating acts of inquiry. *Early Childhood Education Journal, 31*(3), 171–178.

Zigler, E., & Bishop-Josef, S. (2009). Play under siege: A historical overview: *Zero to Three, 30*(1), 4–11.

Index

About the Author

Anita Pandey is professor of linguistics and coordinator of professional communication in the Department of English and Language Arts at Morgan State University. Over the past 22 years, she has taught courses in linguistics, ESL, and business and technical writing.

Born and raised in a bilingual home in Africa, she is fluent in French, Hindi/Urdu, Nigerian Pidgin, Yoruba, and Spanish. During her early years, her family was constantly on the move, so she was forced to skip grades 5 through 8 because English-medium schools were not as accessible. After being home-schooled for a brief period, she entered high school at age 9 and successfully passed the regional West African Examination Council's exit exam (like the SAT) at 13. She gained admission into a 2-year college of arts and sciences the following year, and completed her Bachelor's by age 19. She earned a BA (Hons.) with a 1st Class distinction in linguistics from Ahmadu Bello University, Zaria (Nigeria), and taught at the College of Education, Azare (Nigeria) before pursuing graduate studies. She received her doctorate in linguistics from the University of Illinois at Urbana-Champaign and holds two master's degrees (the 1st in TESOL).

Dr. Pandey was the principal investigator for a large grant from the Administration for Children and Families for a linguistically enhanced training program for ECE professionals. She has participated in and presented at various professional venues, including the NAEYC, IRA, Head Start's National Research Conference, Head Start Grantees' Conference, Association for Childhood Education International (ACEI), TESOL, the American Association for Applied Linguistics, NABE, the International Society for Language Studies, the International Conference on World Englishes, the International Conference on Pragmatics and Language Learning, Georgetown University's Roundtable on Linguistics, and NCTE. All together, she has presented at over 60 international conventions. She is on ACEI's Research and Technical Assistance committees and is working on initiating a forum on increased access to elementary education worldwide. She also serves as education advisor for The UNForgotten Fund (www.unforgotten.org), a nonprofit organization dedicated to educating homeless children who sell trash for a living in Africa and Southeast Asia.

Her research interests include dual language and literacy development, transdisciplinary linguistics, and professional communication. In 2000, she served as lead ontologist for two companies in Silicon Valley, California. This laid the groundwork for her work in professional communication. She was a featured speaker at the 22nd Penn State Conference on Translingual Writing (www.outreach.psu.edu/programs rhetoric/278.html), and her presentation is scheduled to appear in a forthcoming volume from Routledge. She has also been invited to speak at the 2012 Intercultural Communication Conference hosted by Indiana University, and the 2013 NABE Convention.

Dr. Pandey's research has appeared in *Childhood Education, TESOL Quarterly, Critical Inquiry in Language Studies, Africa Today, Business Communication Quarterly,* and *Knowledge Management.* She guest edited the millennium issue of *World Englishes* (London: Blackwell). Her research monograph, *The Child Language Teacher: Intergenerational Language and Literary Enhancement* (Central Institute of Indian Languages), proposes an innovative approach to community language and literacy. She is associate editor of the *Journal of English as an International Language* and guest editor of the 2011 and 2012 issues of the *International Journal of Communication.* She is also on the advisory boards of four international journals.